CELEBRITY CARTOONS OF THE RICH AND FAMOUS

About the Author

JACK ZIEGLER was born in Brooklyn, New York, raised in Queens, and educated in Manhattan and the Bronx. He became a cartoonist to fulfill a need, i.e., to become rich and famous. It was the only way, he felt, that he could get a date with Elizabeth Taylor. Well, that hasn't happened yet, and already this is his fourth collection of cartoons. He has never been to Staten Island.

CELEBRITY CARTOONS OF THE RICH AND FAMOUS

By Jack Ziegler

WARNER BOOKS

A Warner Communications Company

Of the 122 drawings in this collection, 25 originally appeared in *The New Yorker*, and were copyrighted © 1976, 1981, 1982, 1983, 1984, 1985, 1986, and 1987 by The New Yorker Magazine, Inc. One drawing was originally published in *The National Lampoon*, and was copyrighted © 1984 by The National Lampoon, Inc. One drawing originally appeared in *The New York Times*, and was copyrighted © 1984 by The New York Times. Two drawings were originally published in *The Artist's Magazine*, and were copyrighted © 1984 and 1986 by The Artist's Magazine. One drawing originally appeared in *TV Guide*, and was copyrighted © 1983 by Triangle Publications, Inc. One drawing was originally published in *Writer's Digest*, and was copyrighted © 1980 by Writer's Digest. One drawing originally appeared in *The American Bystander*, and was copyrighted © 1982 by The American Bystander Publishing Company.

Copyright © 1987 by Jack Ziegler
All rights reserved.
Warner Books, Inc., 666 Fifth Avenue, New York, NY 10103

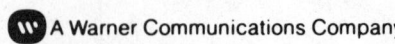 A Warner Communications Company

Printed in the United States of America

First Printing: November 1987

10 9 8 7 6 5 4 3 2 1

Library of Congress Cataloging-in-Publication Data

Ziegler, Jack.
   Celebrity cartoons of the rich and famous.

  1. Celebrities—Caricatures and cartoons.
2. American wit and humor, Pictorial.   I. Title.
NC1429.Z47A4   1987a   741.5′973   87-14240
ISBN 0-446-38524-7 (pbk.) (U.S.A.)
     0-446-38525-5 (pbk.) (Canada)

For my parents

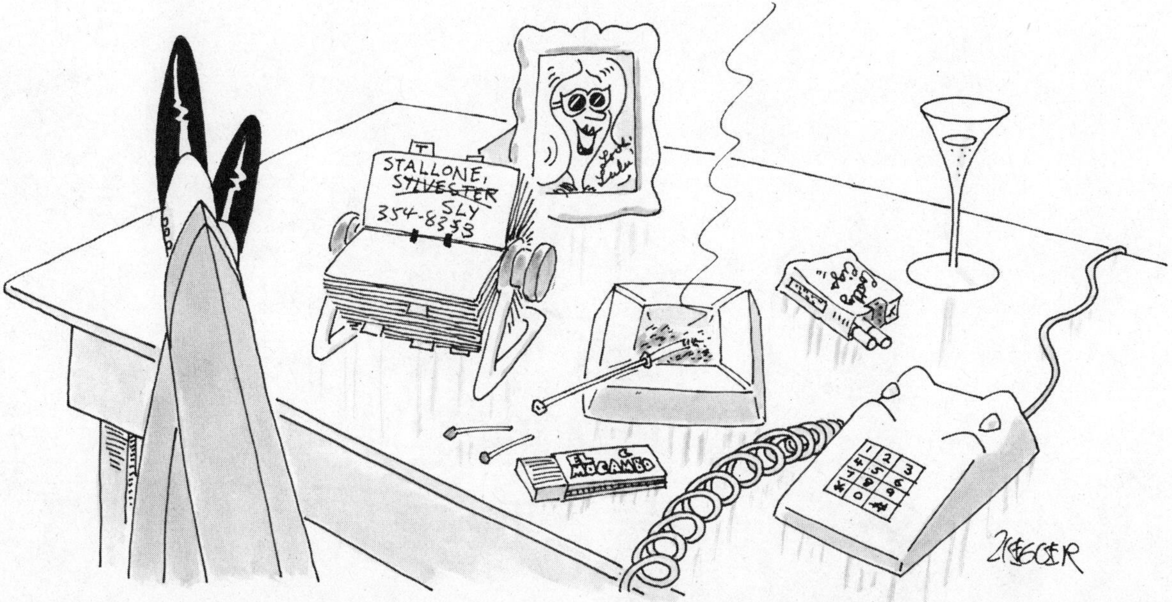
STALLONE, SYLVESTER
SLY
354-8353
EL MOCAMBO
ZIEGLER

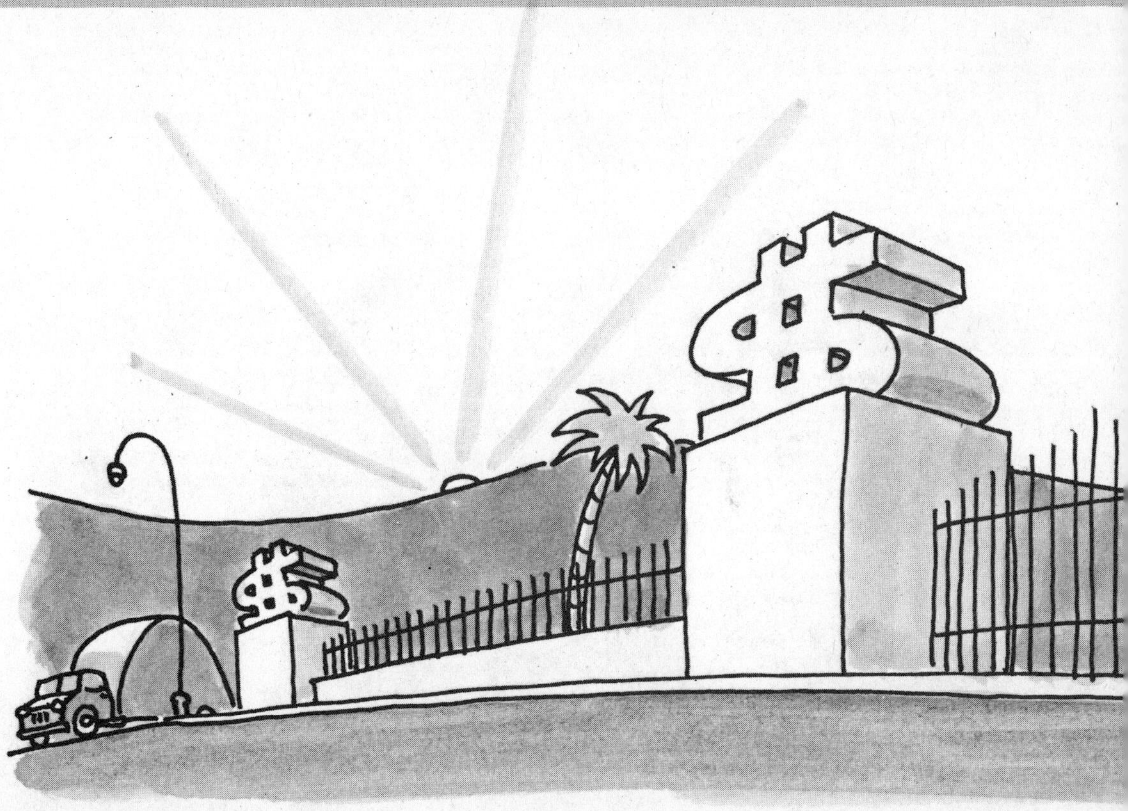

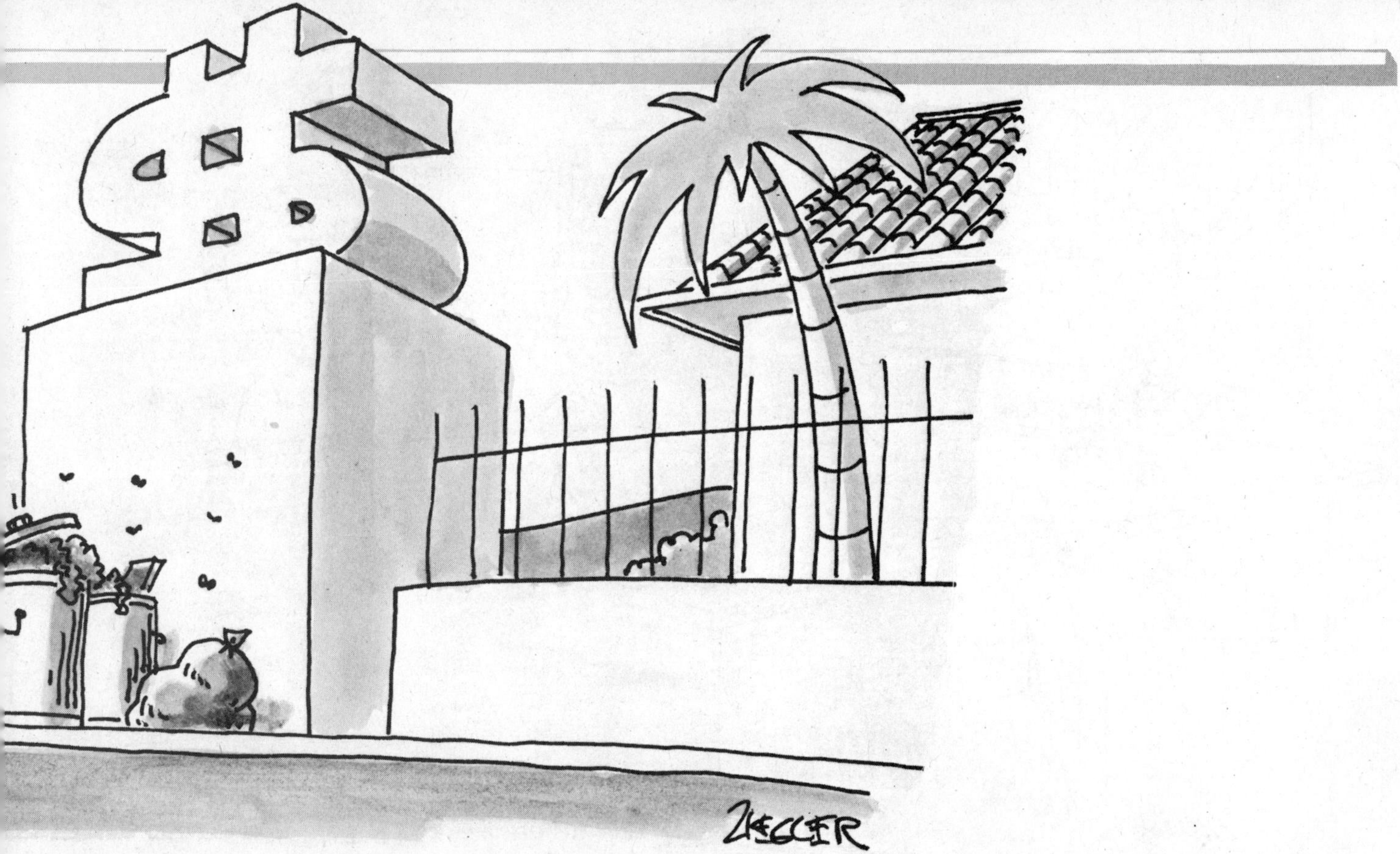
ZIEGLER

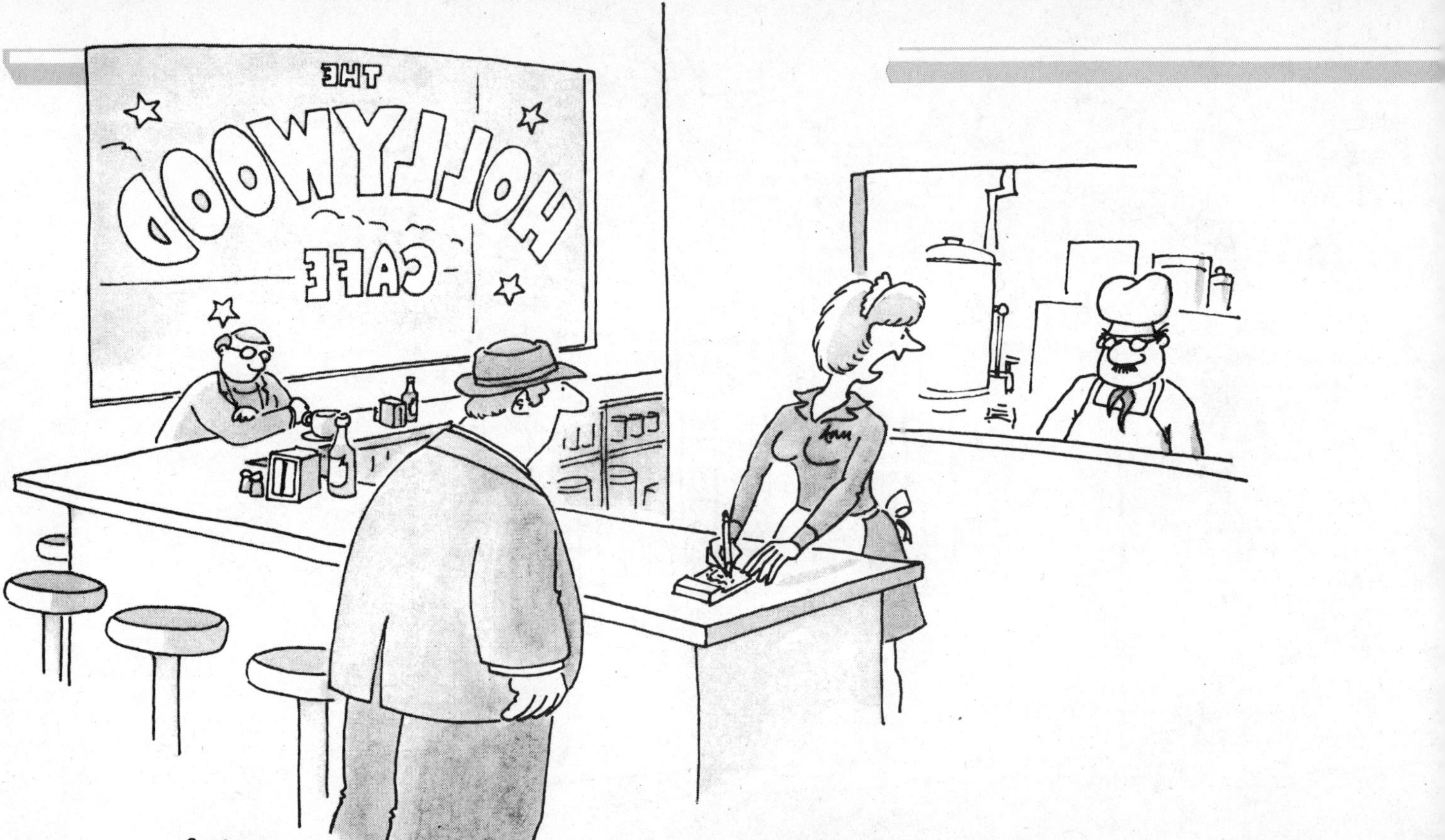
THE
HOLLYWOOD
CAFE

"Two Cagneys and a side of Garbo to go. Hold the Bogart."

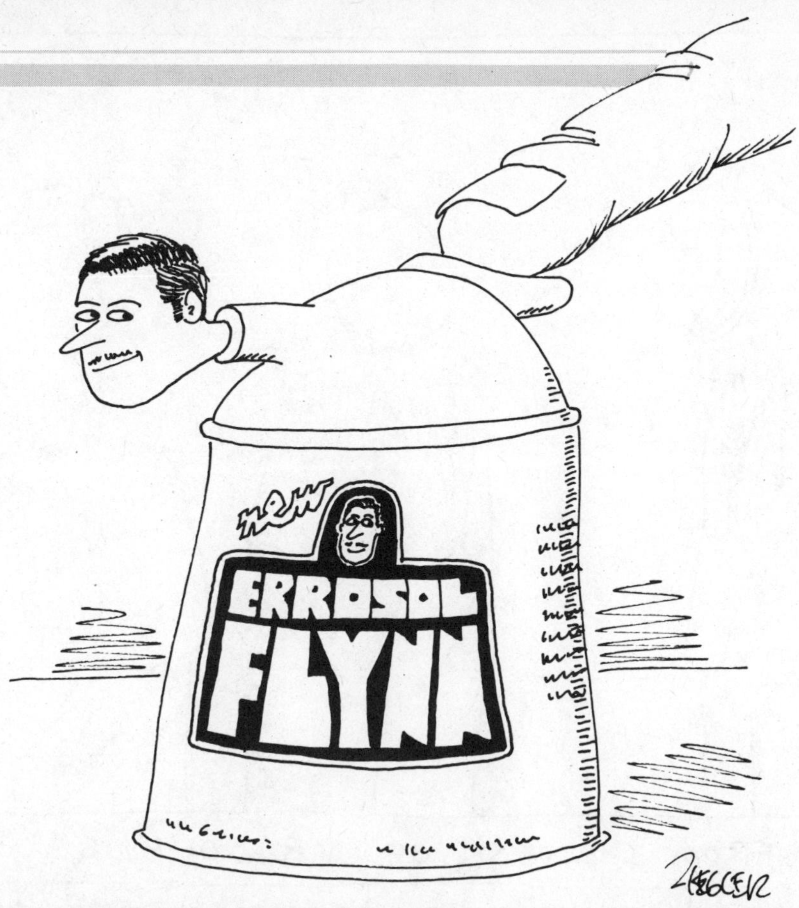
new
ERROSOL
FLYNN
ZIEGLER

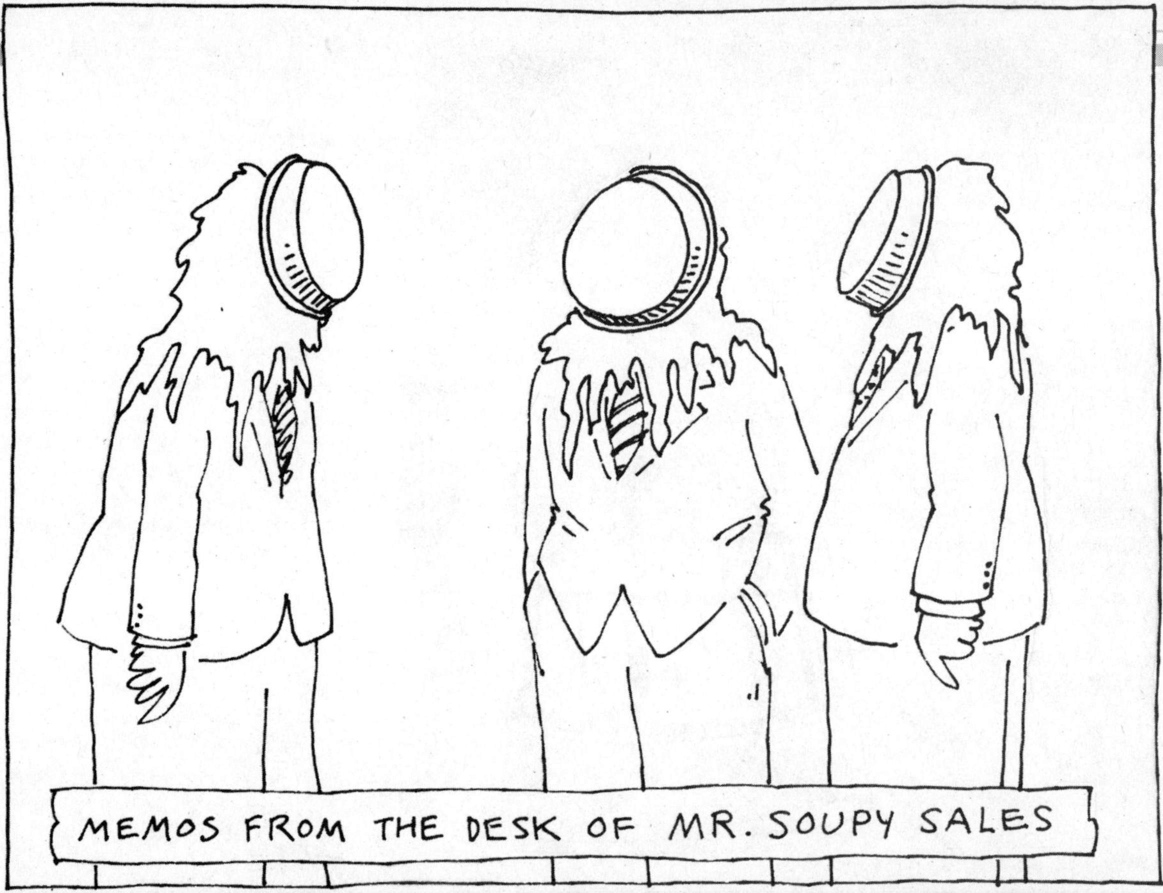
MEMOS FROM THE DESK OF MR. SOUPY SALES
ZIEGLER

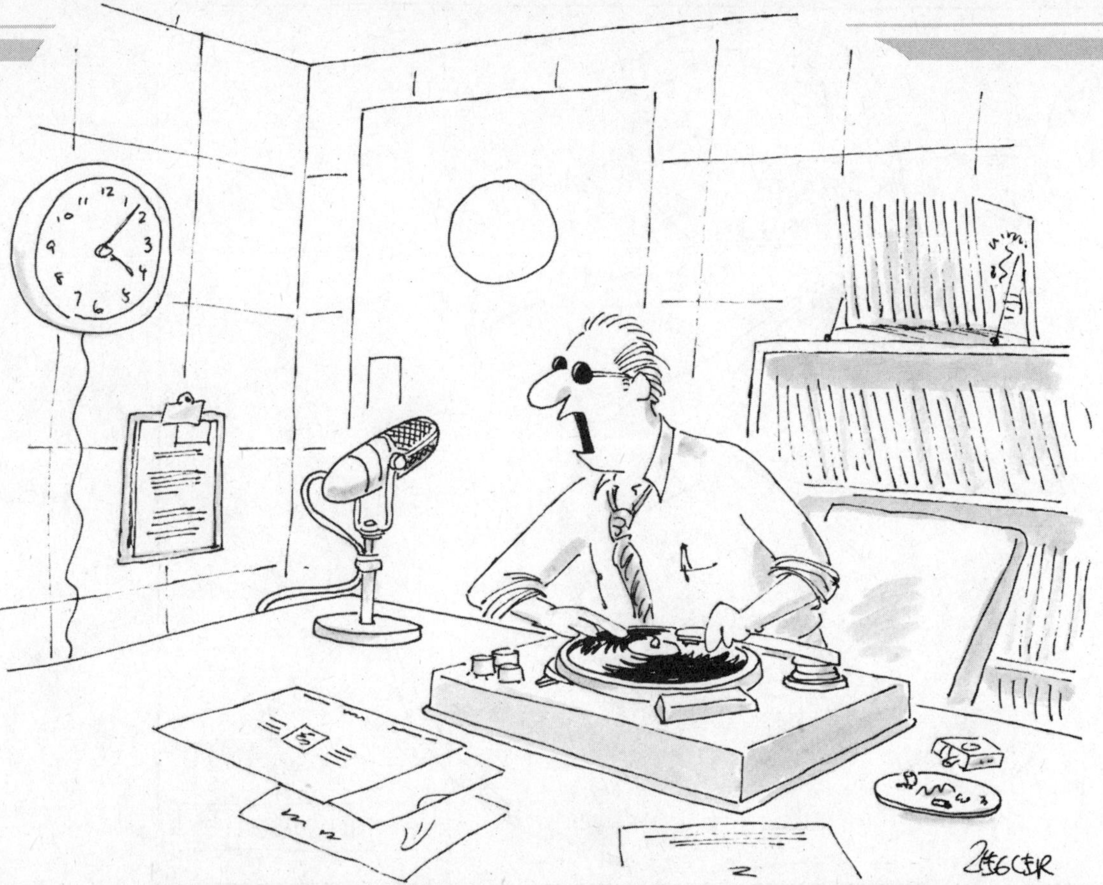

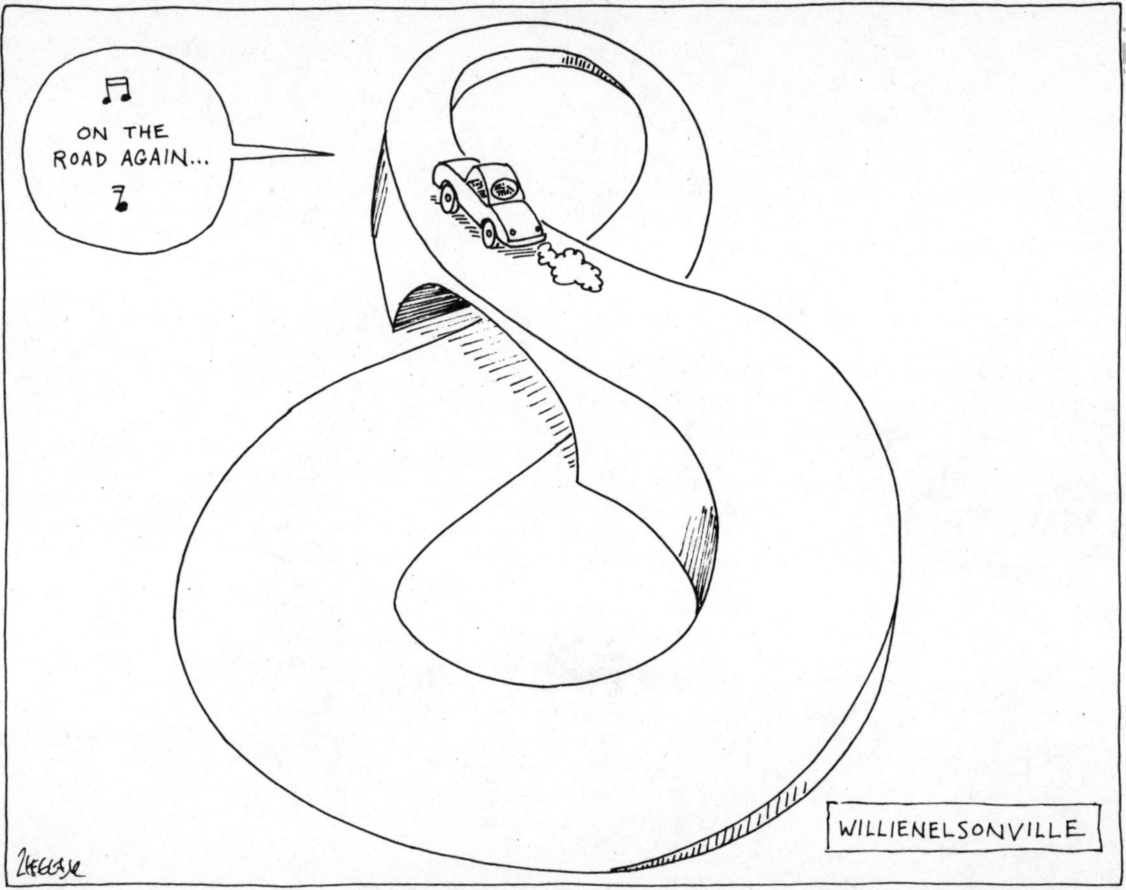
ON THE ROAD AGAIN...
WILLIENELSONVILLE

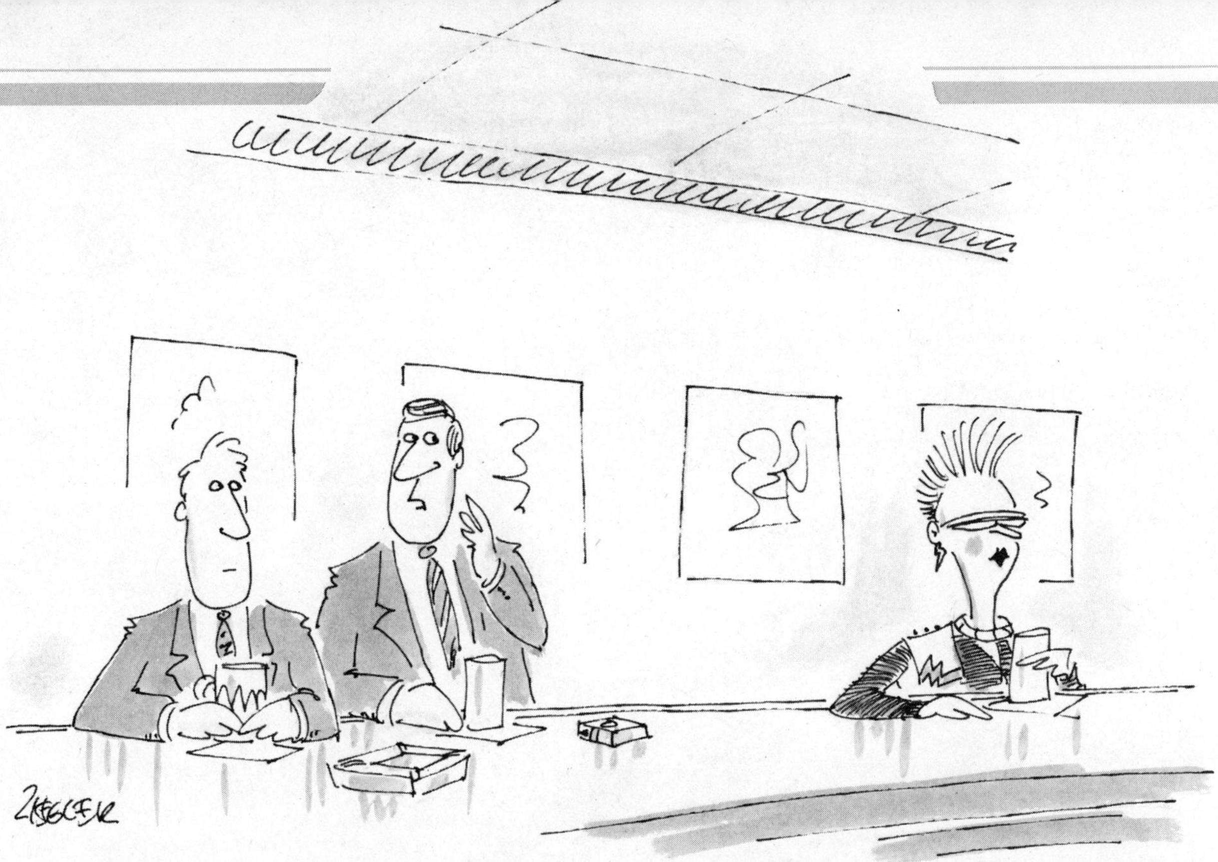

"That's Catherine Deneuve's scent all right, but I don't think that's Catherine Deneuve."

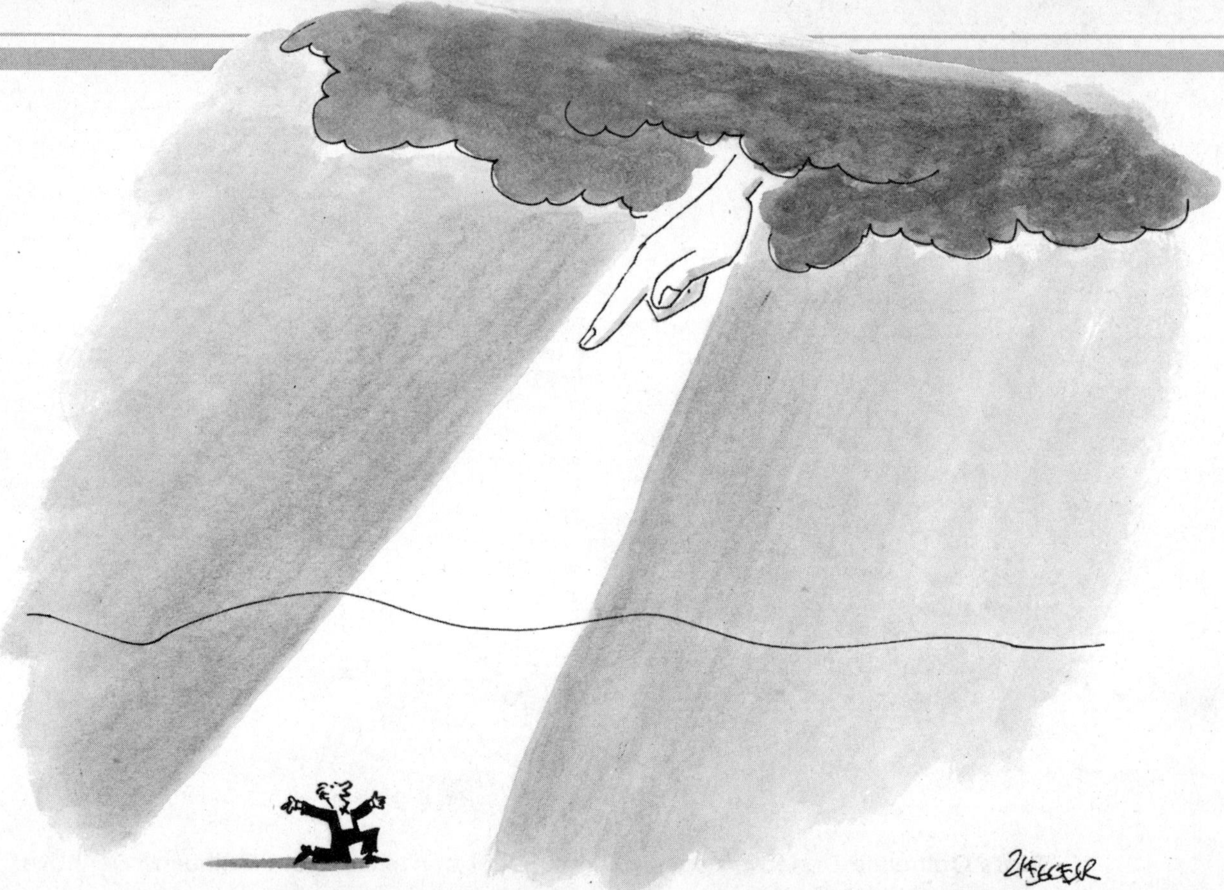

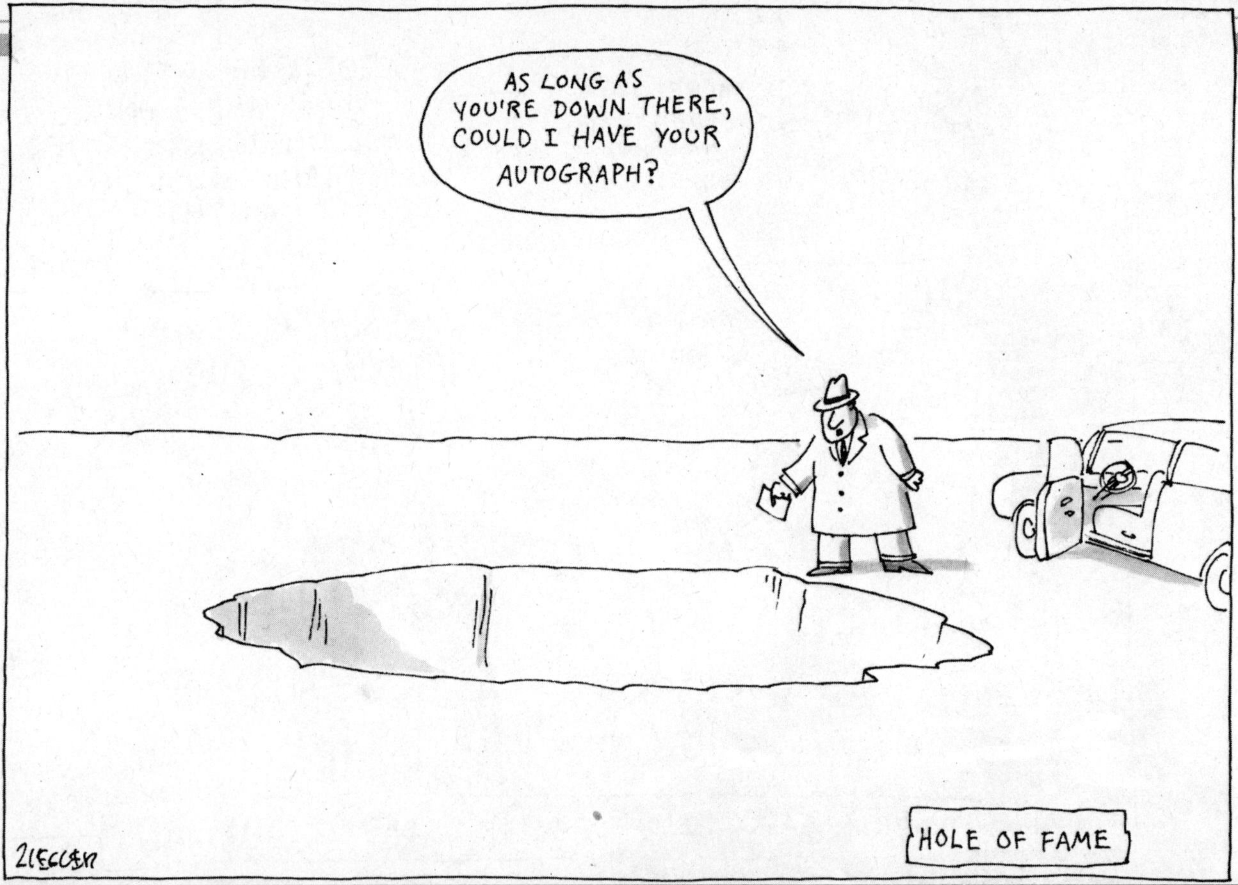
AS LONG AS YOU'RE DOWN THERE, COULD I HAVE YOUR AUTOGRAPH?
HOLE OF FAME
ZIEGLER

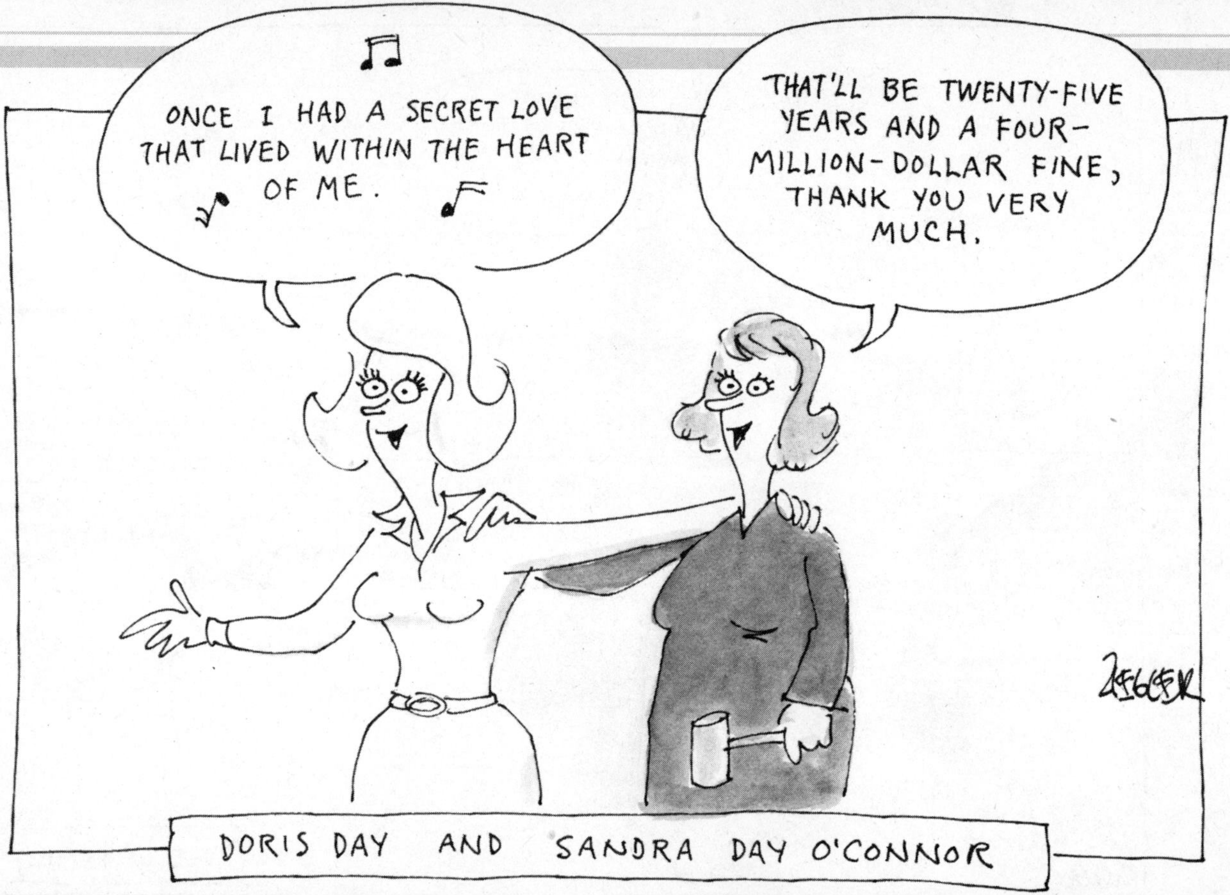
ONCE I HAD A SECRET LOVE THAT LIVED WITHIN THE HEART OF ME.
THAT'LL BE TWENTY-FIVE YEARS AND A FOUR-MILLION-DOLLAR FINE, THANK YOU VERY MUCH.
DORIS DAY AND SANDRA DAY O'CONNOR

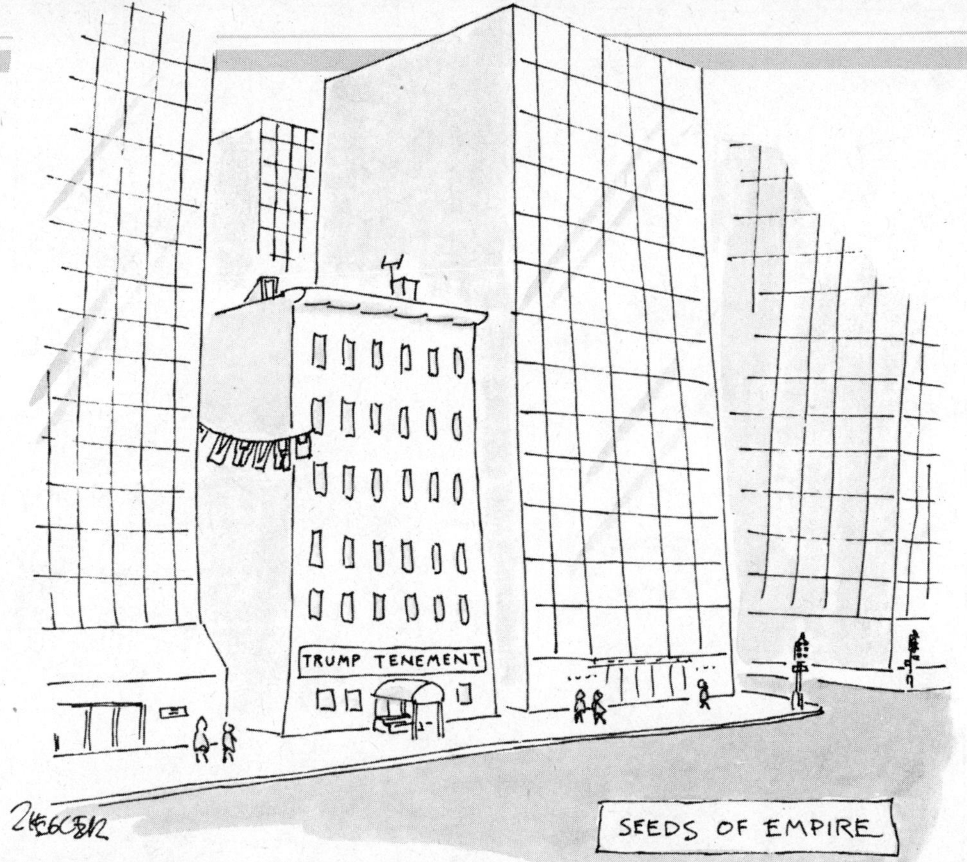
TRUMP TENEMENT
SEEDS OF EMPIRE

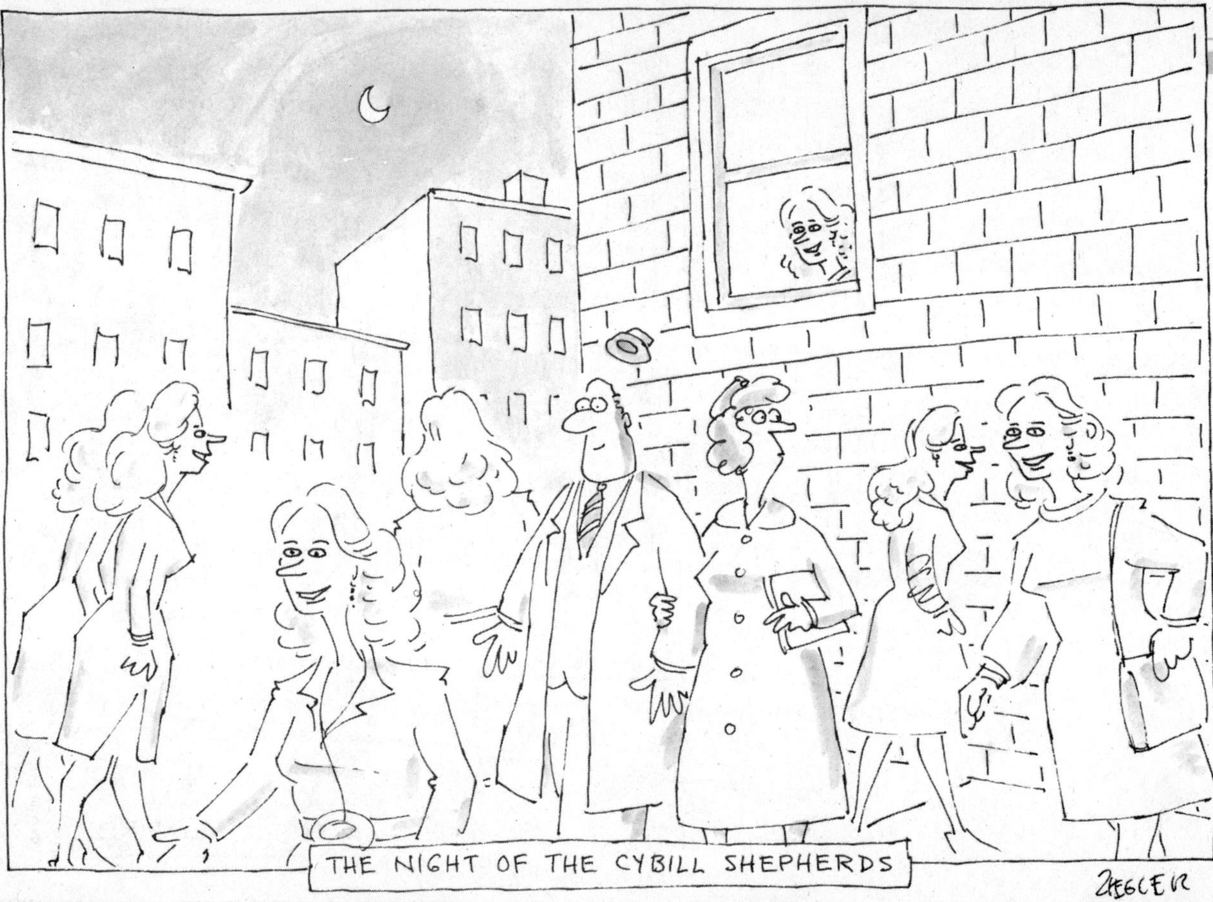
THE NIGHT OF THE CYBILL SHEPHERDS
ZIEGLER

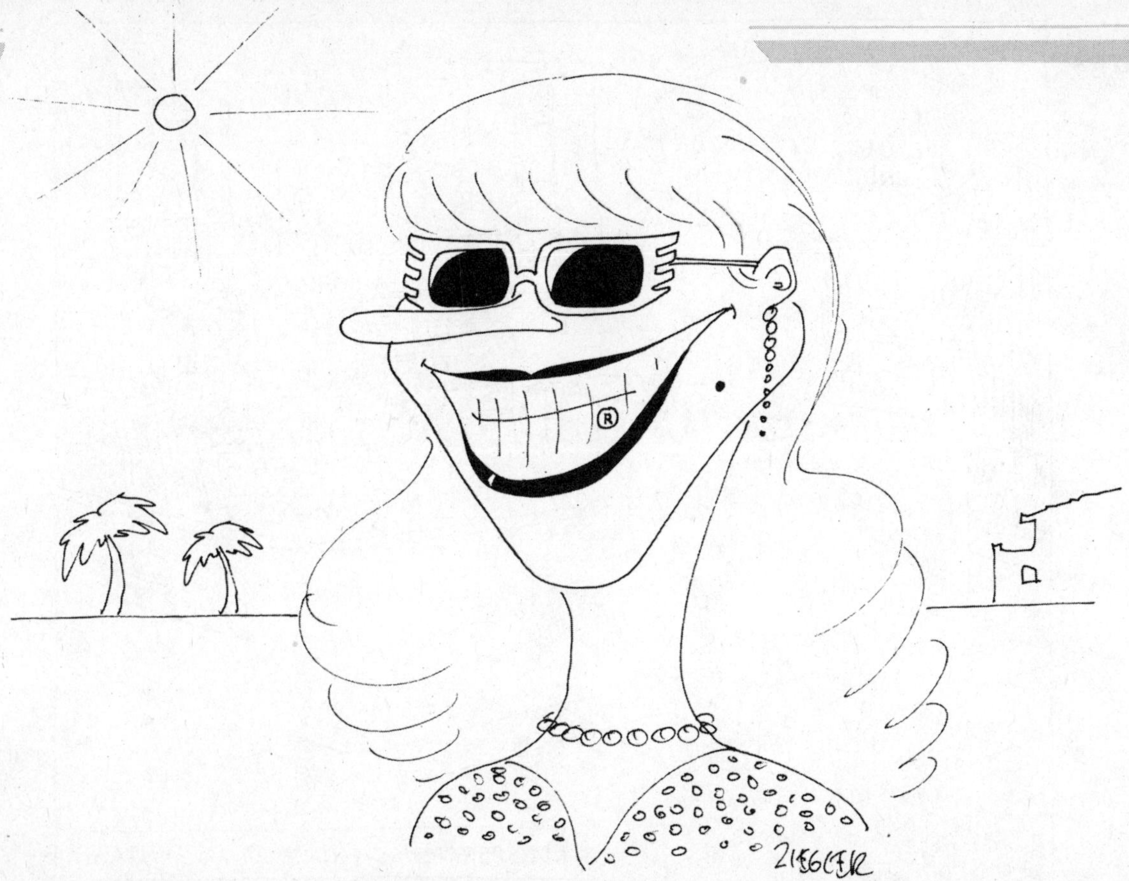

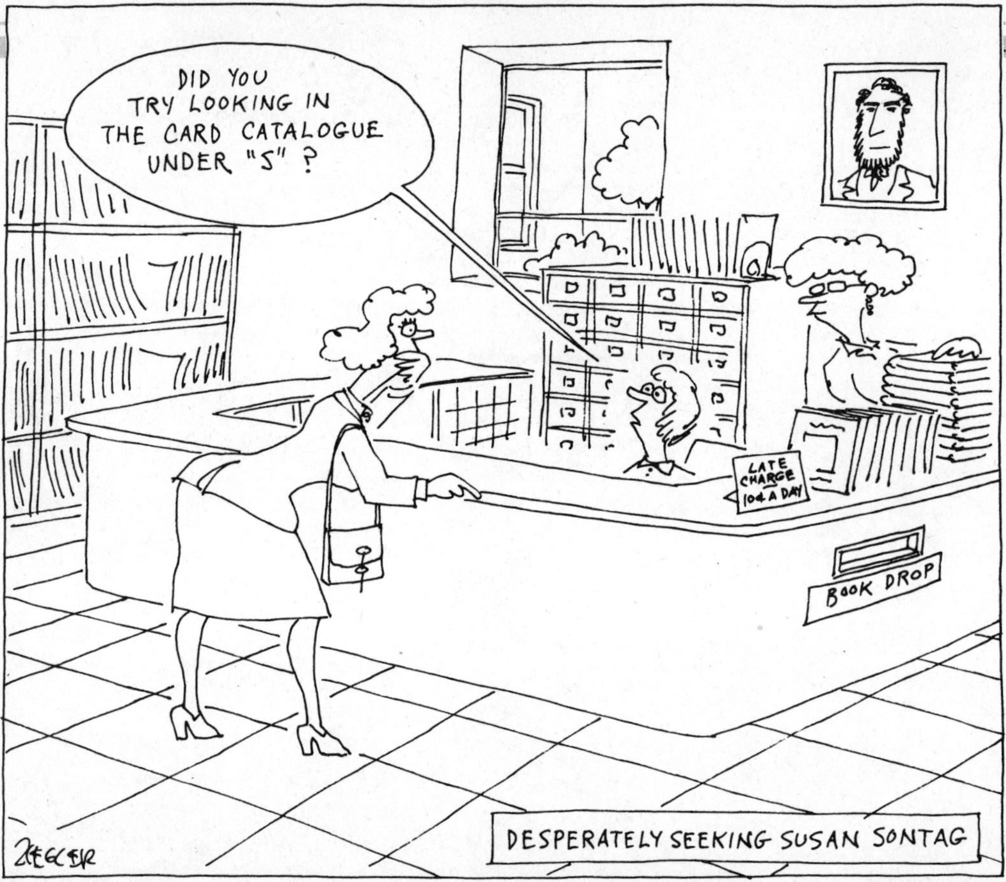
DID YOU TRY LOOKING IN THE CARD CATALOGUE UNDER "S" ?
LATE CHARGE 10¢ A DAY
BOOK DROP
DESPERATELY SEEKING SUSAN SONTAG

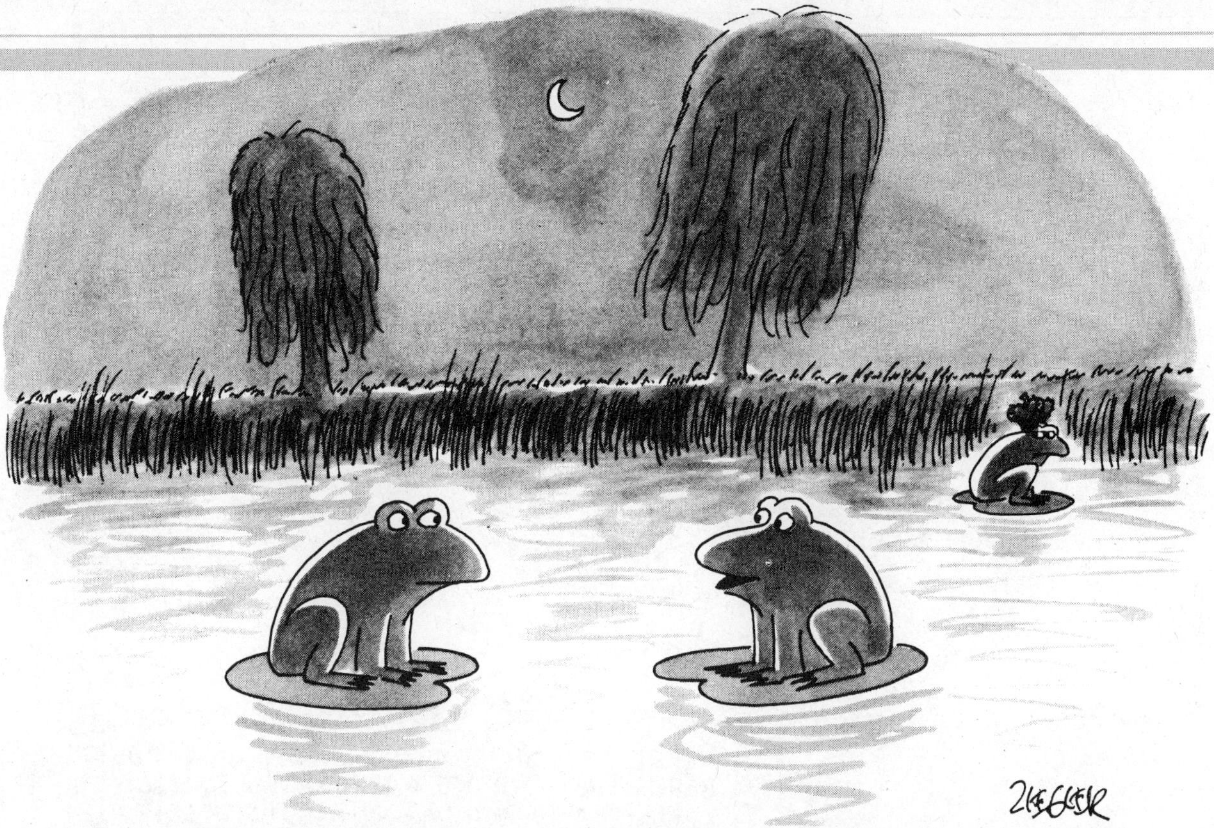

"I'm a frog. You're a frog. Hell, we're all frogs. Except, of course, for Prince Charming over there."

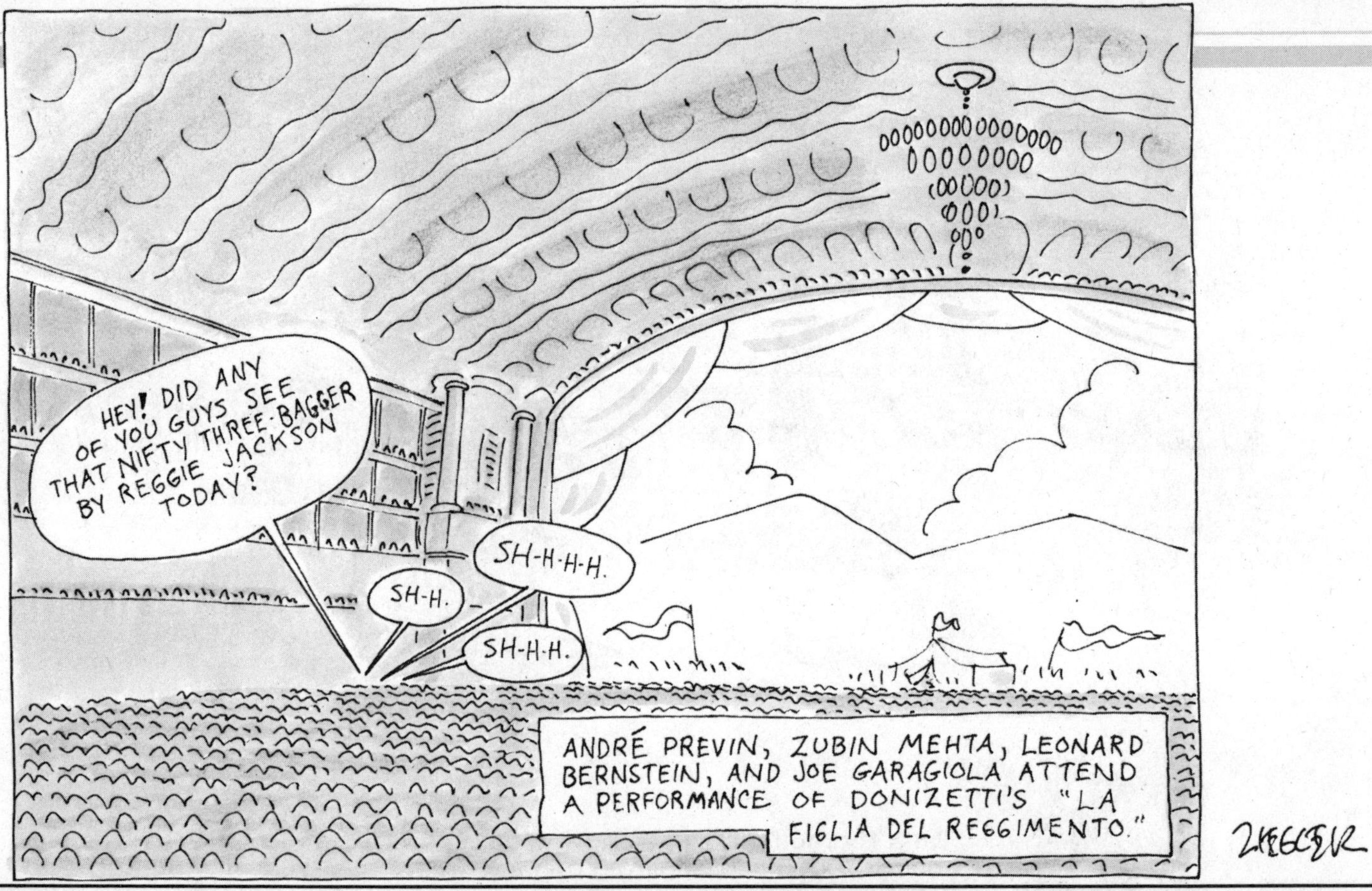
HEY! DID ANY OF YOU GUYS SEE THAT NIFTY THREE-BAGGER BY REGGIE JACKSON TODAY?
SH-H-H-H.
SH-H.
SH-H-H.
ANDRÉ PREVIN, ZUBIN MEHTA, LEONARD BERNSTEIN, AND JOE GARAGIOLA ATTEND A PERFORMANCE OF DONIZETTI'S "LA FIGLIA DEL REGGIMENTO."

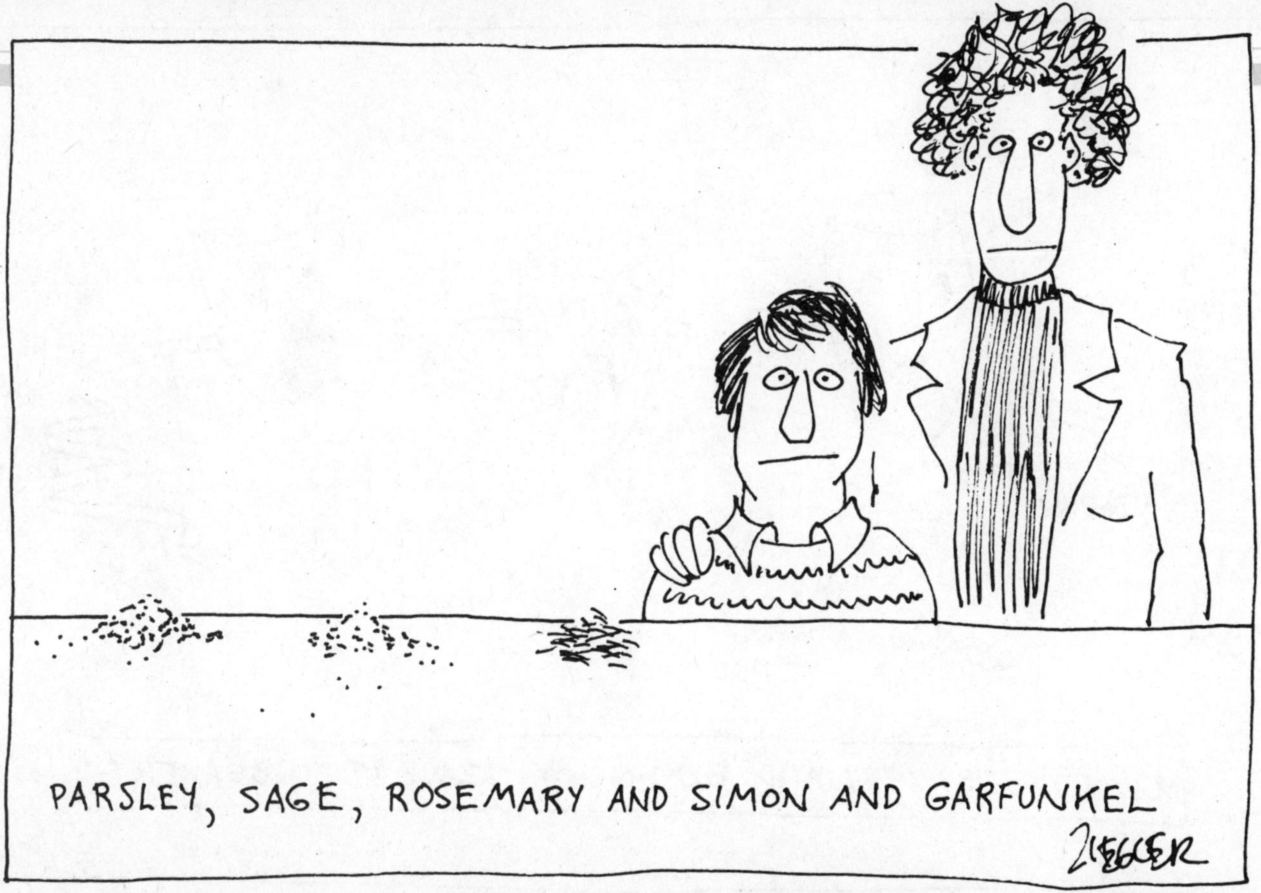
PARSLEY, SAGE, ROSEMARY AND SIMON AND GARFUNKEL
ZIEGLER

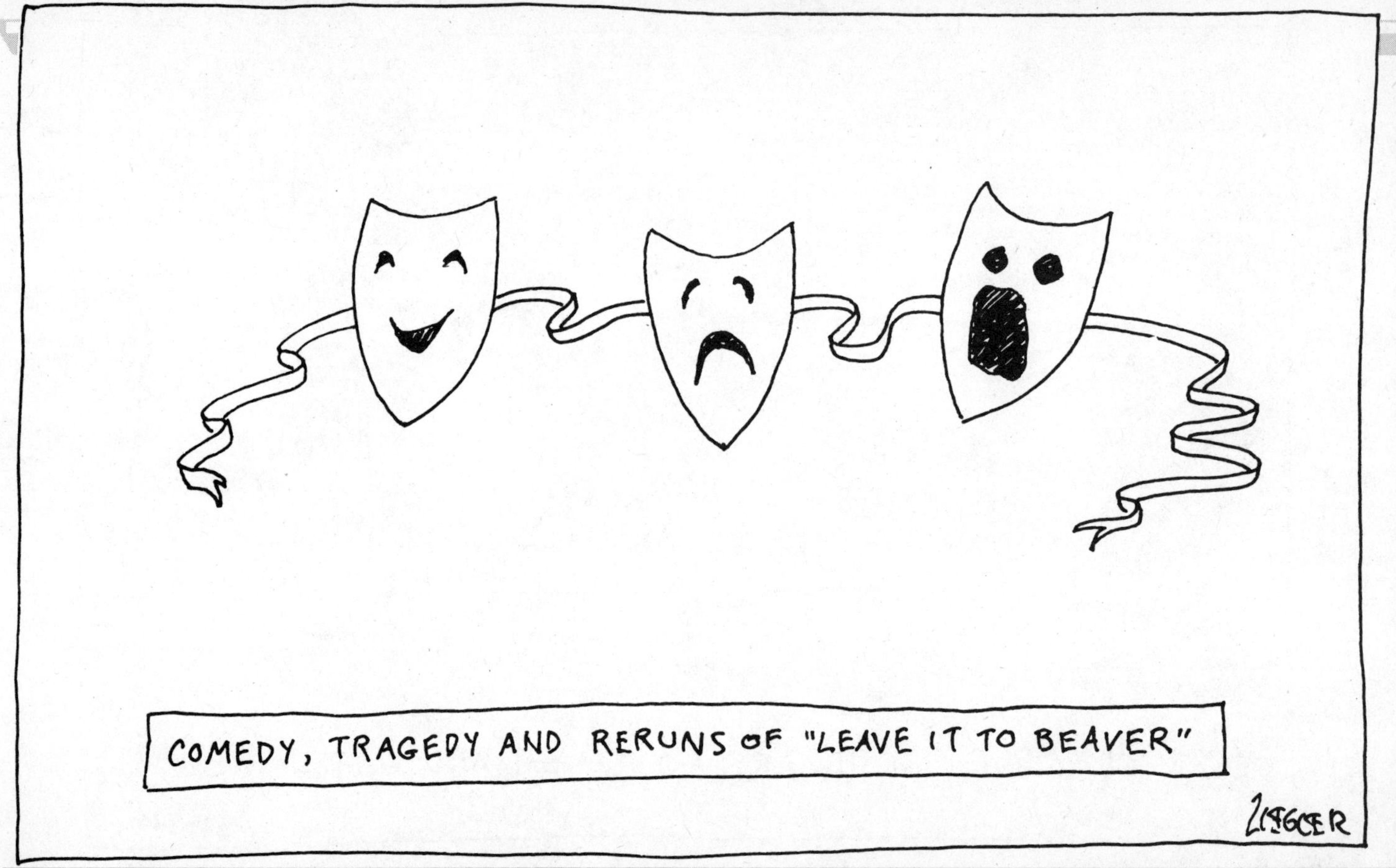
COMEDY, TRAGEDY AND RERUNS OF "LEAVE IT TO BEAVER"
ZIEGLER

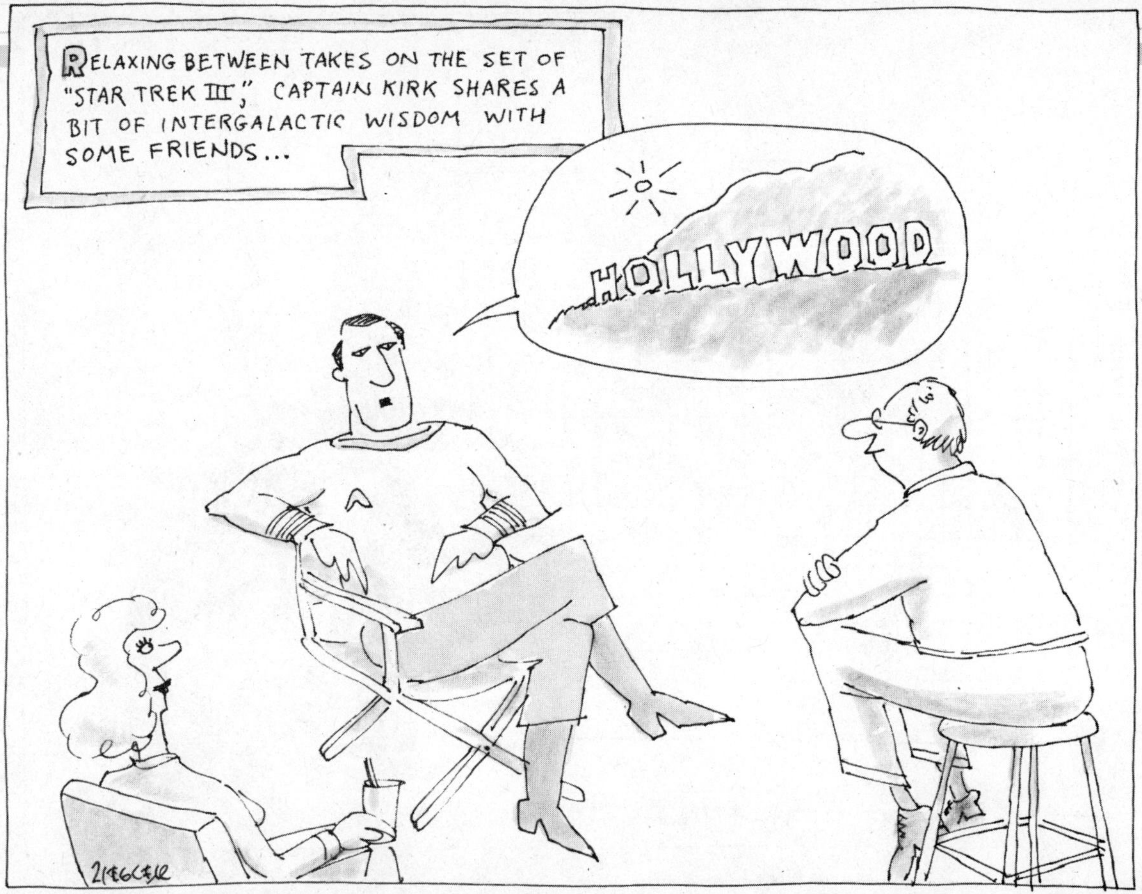
RELAXING BETWEEN TAKES ON THE SET OF "STAR TREK III," CAPTAIN KIRK SHARES A BIT OF INTERGALACTIC WISDOM WITH SOME FRIENDS...
HOLLYWOOD
ZIEGLER

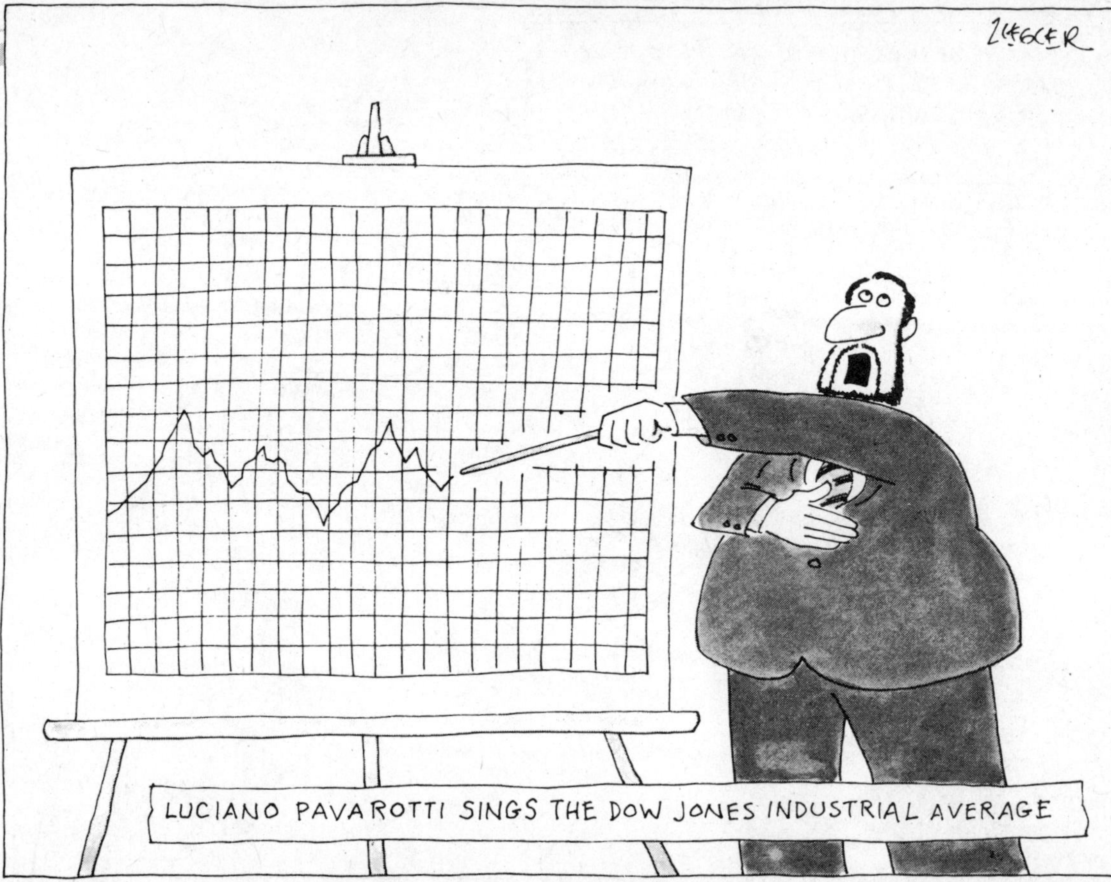
LUCIANO PAVAROTTI SINGS THE DOW JONES INDUSTRIAL AVERAGE

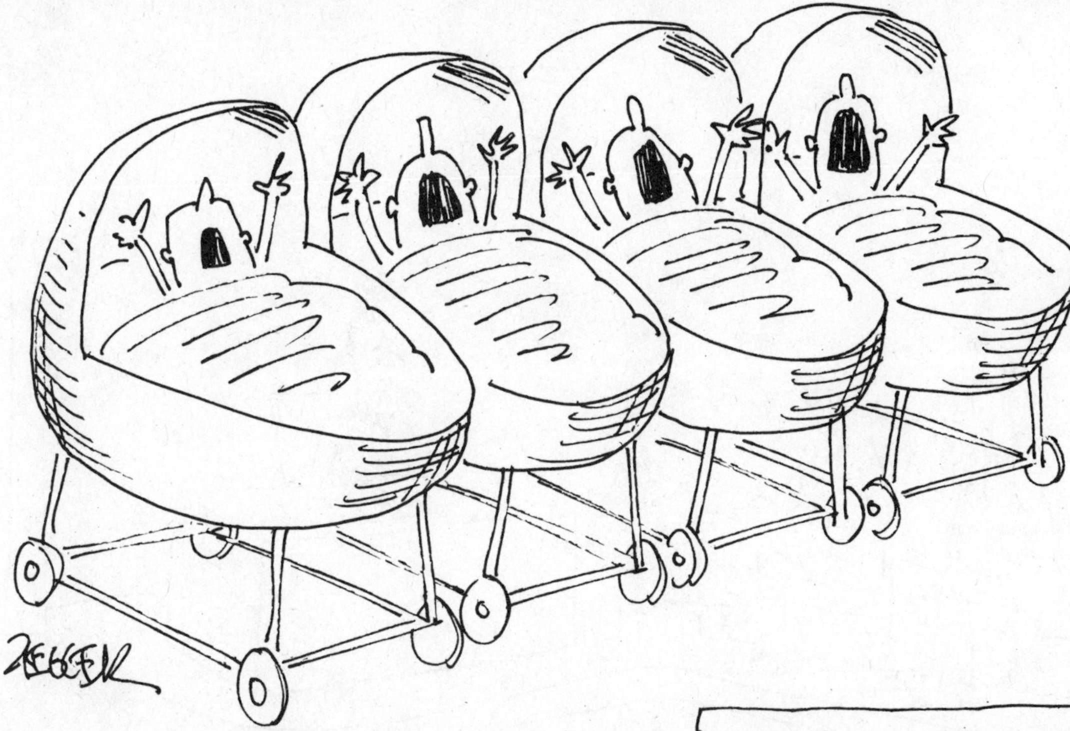

VERY EARLY BEATLES

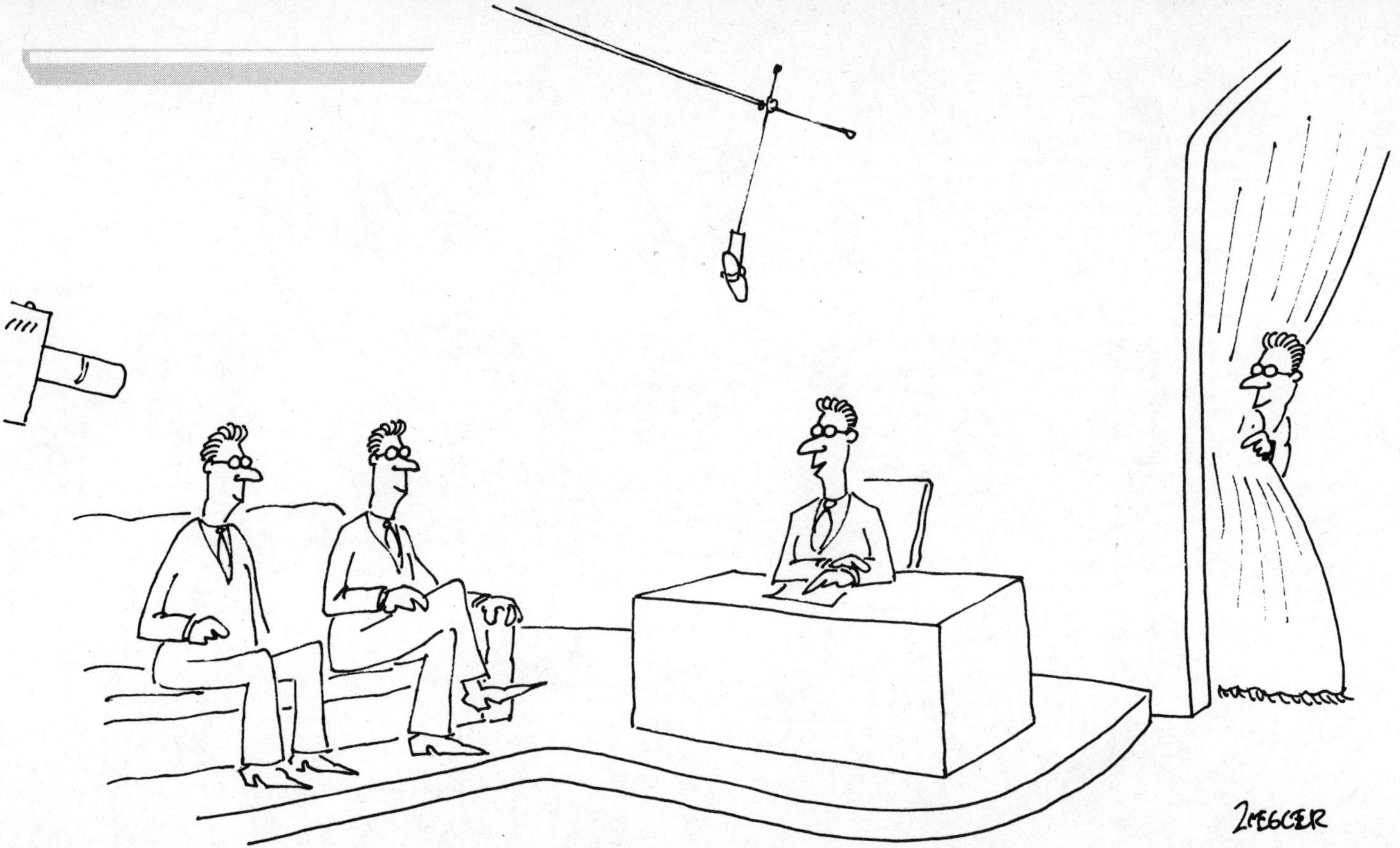
ZIEGLER

"My next guest is a man who needs no introduction."

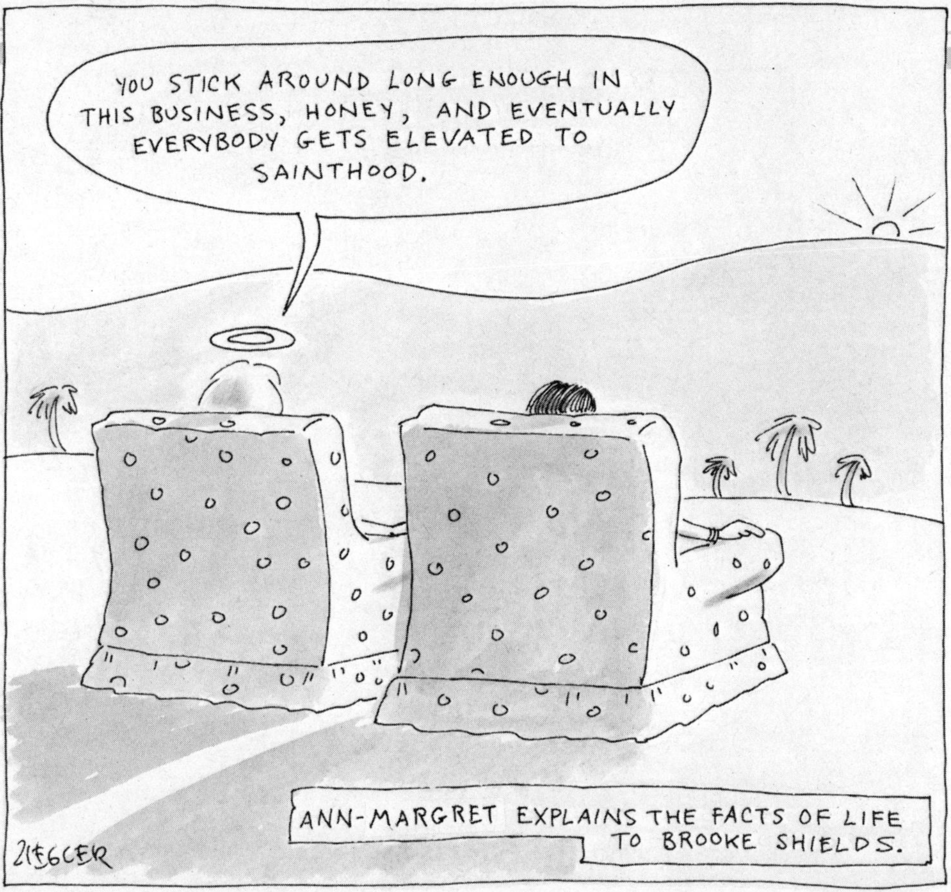
YOU STICK AROUND LONG ENOUGH IN THIS BUSINESS, HONEY, AND EVENTUALLY EVERYBODY GETS ELEVATED TO SAINTHOOD.
ANN-MARGRET EXPLAINS THE FACTS OF LIFE TO BROOKE SHIELDS.
ZIEGLER

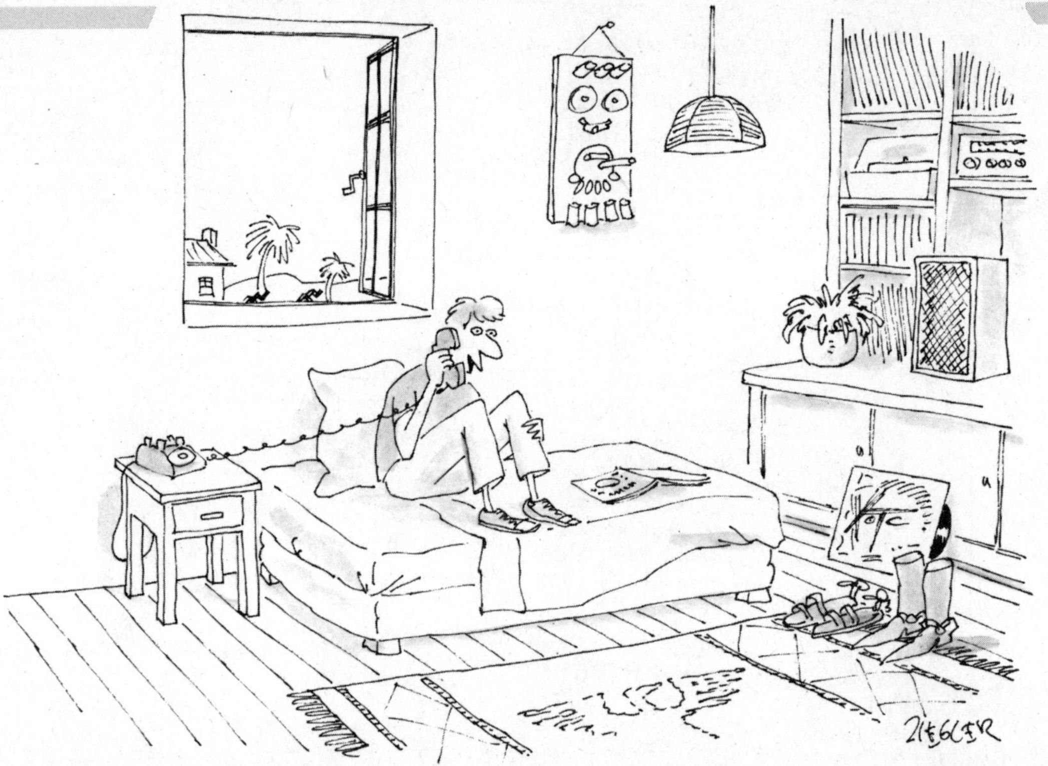

"It's all very exciting, Mom. I'm on a first-name basis with Cher."

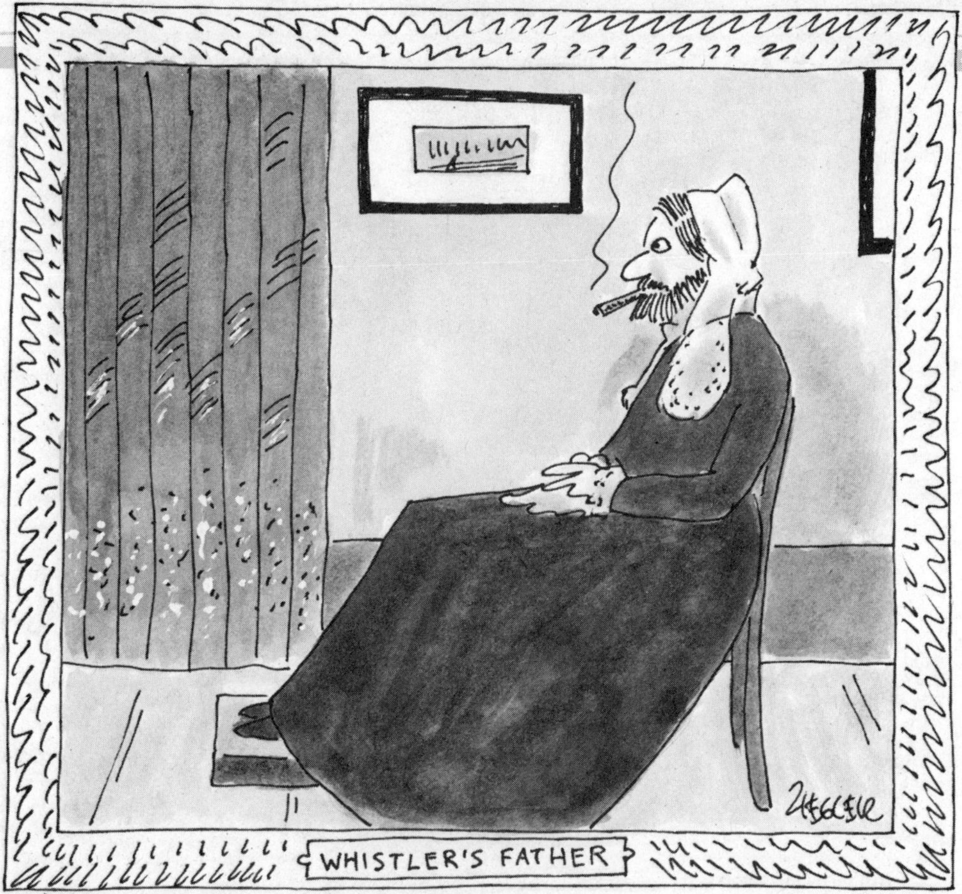
WHISTLER'S FATHER

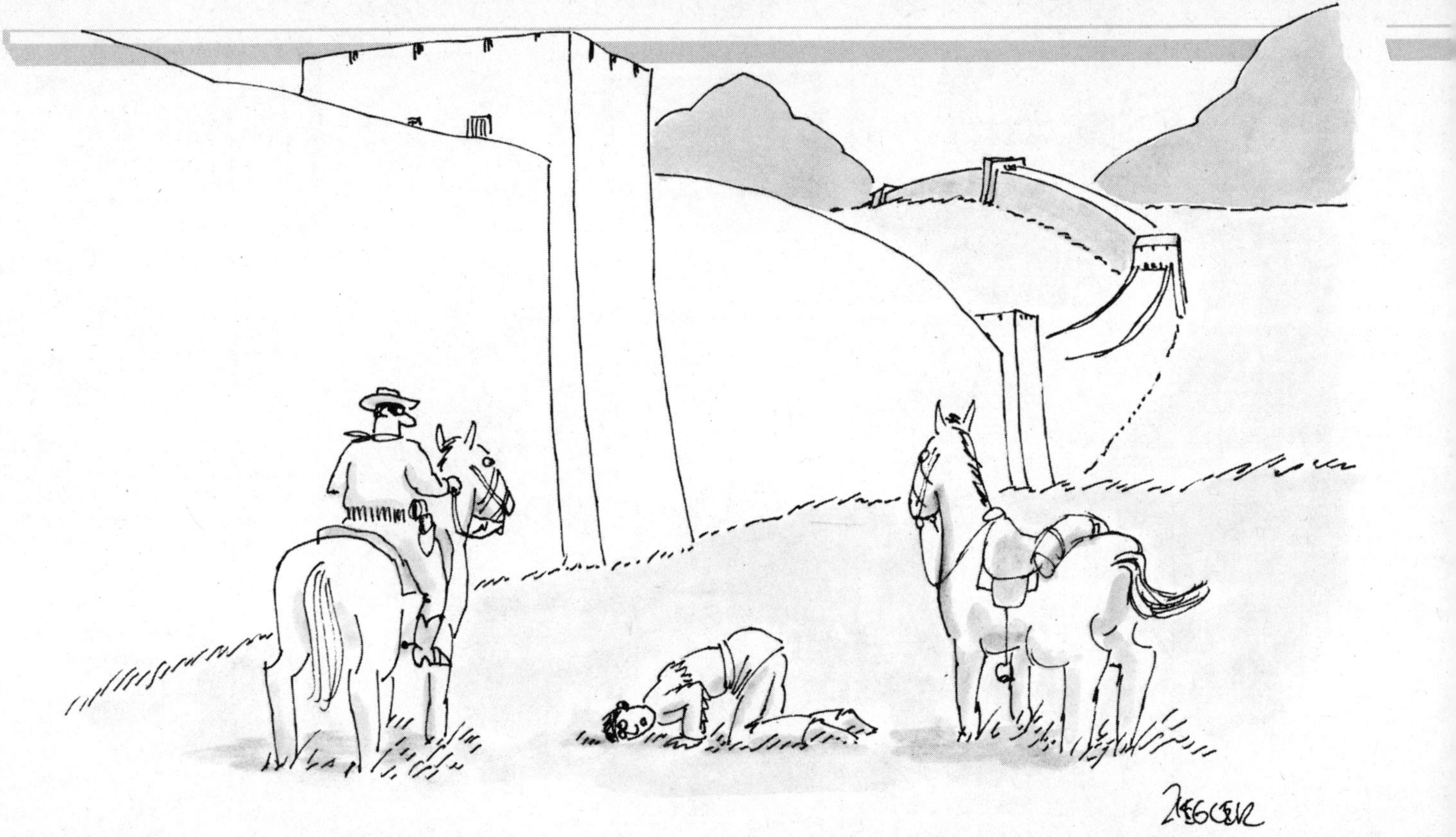
ZIEGLER

"Chinese, Kemo-sabe! Billions of them!"

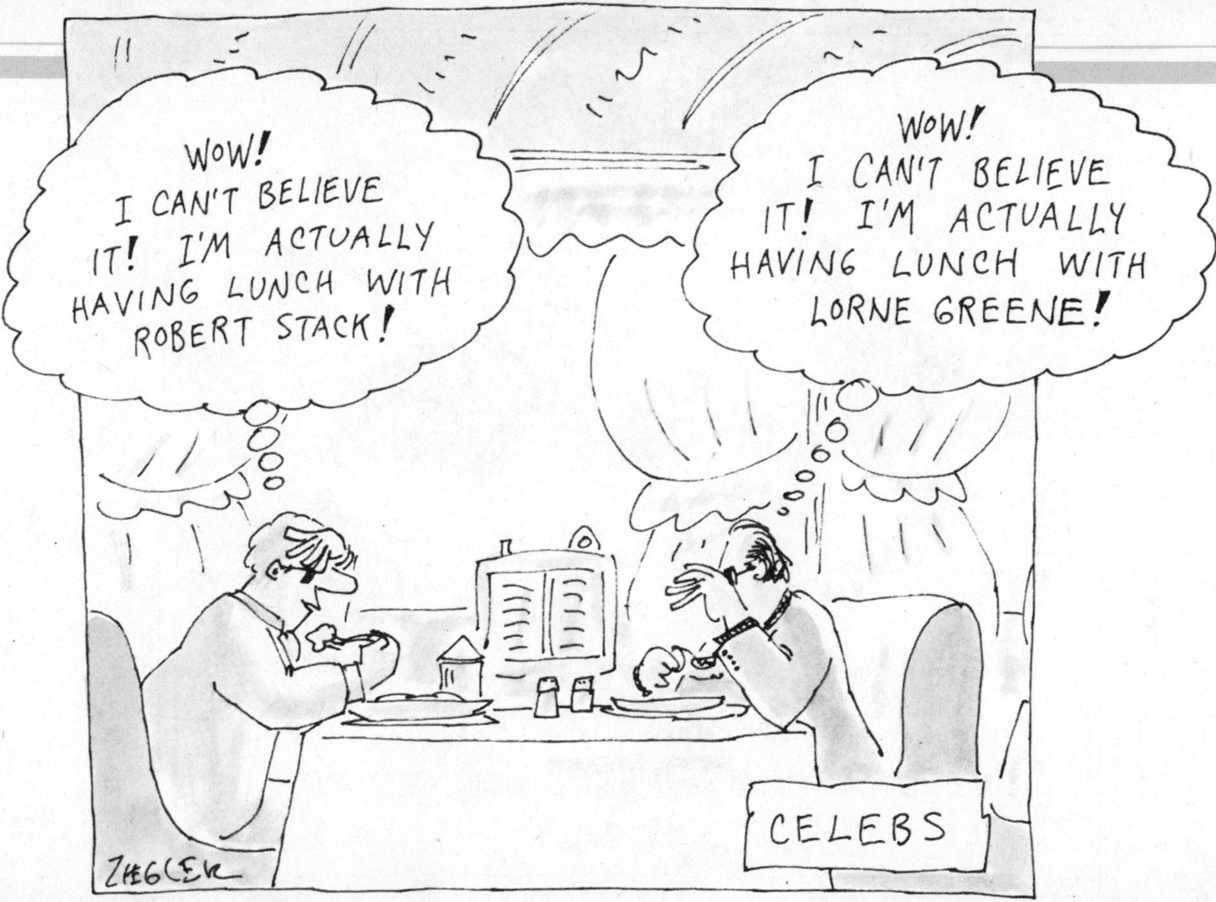
WOW!
I CAN'T BELIEVE IT! I'M ACTUALLY HAVING LUNCH WITH ROBERT STACK!
WOW!
I CAN'T BELIEVE IT! I'M ACTUALLY HAVING LUNCH WITH LORNE GREENE!
CELEBS
ZIEGLER

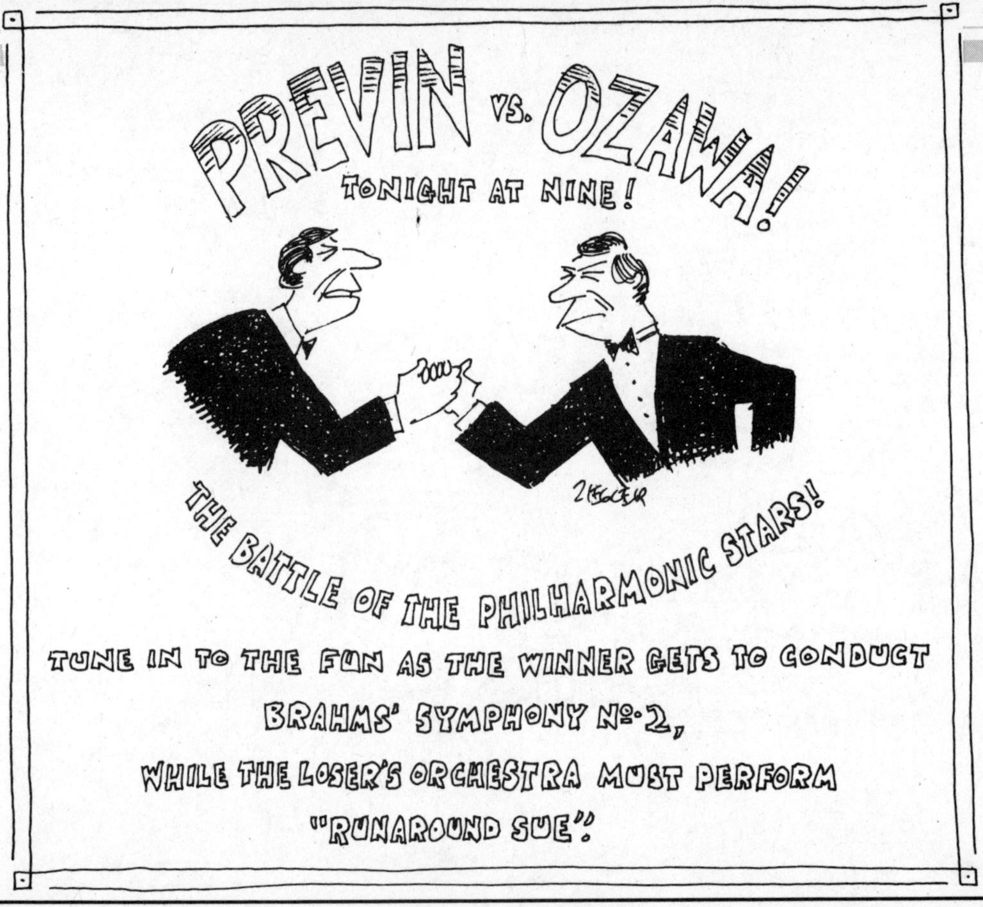
PREVIN VS. OZAWA!
TONIGHT AT NINE!
THE BATTLE OF THE PHILHARMONIC STARS!
TUNE IN TO THE FUN AS THE WINNER GETS TO CONDUCT
BRAHMS' SYMPHONY NO. 2,
WHILE THE LOSER'S ORCHESTRA MUST PERFORM
"RUNAROUND SUE"!

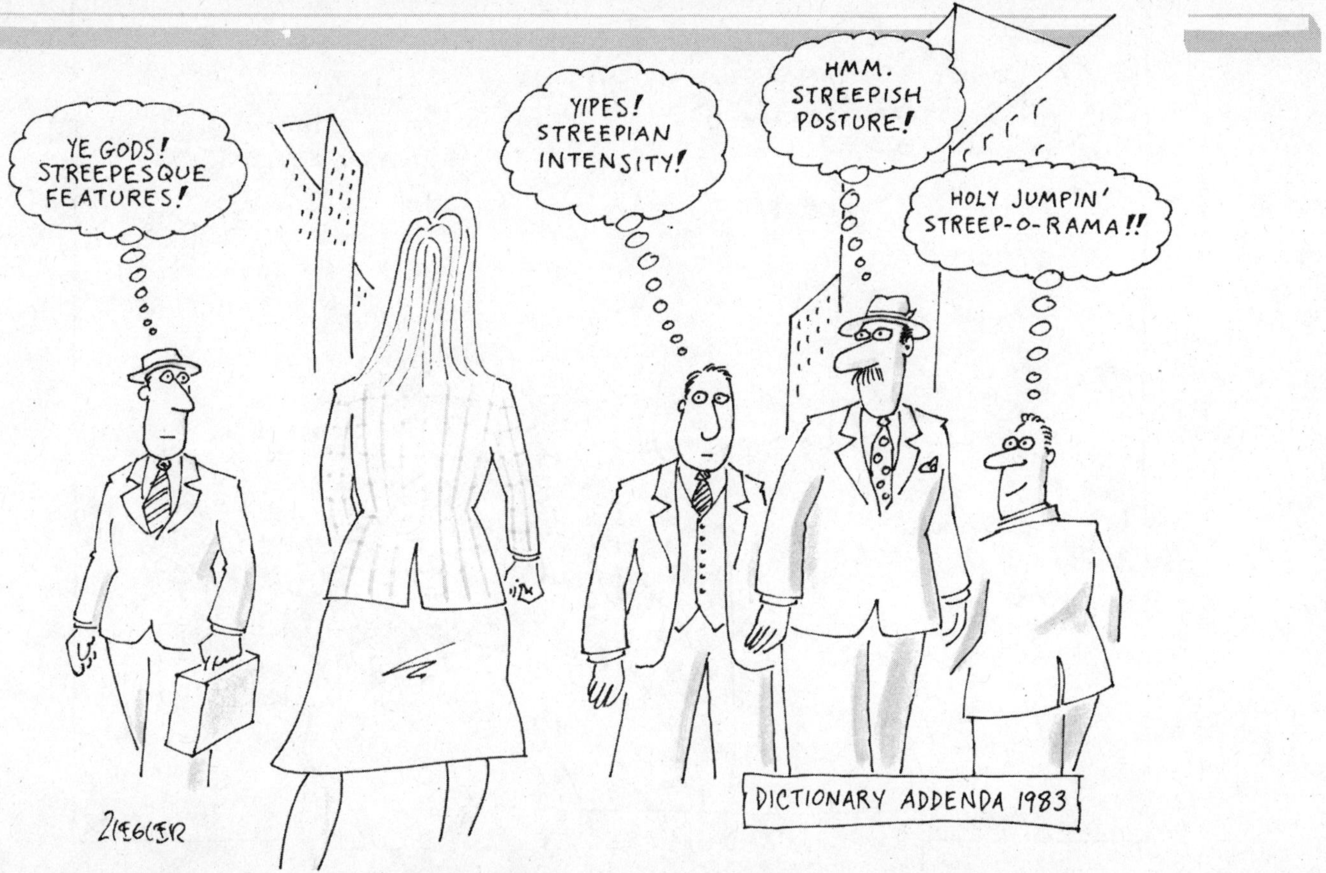
YE GODS! STREEPESQUE FEATURES!
YIPES! STREEPIAN INTENSITY!
HMM. STREEPISH POSTURE!
HOLY JUMPIN' STREEP-O-RAMA!!
DICTIONARY ADDENDA 1983
ZIEGLER

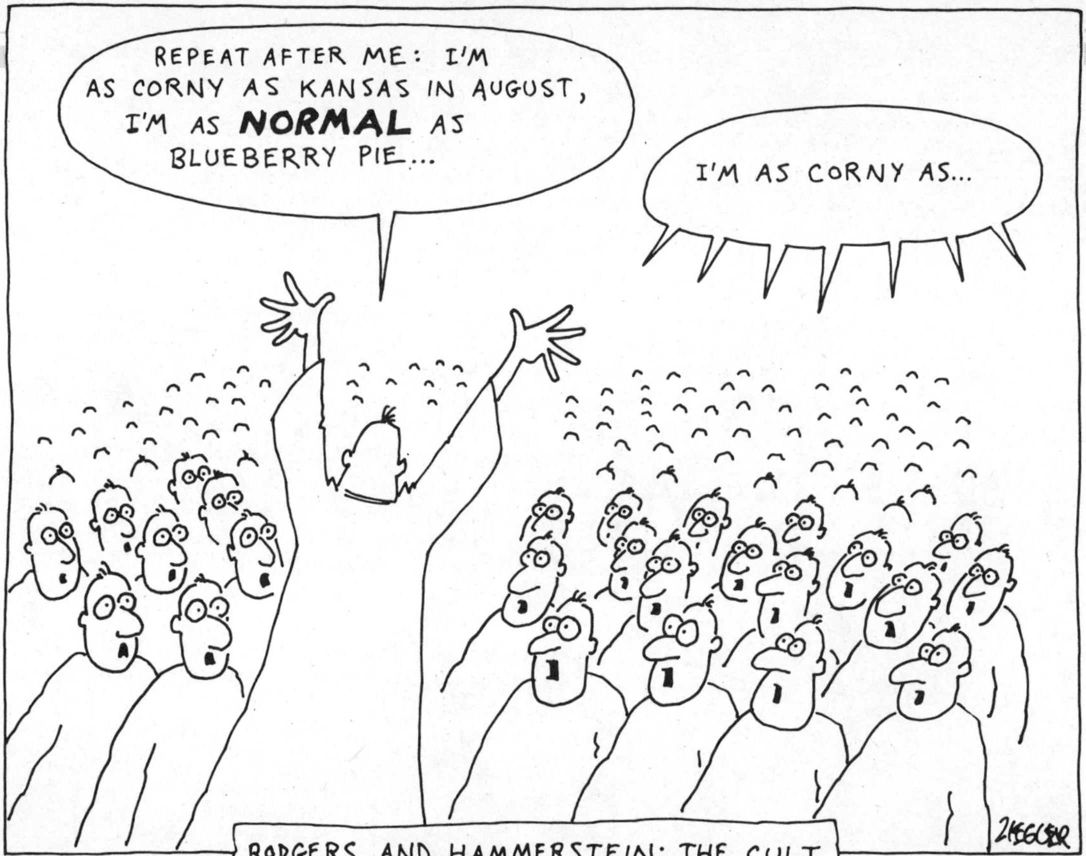
REPEAT AFTER ME: I'M AS CORNY AS KANSAS IN AUGUST, I'M AS **NORMAL** AS BLUEBERRY PIE...
I'M AS CORNY AS...
ZIEGLER

RODGERS AND HAMMERSTEIN: THE CULT

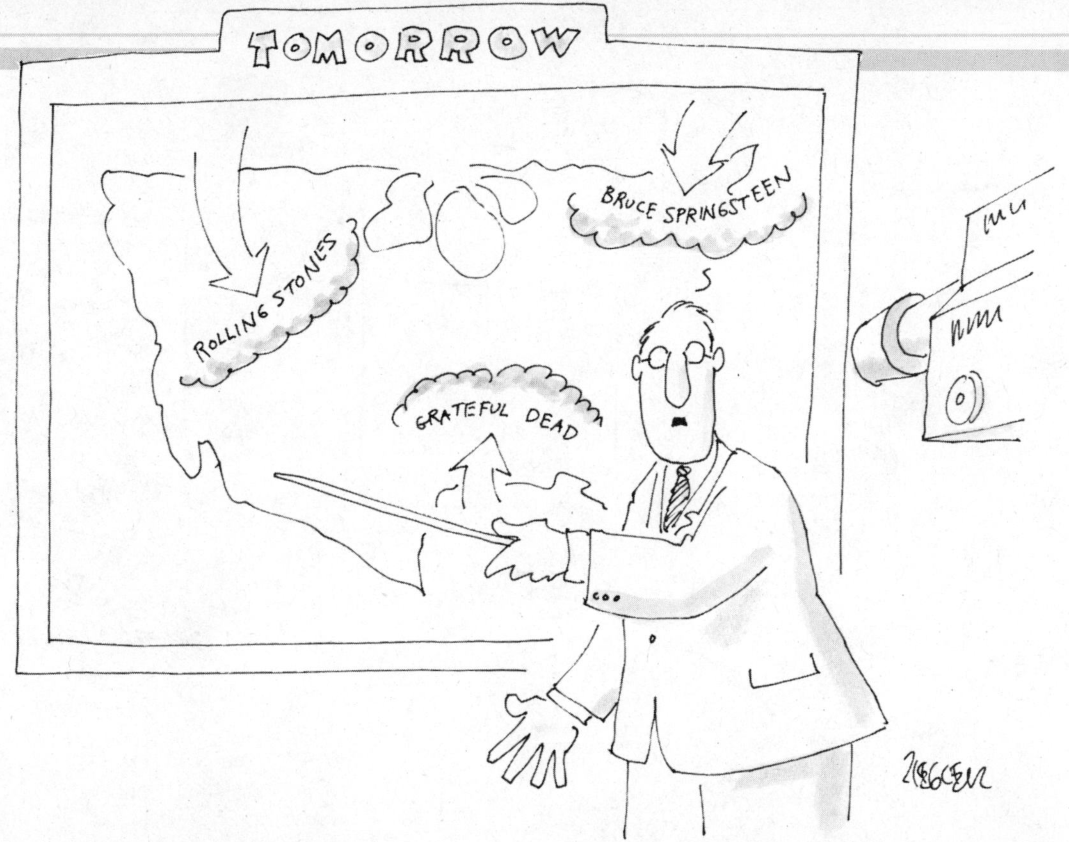
TOMORROW
ROLLING STONES
BRUCE SPRINGSTEEN
GRATEFUL DEAD

"I'm afraid I don't have very good news for all you opera lovers out there."

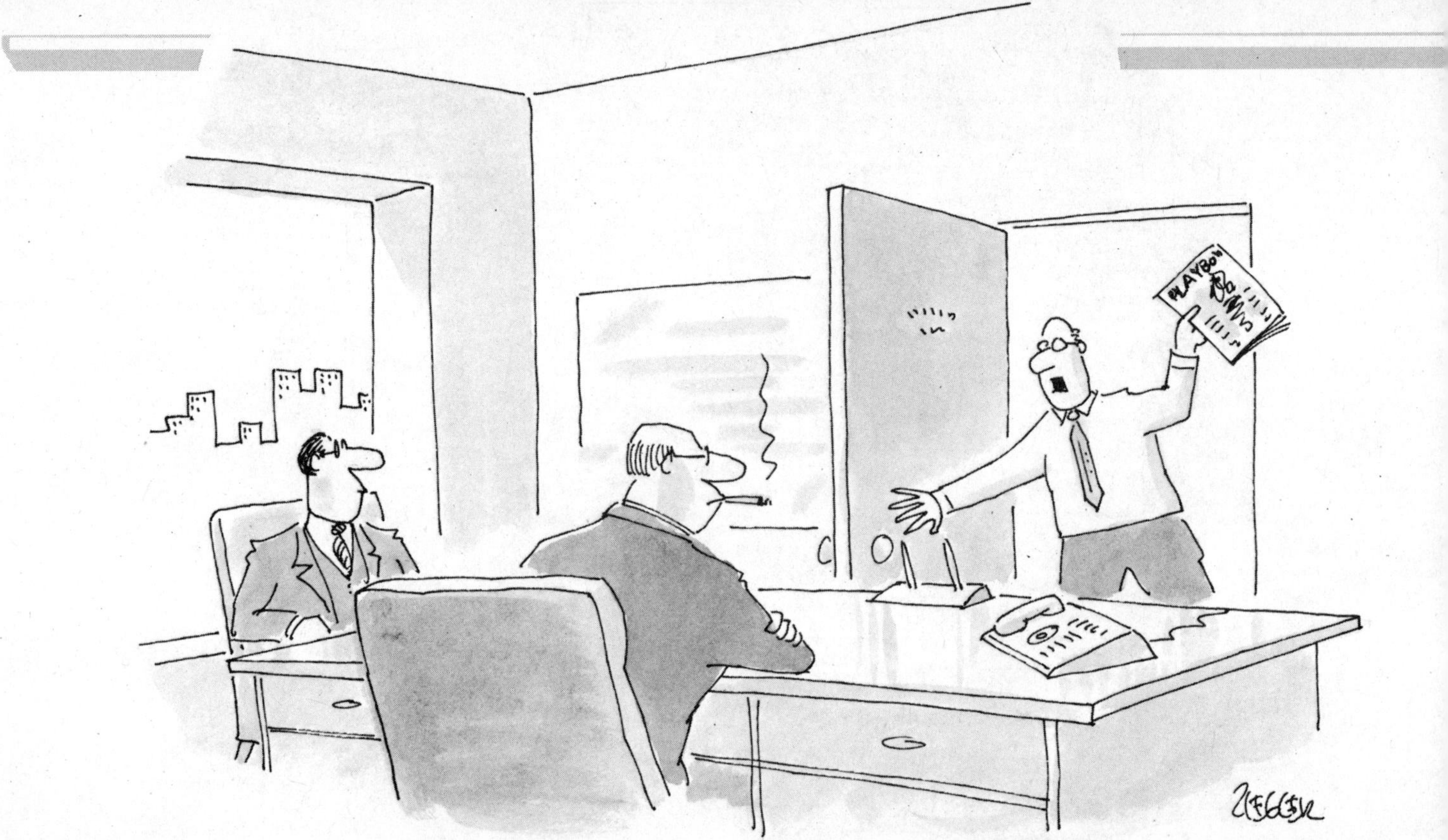
PLAYBOY

"Bad news, boss. The latest issue of *Playboy.* Nude photos of the whole damned accounting department."

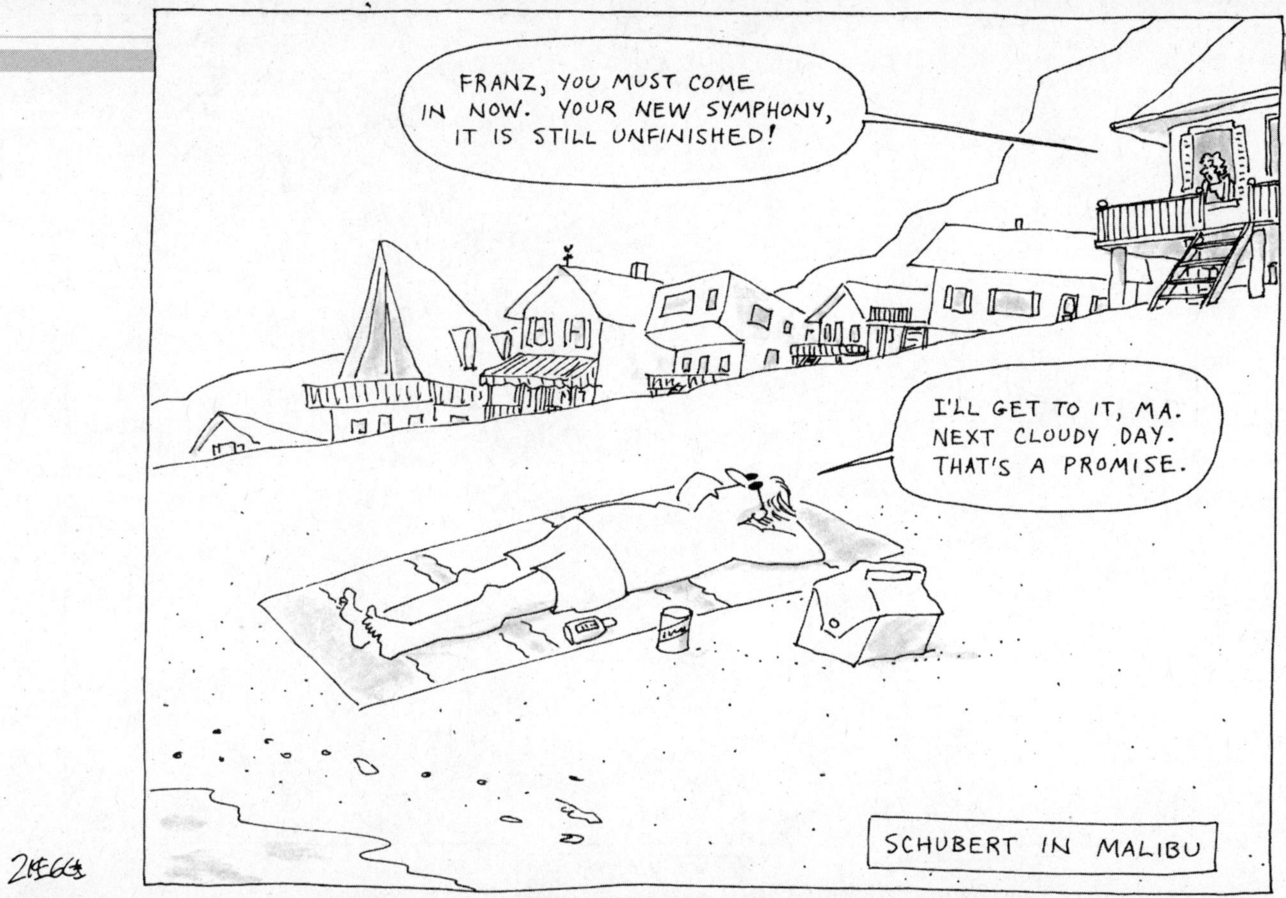
FRANZ, YOU MUST COME IN NOW. YOUR NEW SYMPHONY, IT IS STILL UNFINISHED!
I'LL GET TO IT, MA. NEXT CLOUDY DAY. THAT'S A PROMISE.

SCHUBERT IN MALIBU

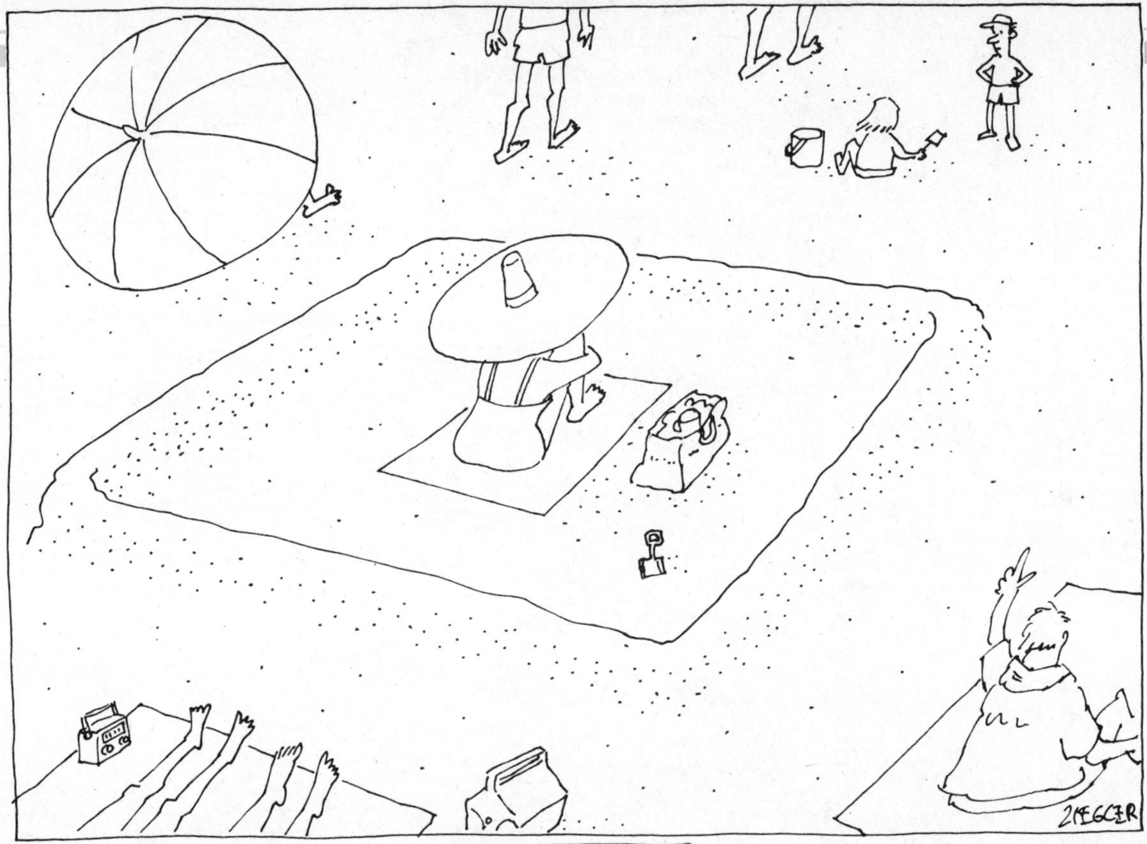
ZIEGLER

GARBO AT CONEY

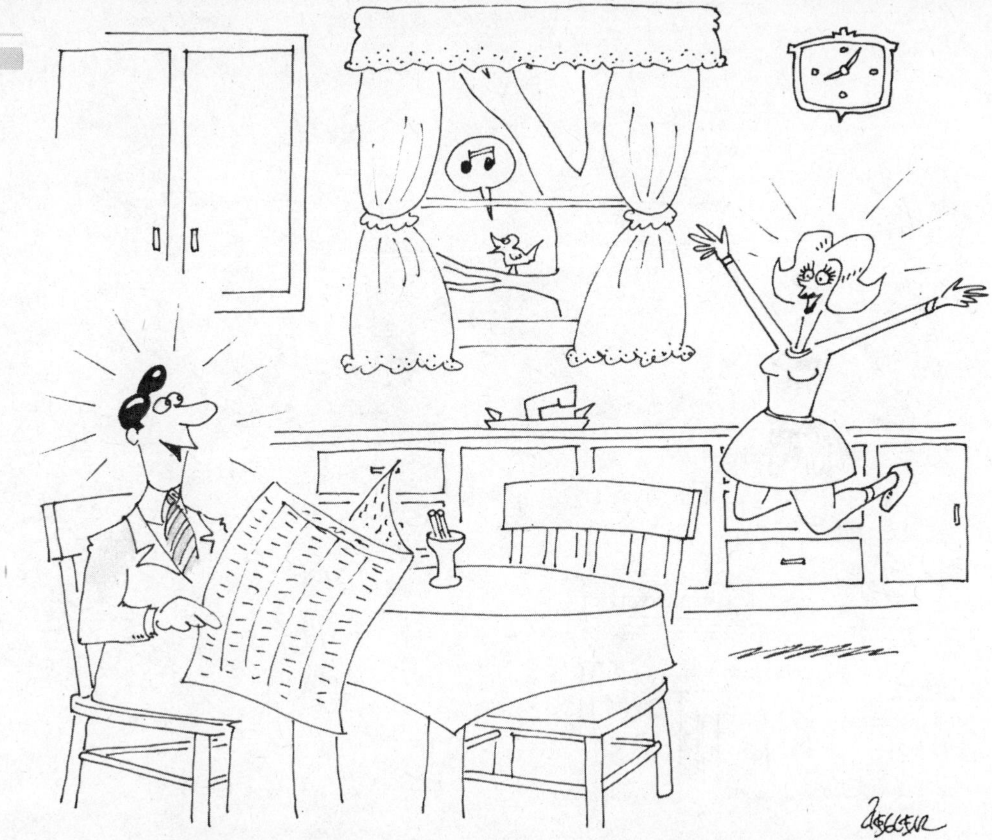

"Jeepers, honey, my Donny Osmond stock is doing just neat-o!"

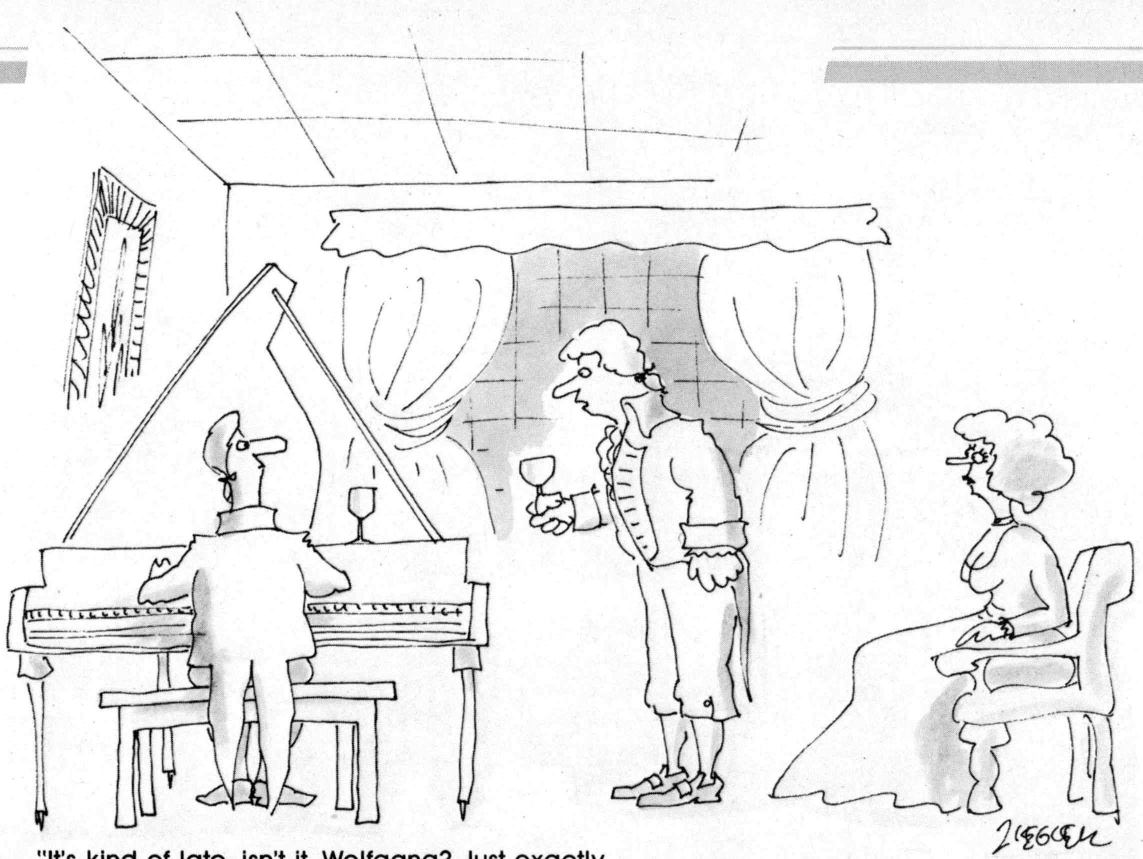

"It's kind of late, isn't it, Wolfgang? Just exactly how Kleine is this Nachtmusik going to be?"

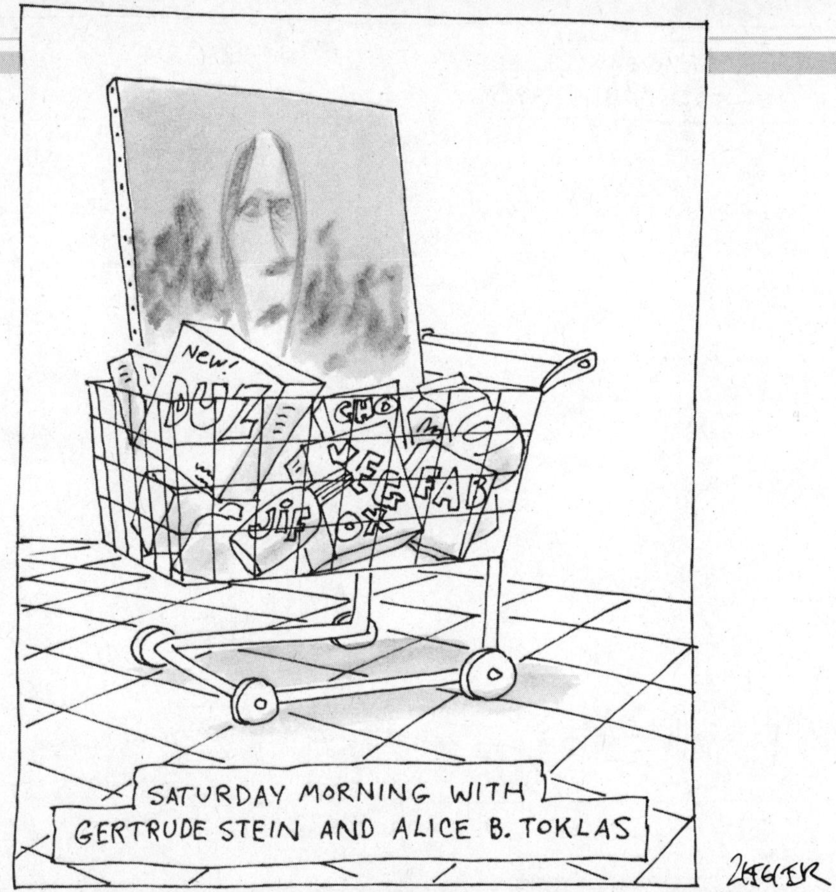
New!
DUZ
CHO
VEG
FAB
JIF
OX
SATURDAY MORNING WITH
GERTRUDE STEIN AND ALICE B. TOKLAS
ZIEGLER

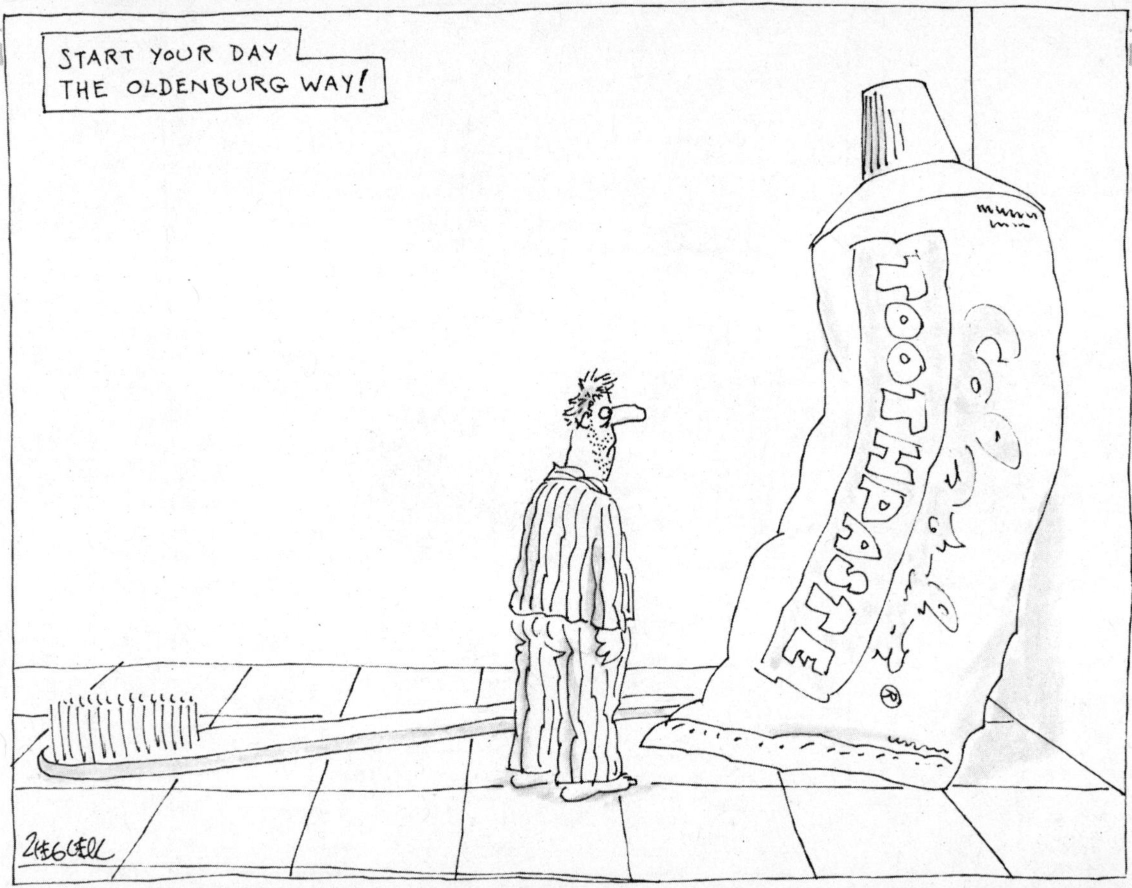
START YOUR DAY
THE OLDENBURG WAY!
TOOTHPASTE
ZIEGLER

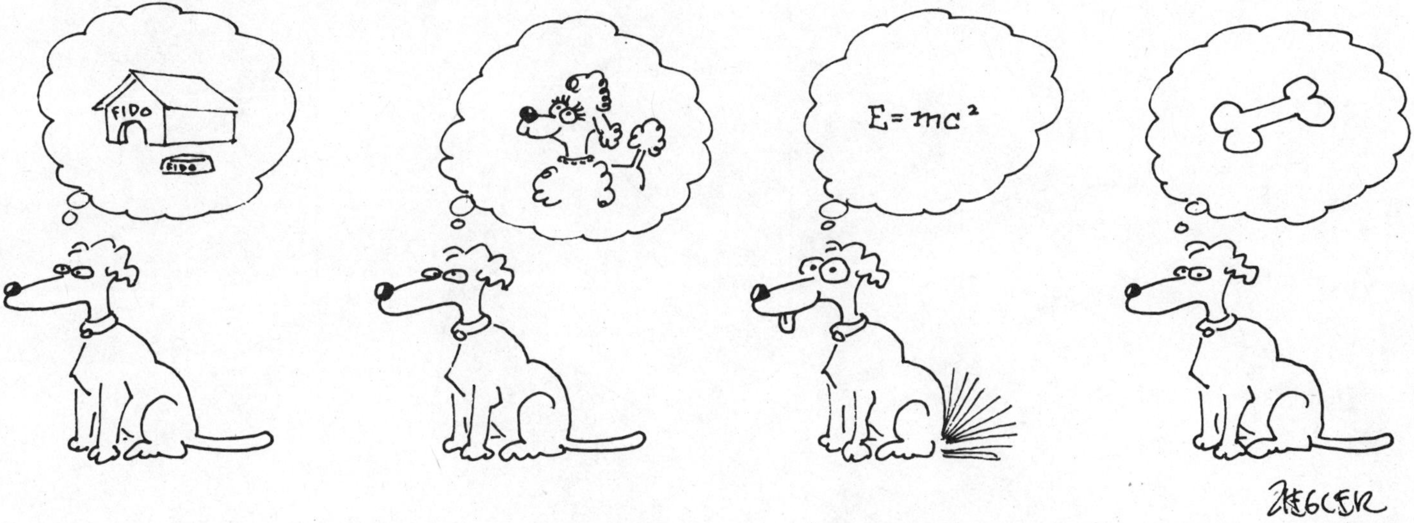

FIDO
FIDO
E = mc²
ZIEGLER

The Reincarnation of Albert Einstein

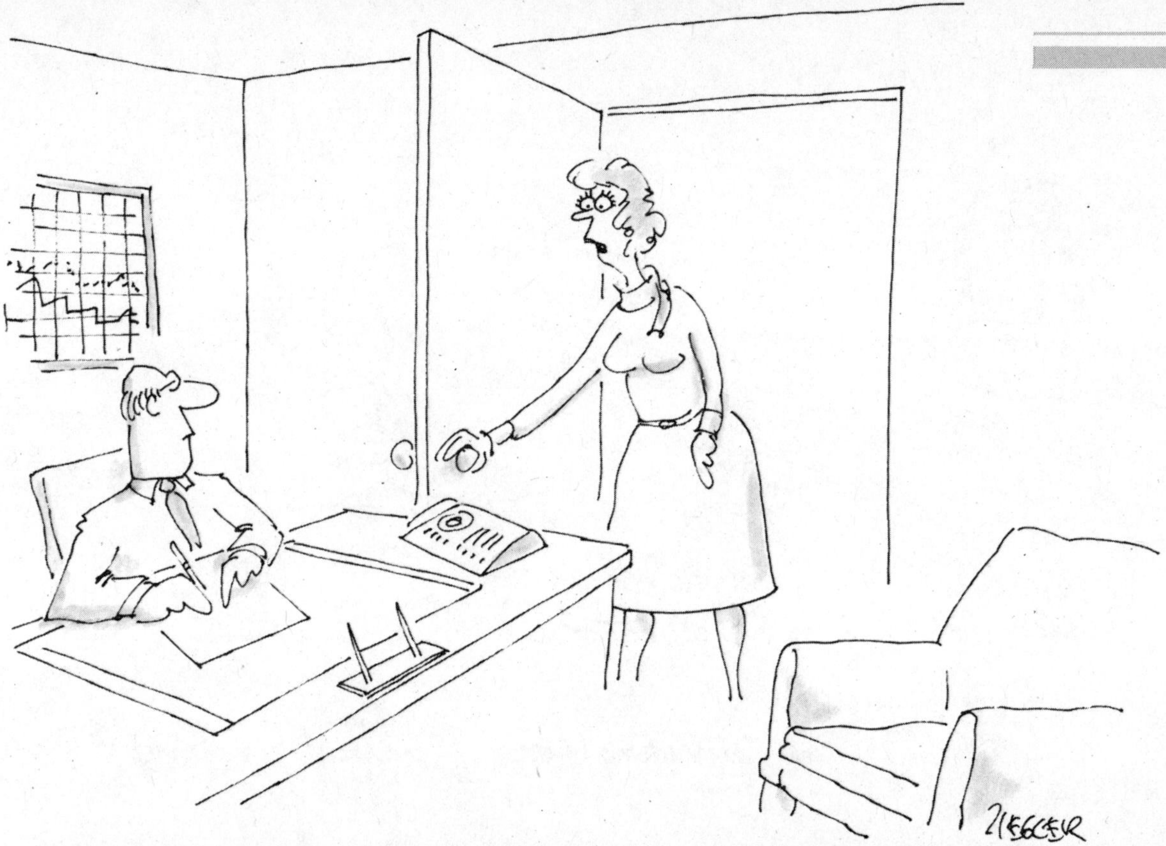

"Mr. T. Boone Pickens and an incredibly large amount of cash to see you, sir."

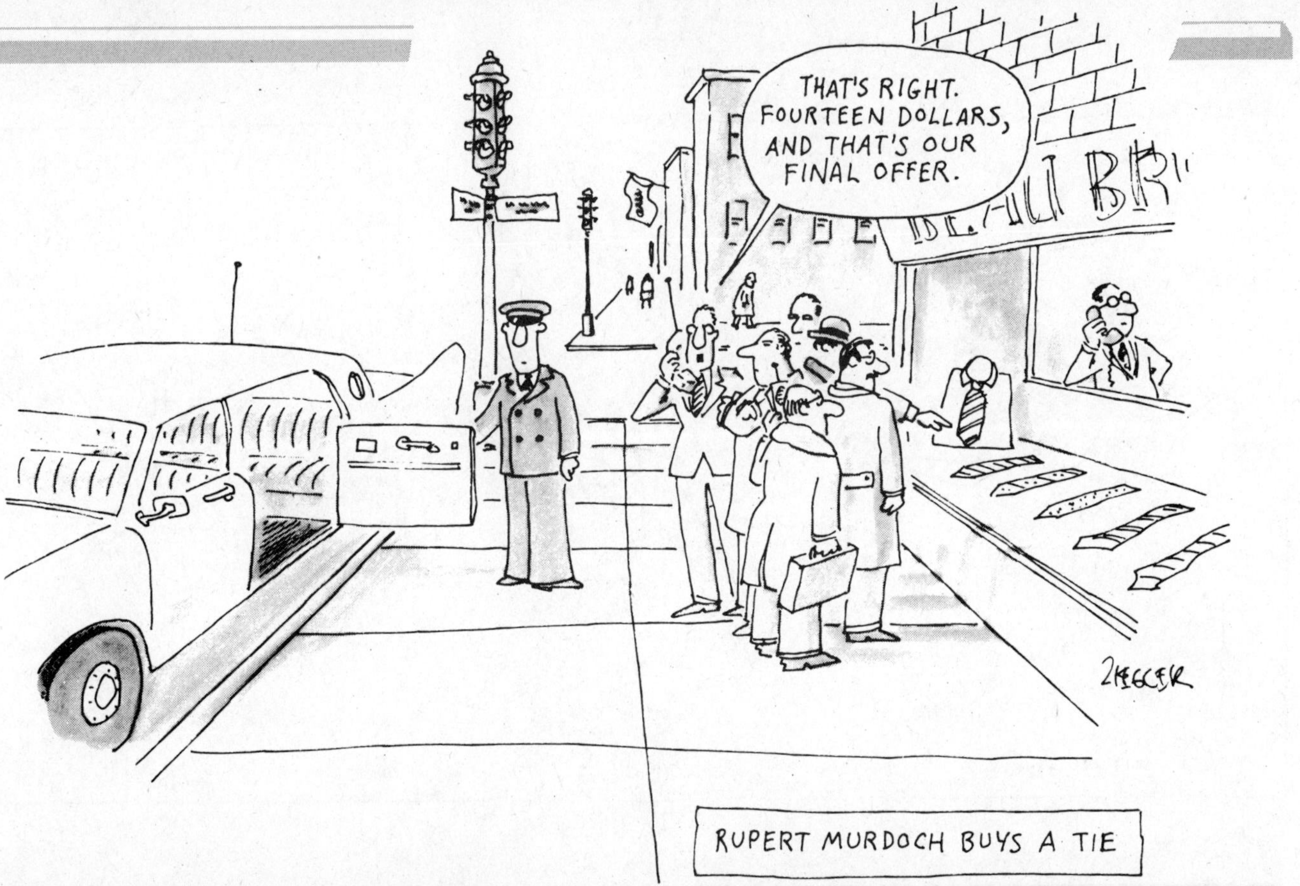
THAT'S RIGHT. FOURTEEN DOLLARS, AND THAT'S OUR FINAL OFFER.
RUPERT MURDOCH BUYS A TIE

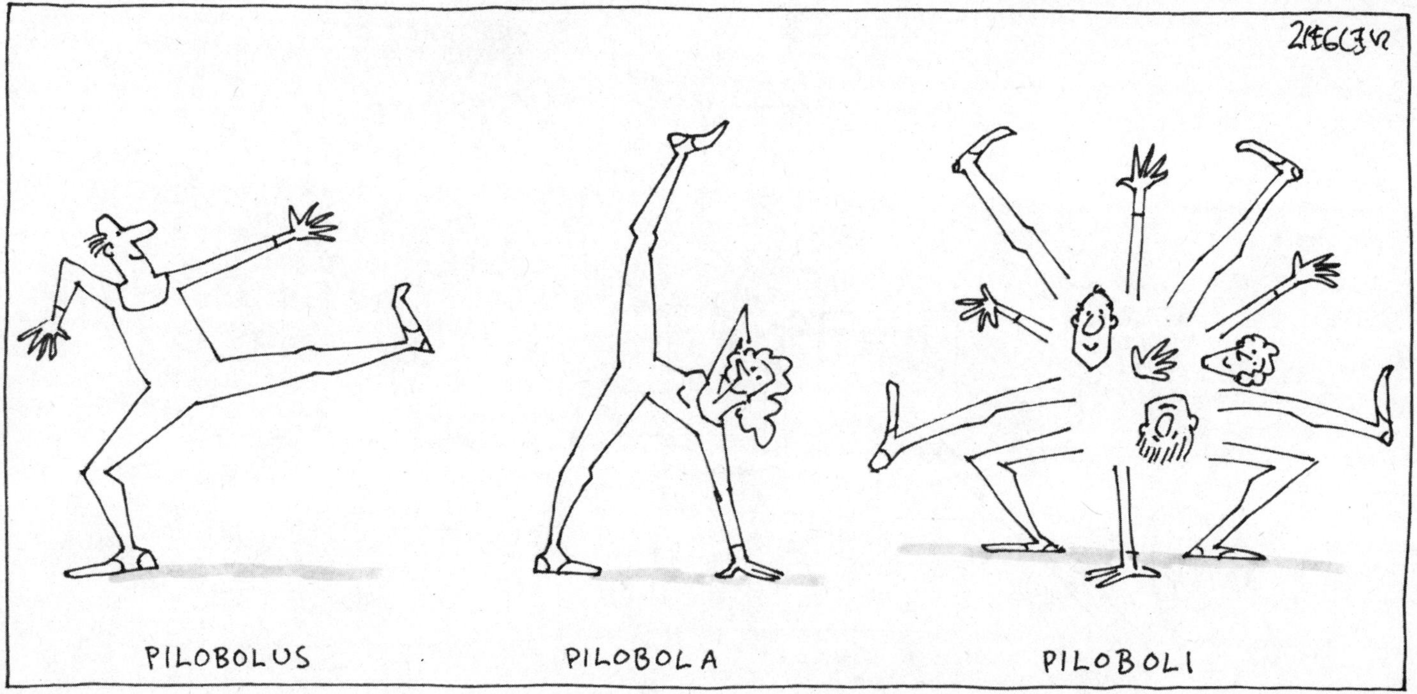

PILOBOLUS
PILOBOLA
PILOBOLI

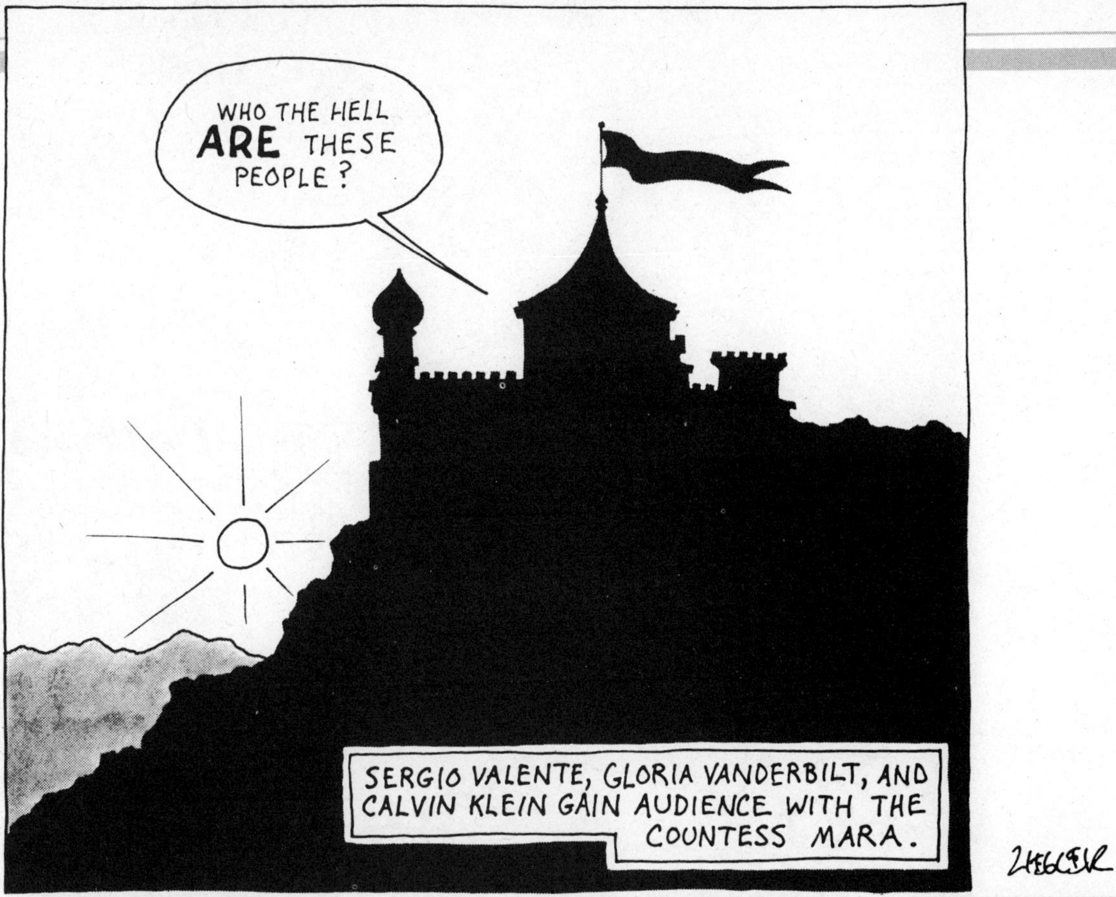
WHO THE HELL **ARE** THESE PEOPLE?
SERGIO VALENTE, GLORIA VANDERBILT, AND CALVIN KLEIN GAIN AUDIENCE WITH THE COUNTESS MARA.

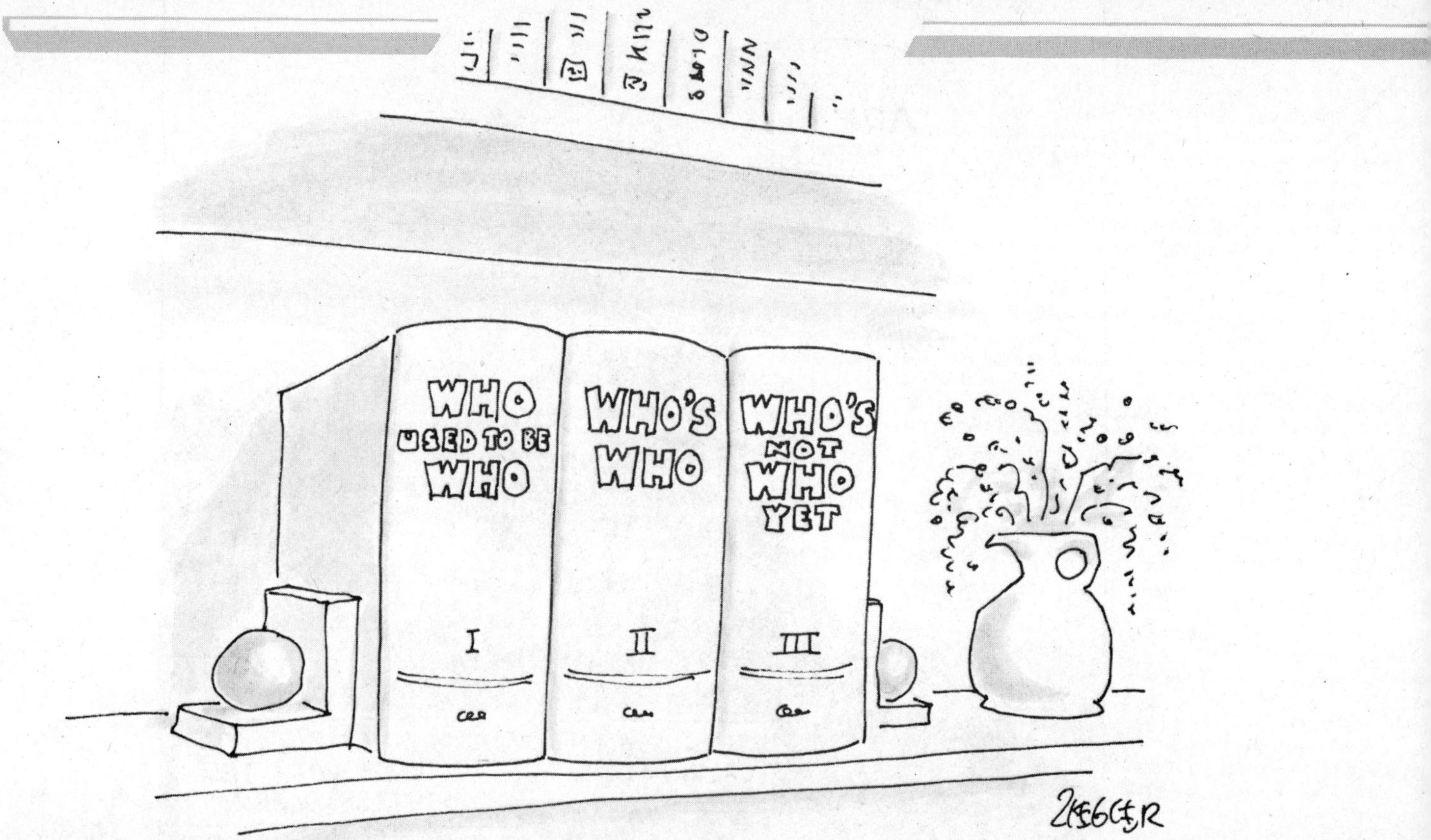
WHO USED TO BE WHO
I
WHO'S WHO
II
WHO'S NOT WHO YET
III
ZIEGLER

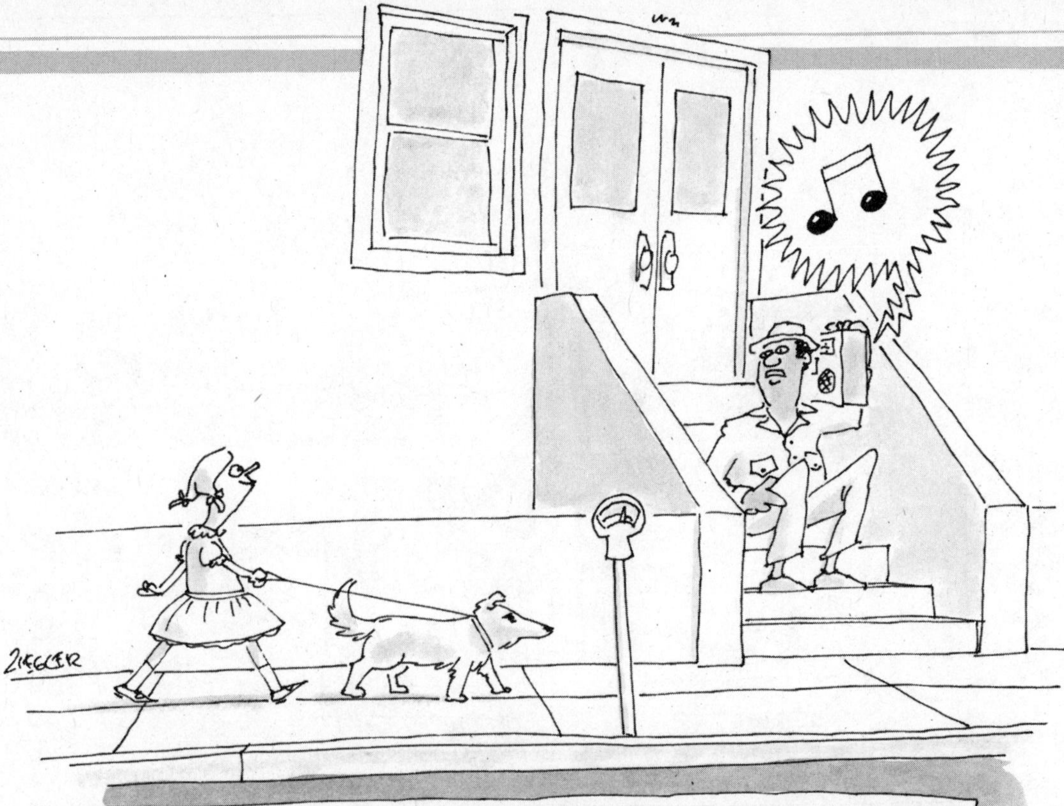
ZIEGLER

Rebecca of Sunnybrook Farm and Lad of Sunnybank meet the Duke of Earl

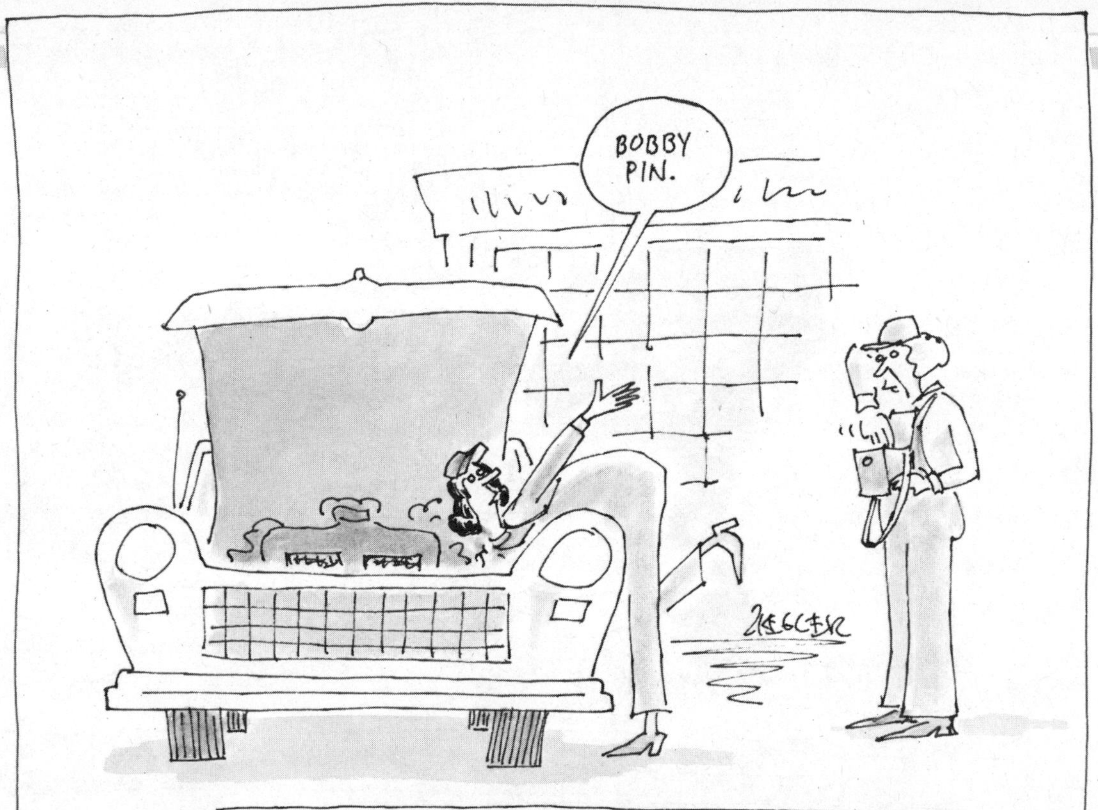
BOBBY PIN.
ZIEGLER

THE CAGNEY & LACEY SCHOOL OF AUTO REPAIR

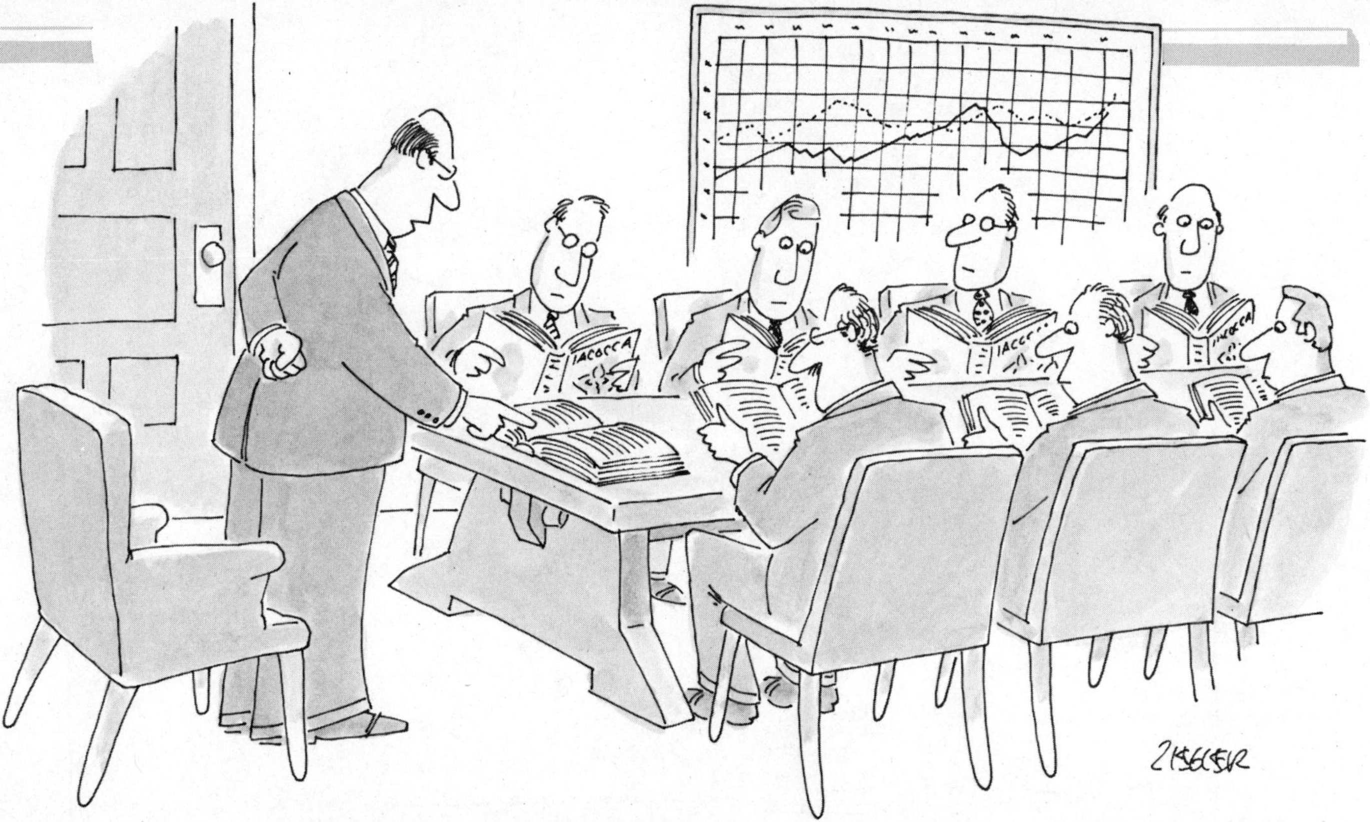
IACOCCA

"Gentlemen, let us open to page 82 of our Iacoccas."

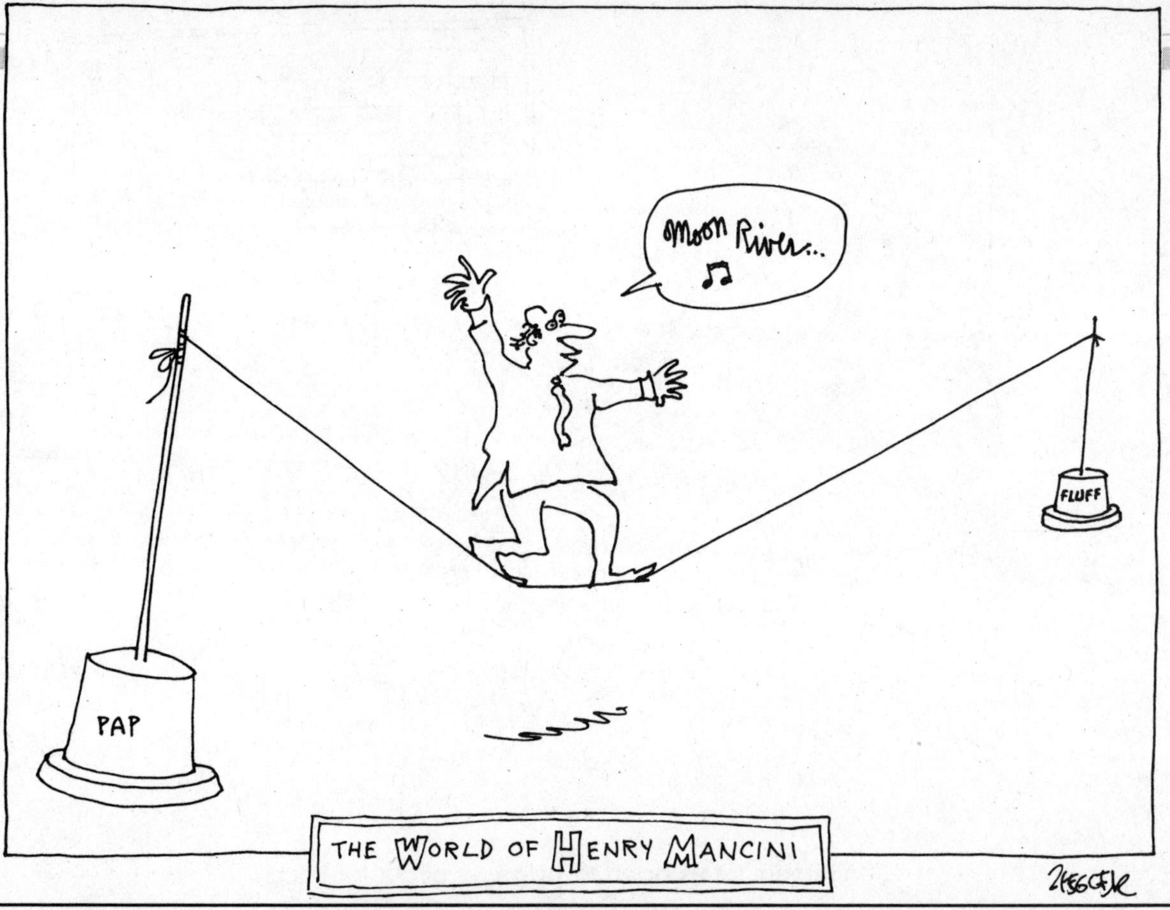
Moon River...
PAP
FLUFF
THE WORLD OF HENRY MANCINI

"Ah, spring! To be outdoors once again as the cooling breeze wafts from across the street the gentle strains of Bruce Springsteen's latest hit. Or, hush! is it Duran Duran?"

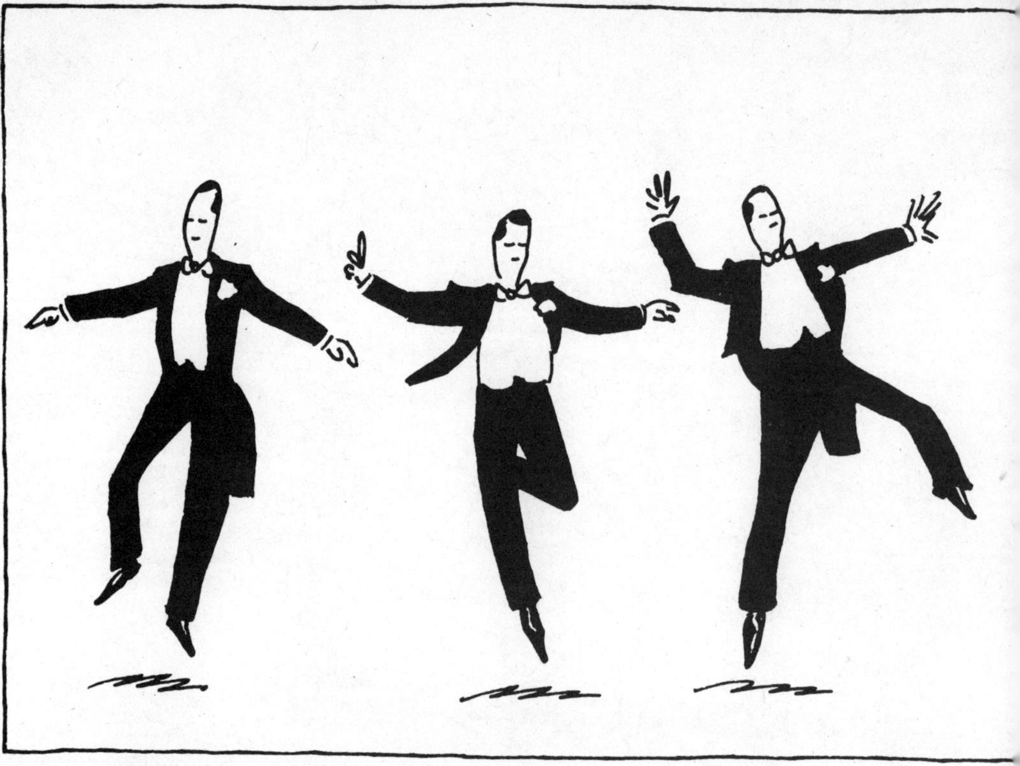

"SWINGTIME": THE CUTTING ROOM FLOOR

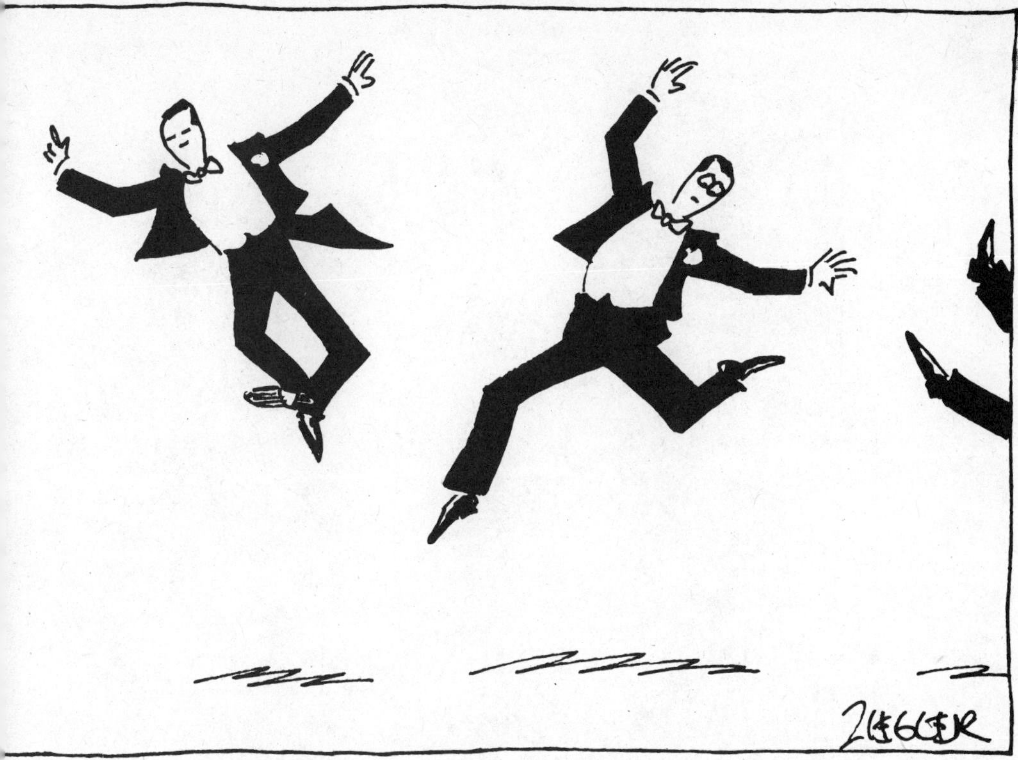
ZIEGLER

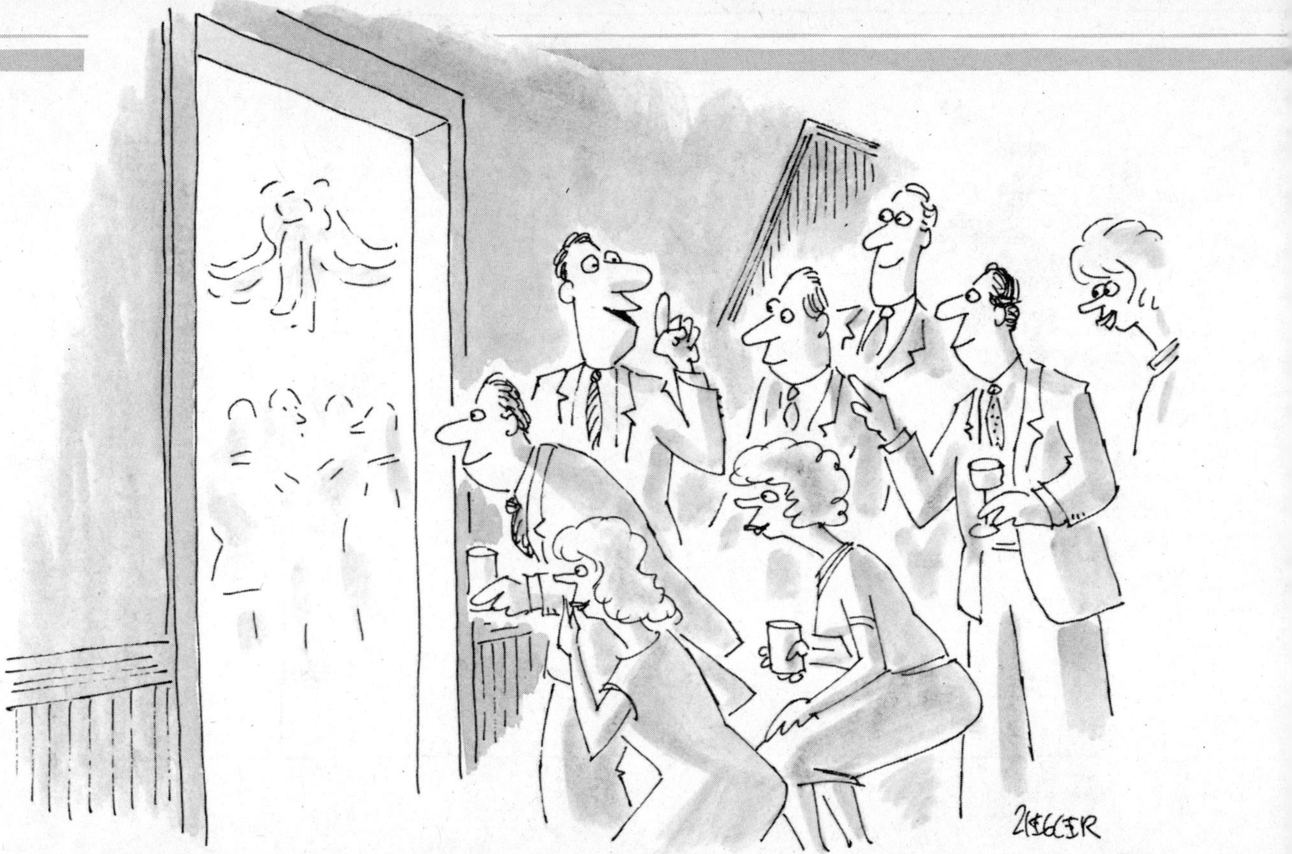

"Quiet, everybody. Let's see what happens. She thinks she's talking to the *real* Henry Kissinger."

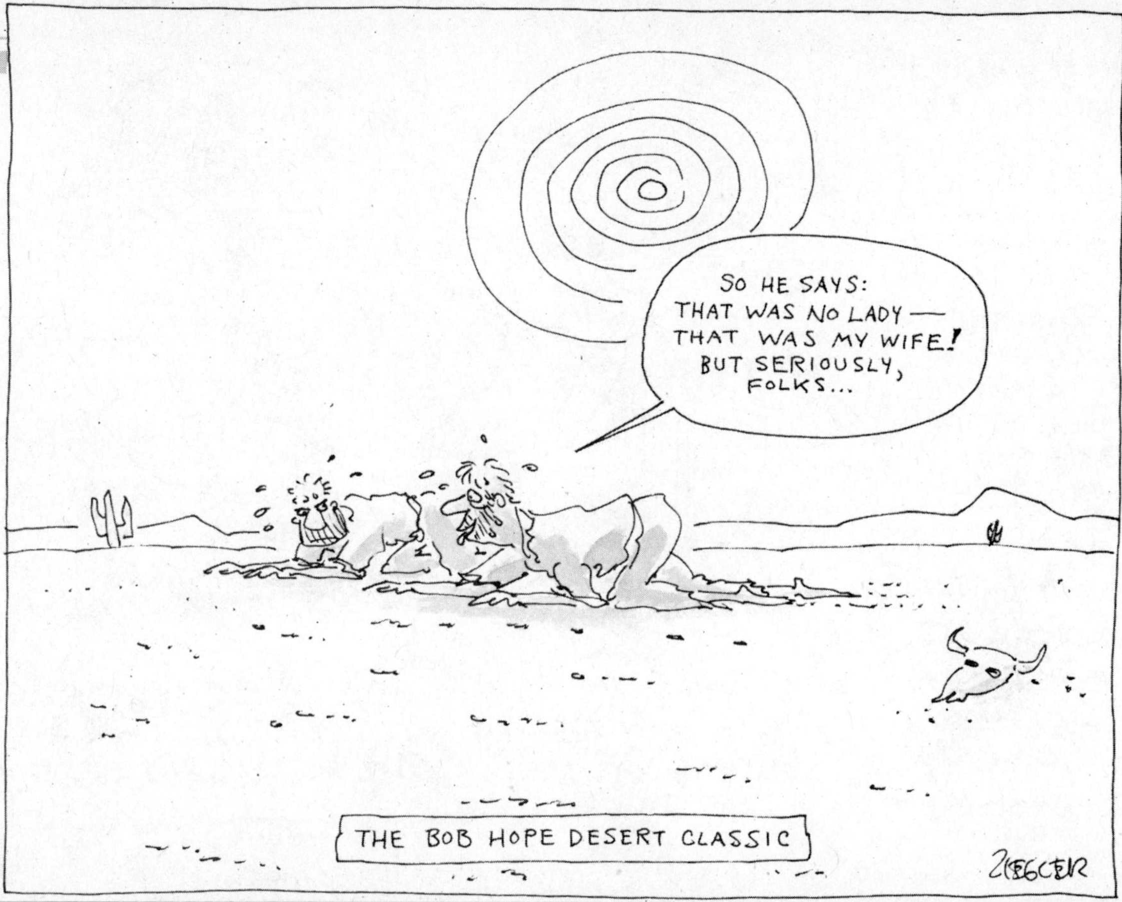
SO HE SAYS:
THAT WAS NO LADY —
THAT WAS MY WIFE!
BUT SERIOUSLY,
FOLKS...
THE BOB HOPE DESERT CLASSIC
ZIEGLER

AT HIS HOME ON THE PLANET MONGO, FLASH GORDON RECEIVES WORD THAT THE L.A. PIX CRIX INSTITUTE HAS JUST NAMED "FLASHDANCE" AS COMEBACK OF THE YEAR. MR. GORDON IS MORE ANNOYED THAN PLEASED AND FIRES OFF THE FOLLOWING REPLY:

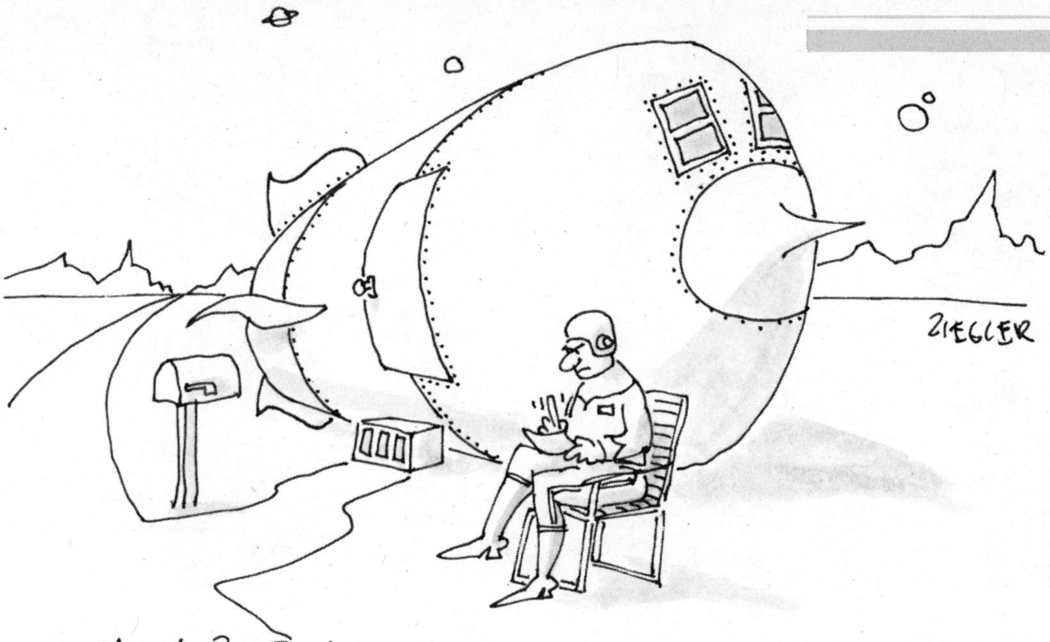
ZIEGLER

"Dear Sirs,

"Your tribute comes a little late in the game, don't you think? Zarkov is gone. Ming is gone. Even the Clay People, for God's sake, are gone. And Dale and I haven't done the Flashdance in years! Nor do we intend to take it up again now!

"Yours truly,

F. Gordon"

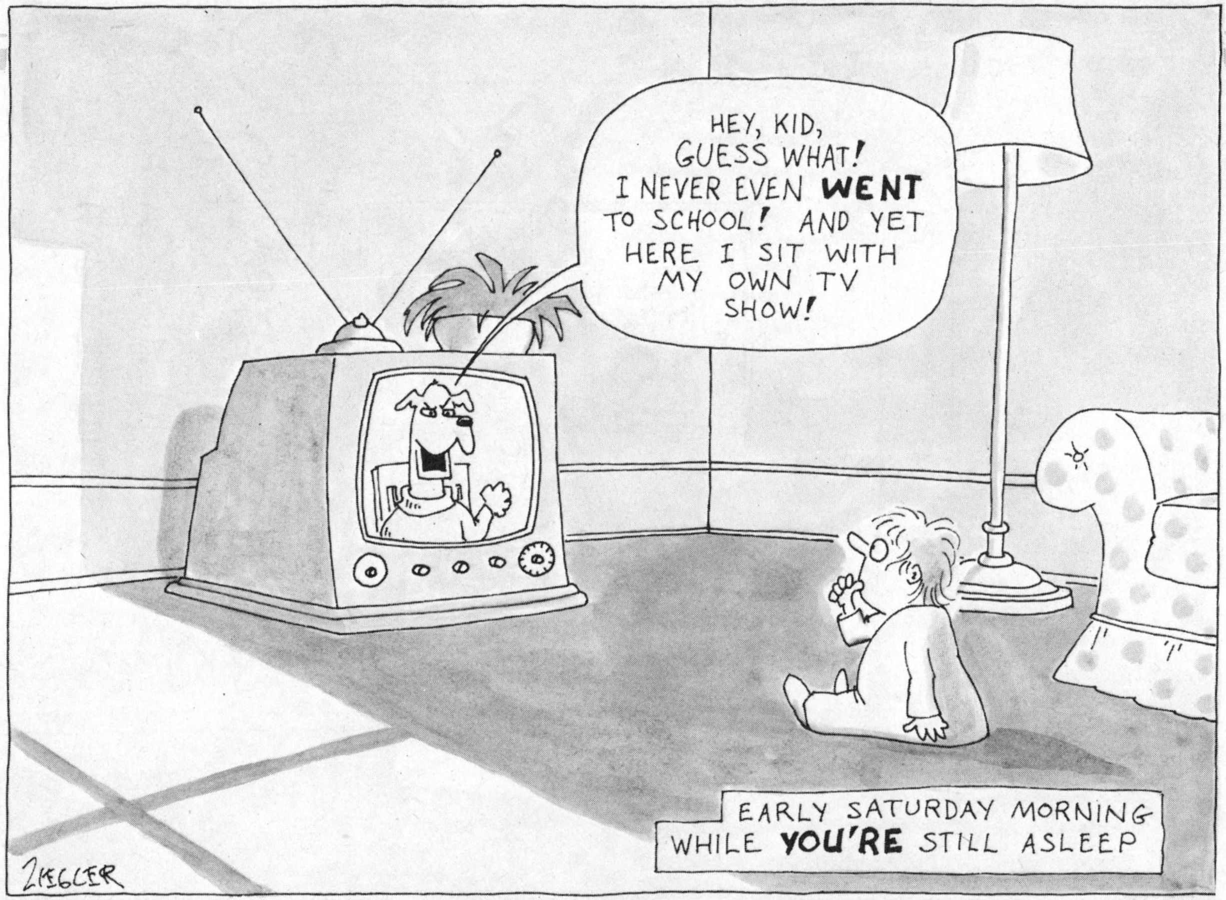
HEY, KID, GUESS WHAT! I NEVER EVEN **WENT** TO SCHOOL! AND YET HERE I SIT WITH MY OWN TV SHOW!
EARLY SATURDAY MORNING WHILE **YOU'RE** STILL ASLEEP
ZIEGLER

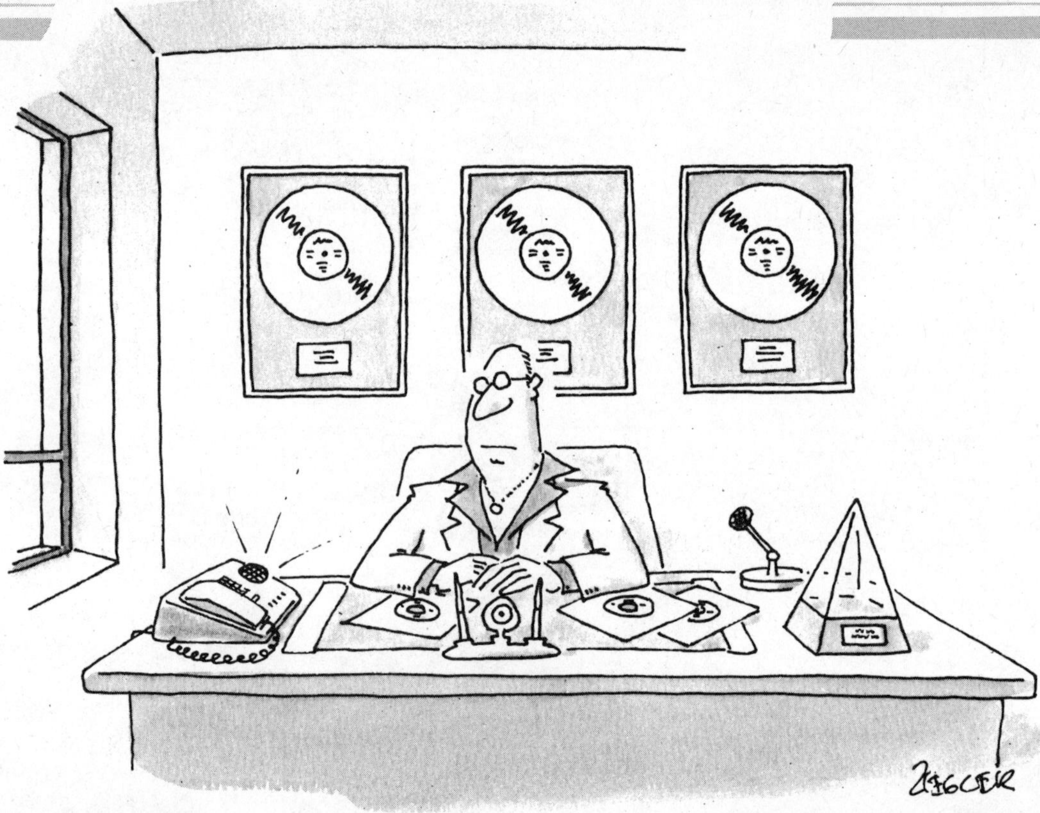
ZIEGLER

"Cyndi Lauper on four, sir, with a bullet."

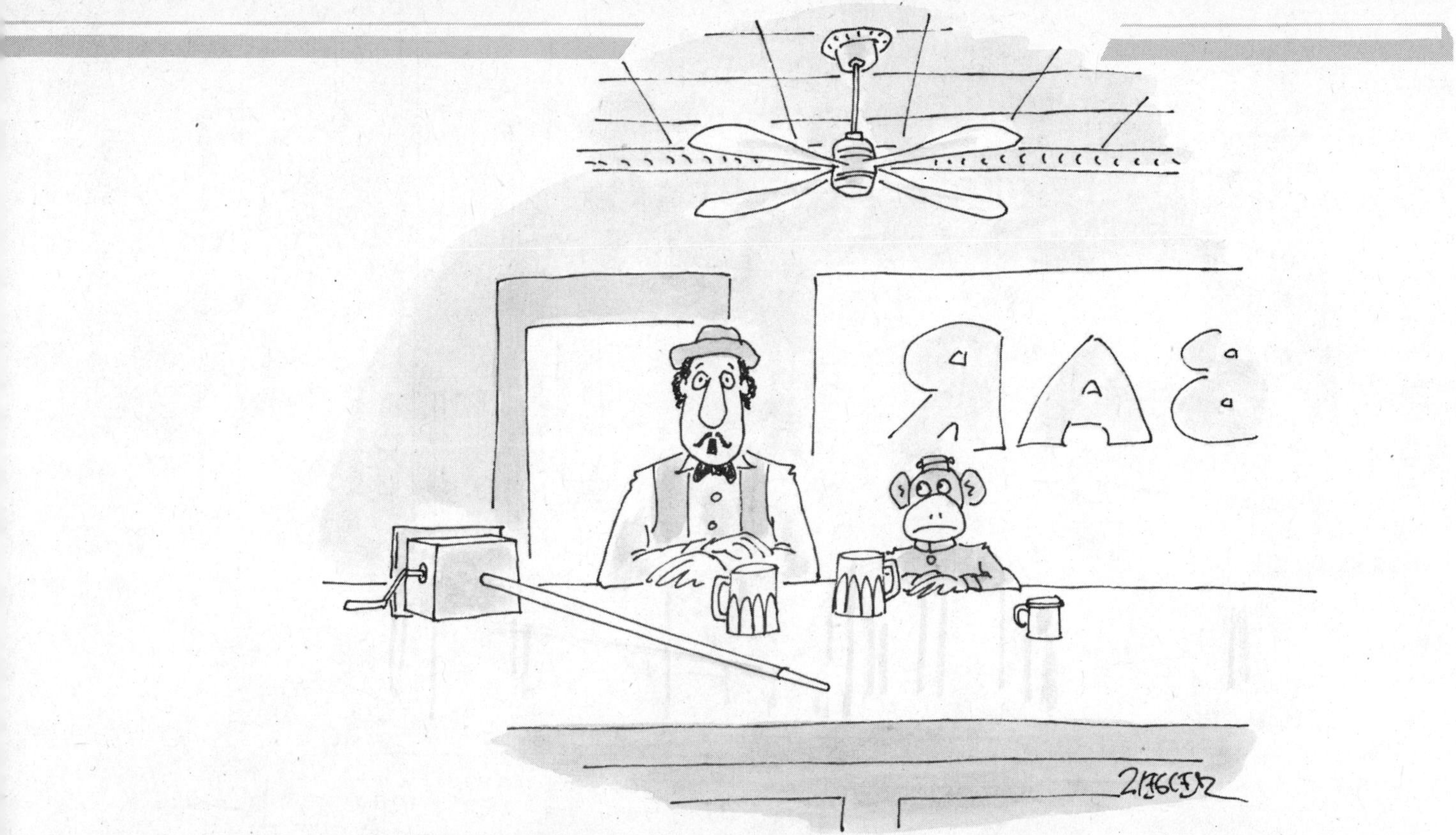

"The economy is in a mess, Cheetah. I'm afraid I'm going to have to send you back to Tarzan for a while."

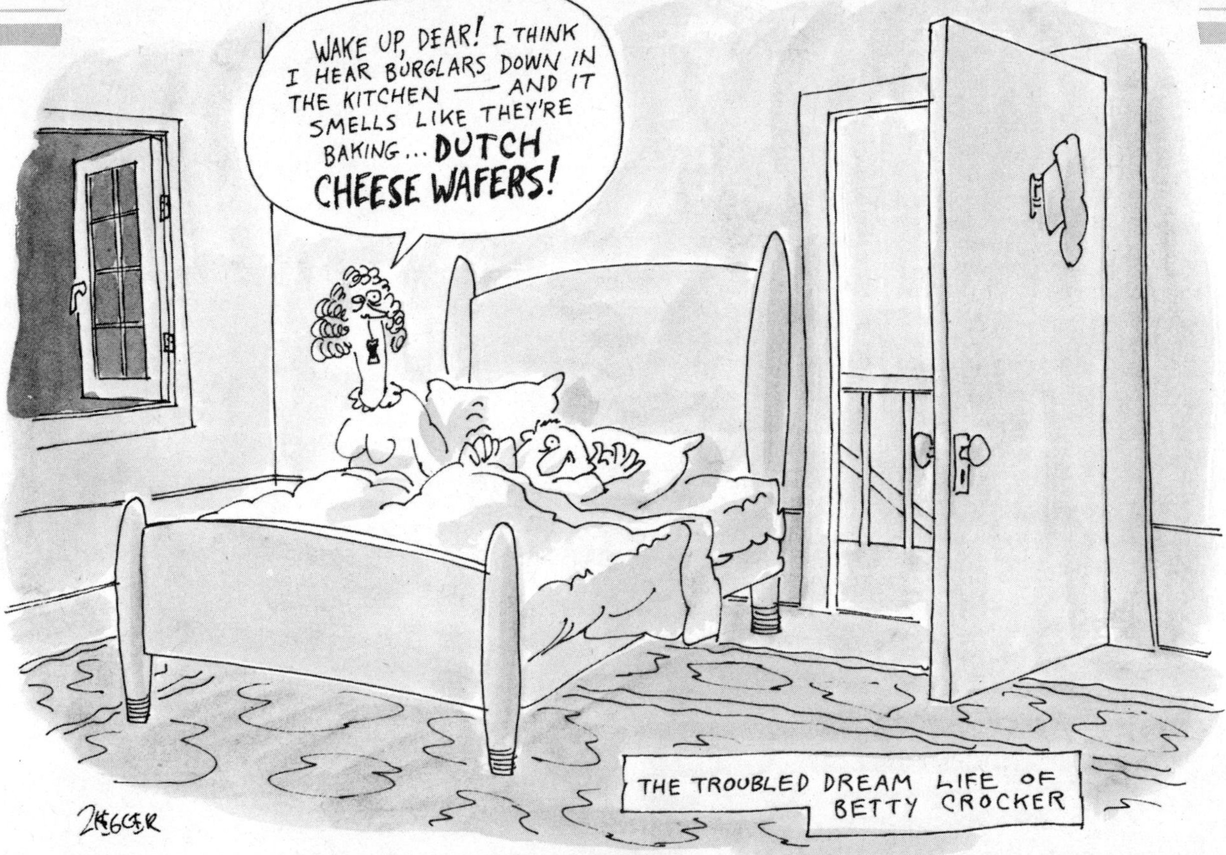
WAKE UP, DEAR! I THINK I HEAR BURGLARS DOWN IN THE KITCHEN — AND IT SMELLS LIKE THEY'RE BAKING... DUTCH CHEESE WAFERS!
THE TROUBLED DREAM LIFE OF BETTY CROCKER
ZIEGLER

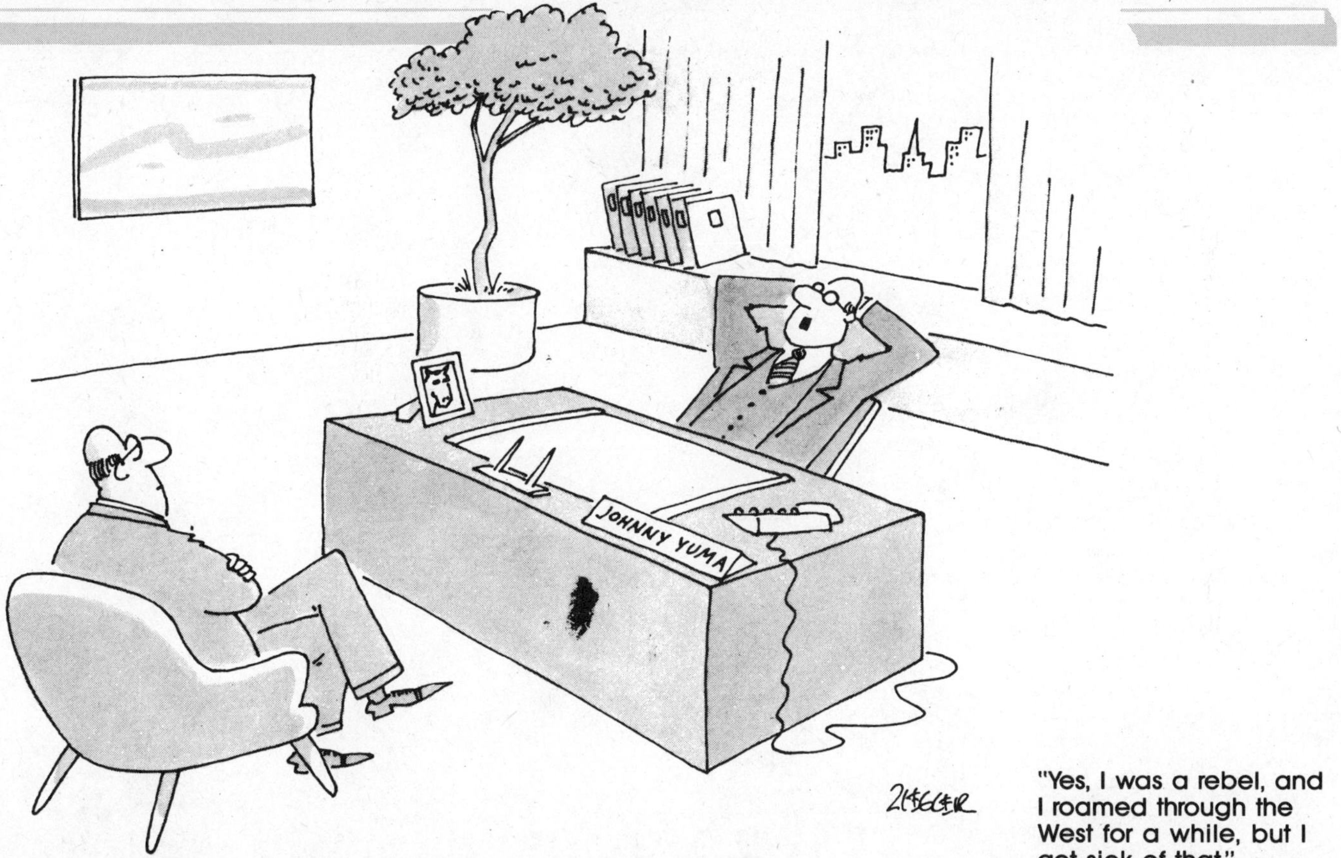
JOHNNY YUMA

"Yes, I was a rebel, and I roamed through the West for a while, but I got sick of that."

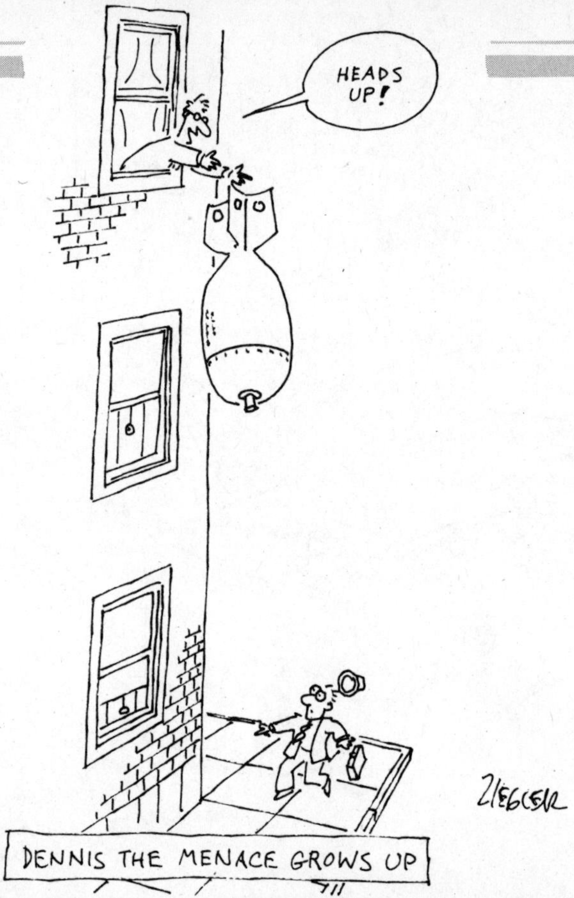
HEADS UP!
ZIEGLER
DENNIS THE MENACE GROWS UP

ZIEGLER

"That's *Ms.* Wonder Woman to you, fella!"

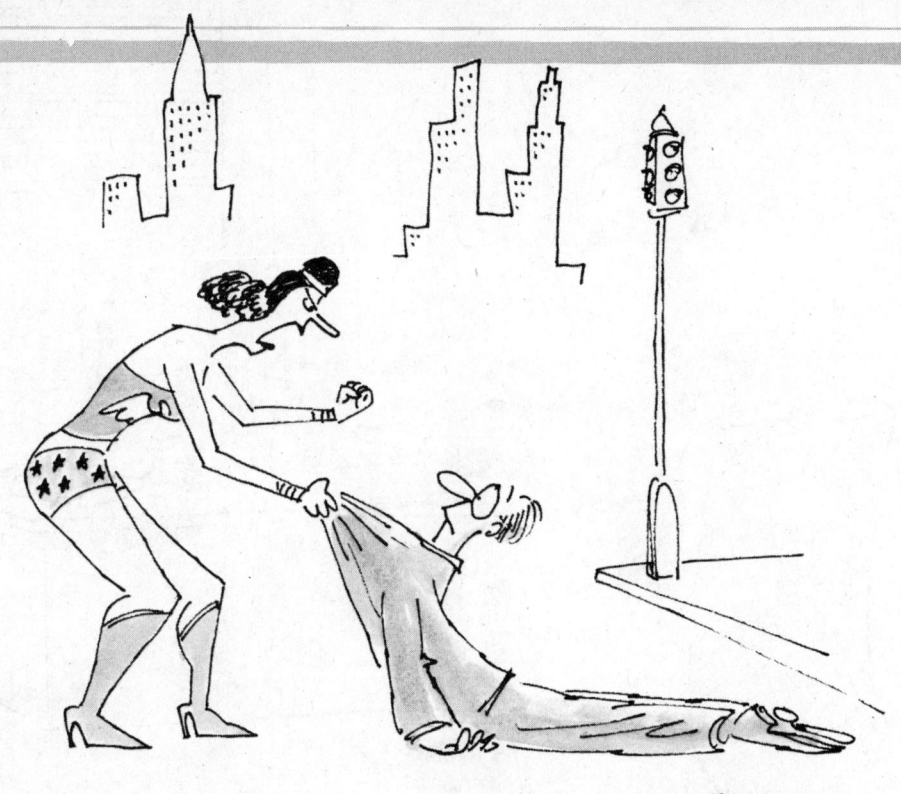

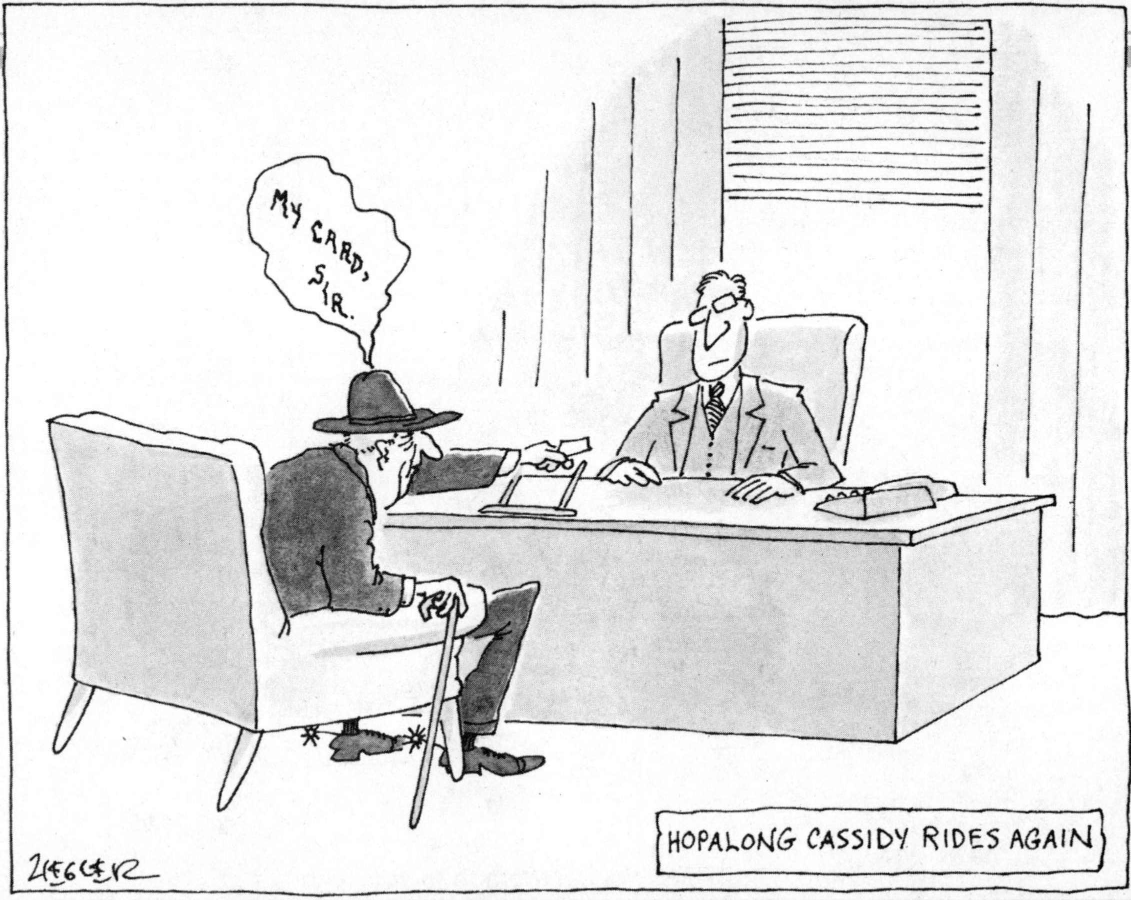

MY CARD, SIR.
HOPALONG CASSIDY RIDES AGAIN
ZIEGLER

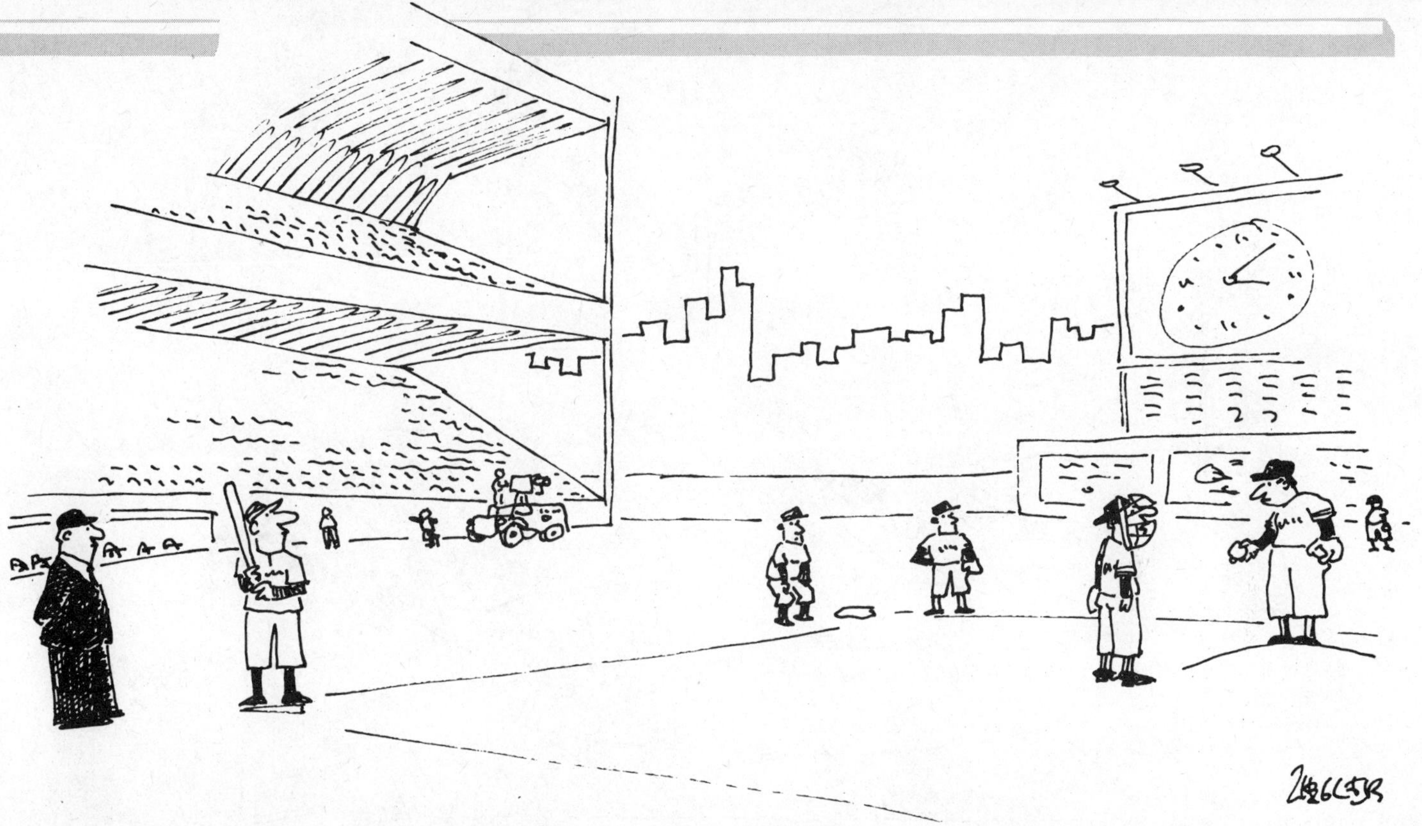

"Mister Steinbrenner wants you to stop spitting during those close-ups."

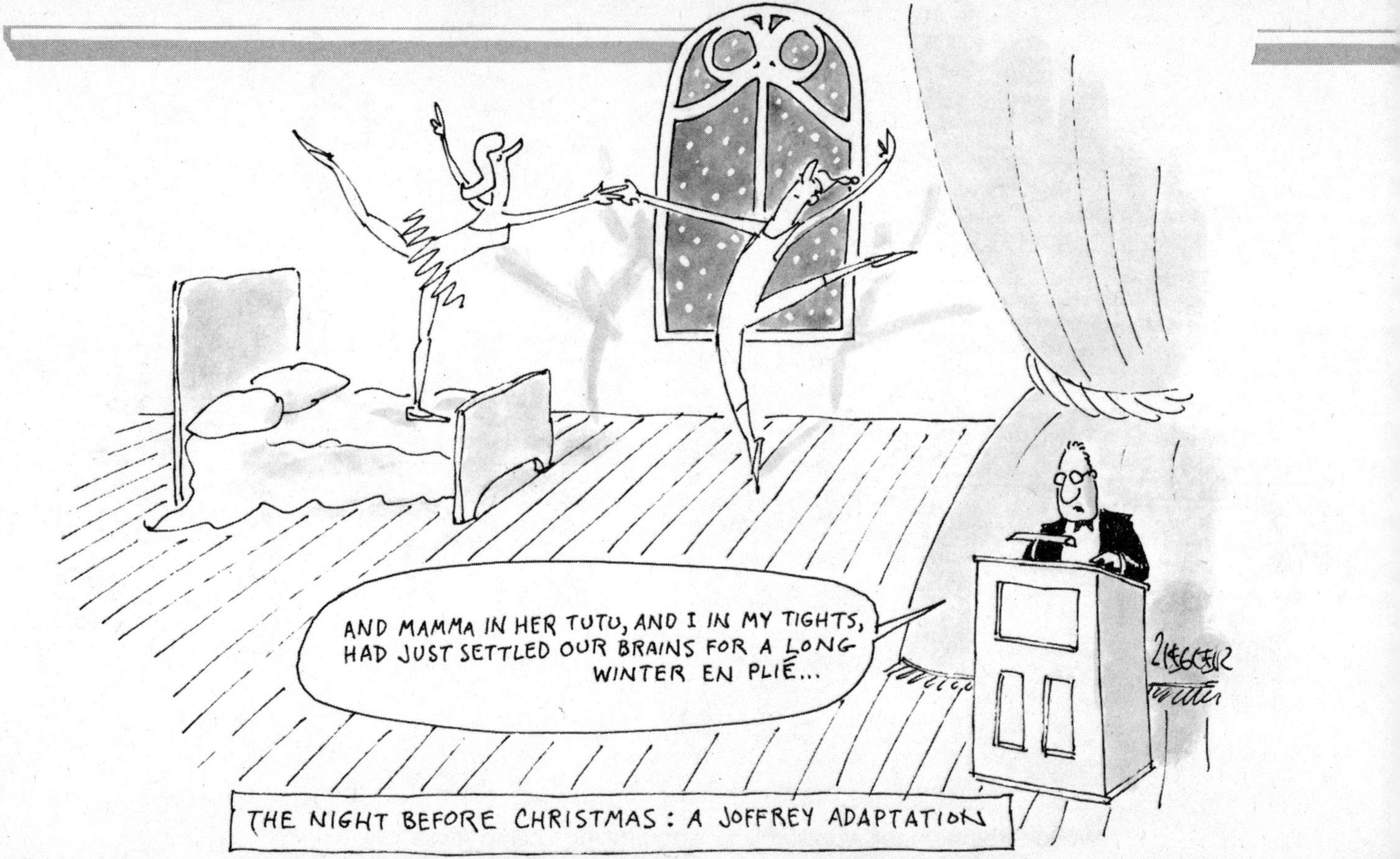
AND MAMMA IN HER TUTU, AND I IN MY TIGHTS, HAD JUST SETTLED OUR BRAINS FOR A LONG WINTER EN PLIÉ...
ZIEGLER
THE NIGHT BEFORE CHRISTMAS: A JOFFREY ADAPTATION

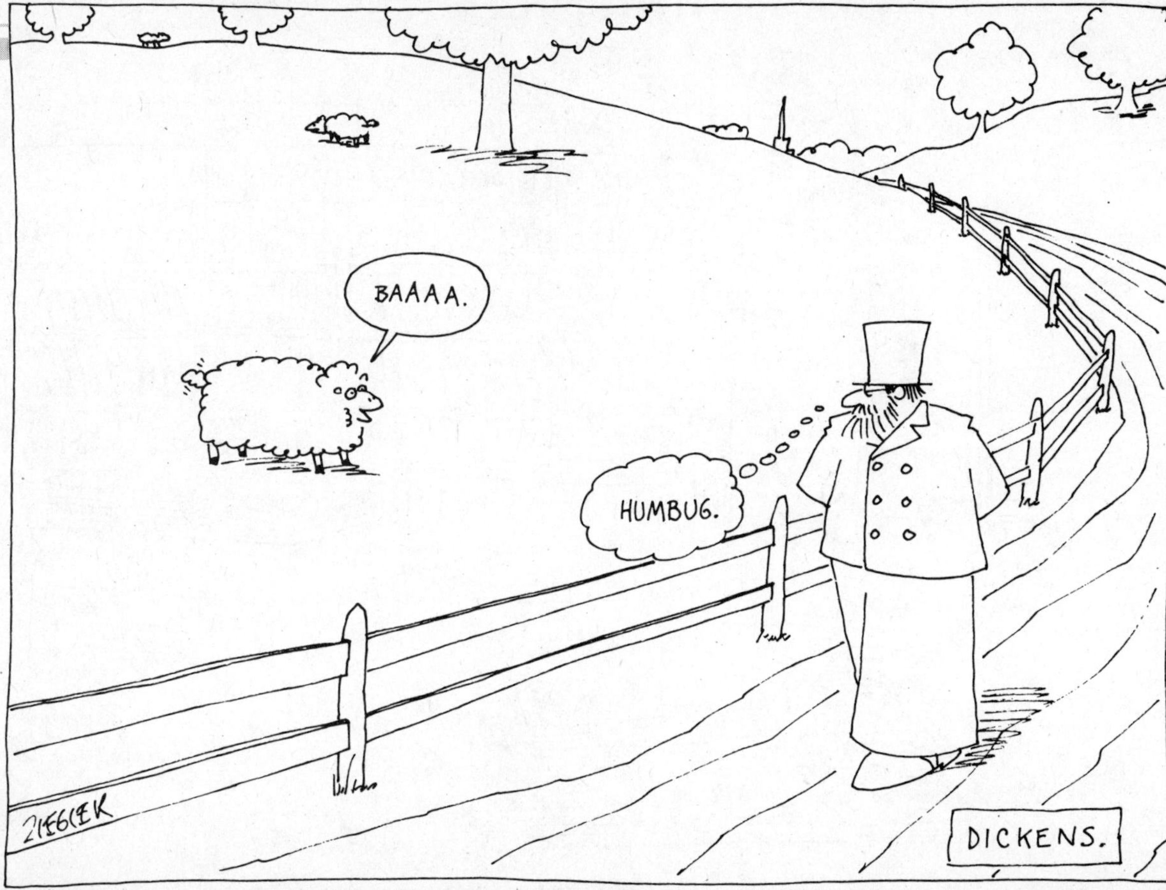
BAAAA.
HUMBUG.
ZIEGLER
DICKENS.

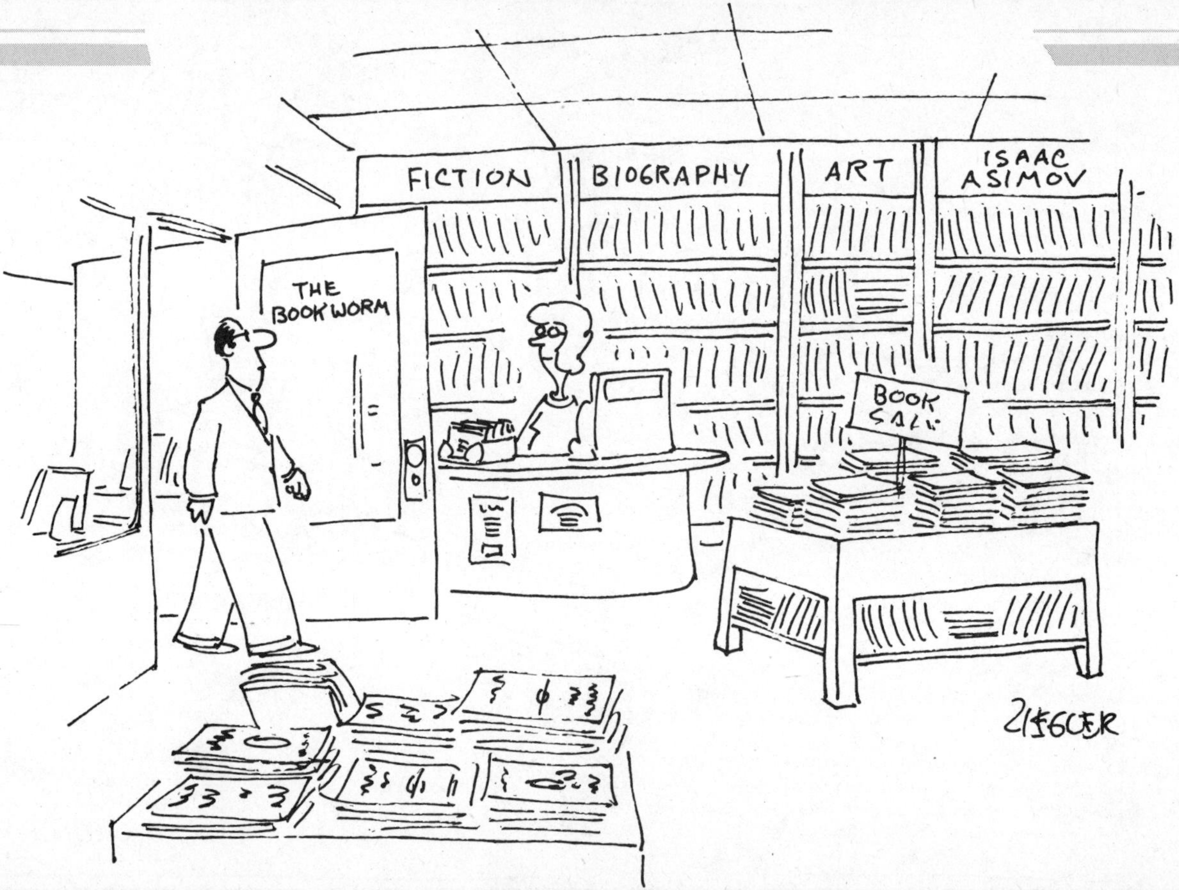
FICTION
BIOGRAPHY
ART
ISAAC ASIMOV
THE BOOKWORM
BOOK
ZIEGLER

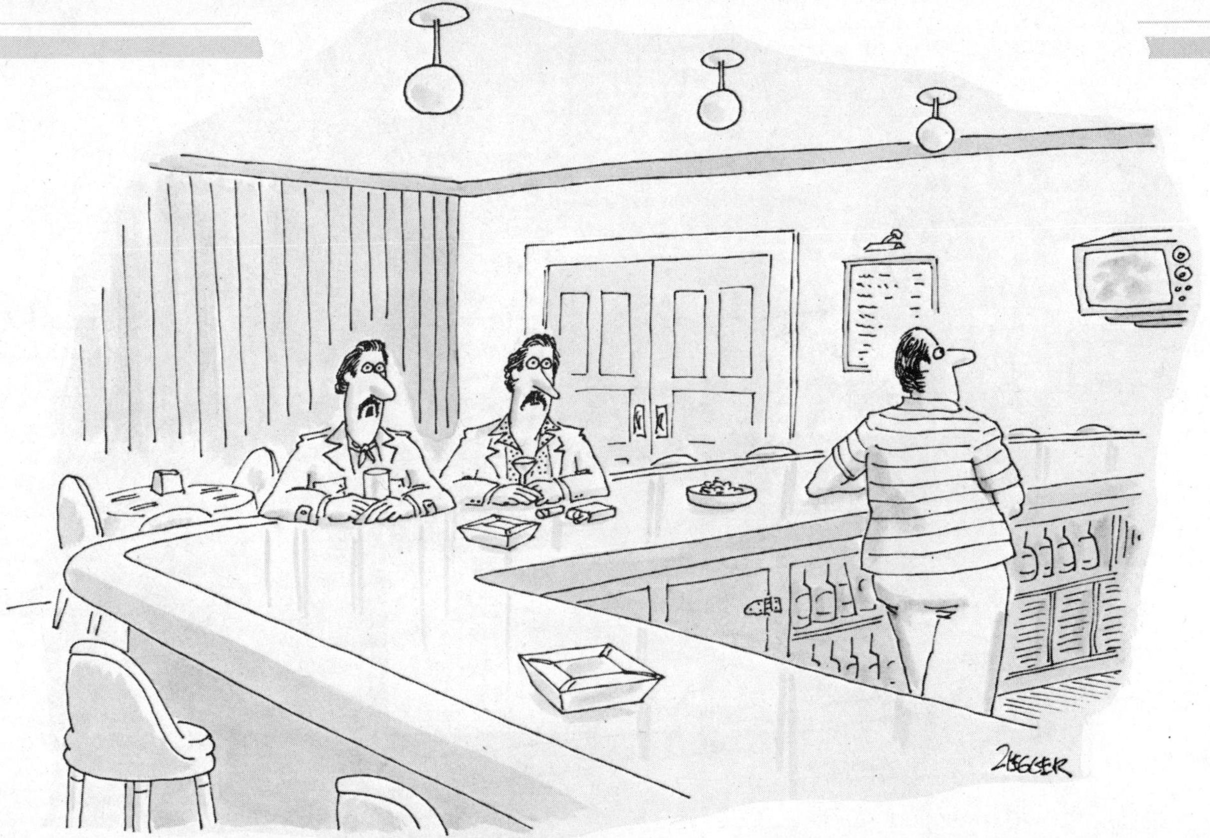
ZIEGLER

"I wonder whether Sonny Bono is having a good time tonight."

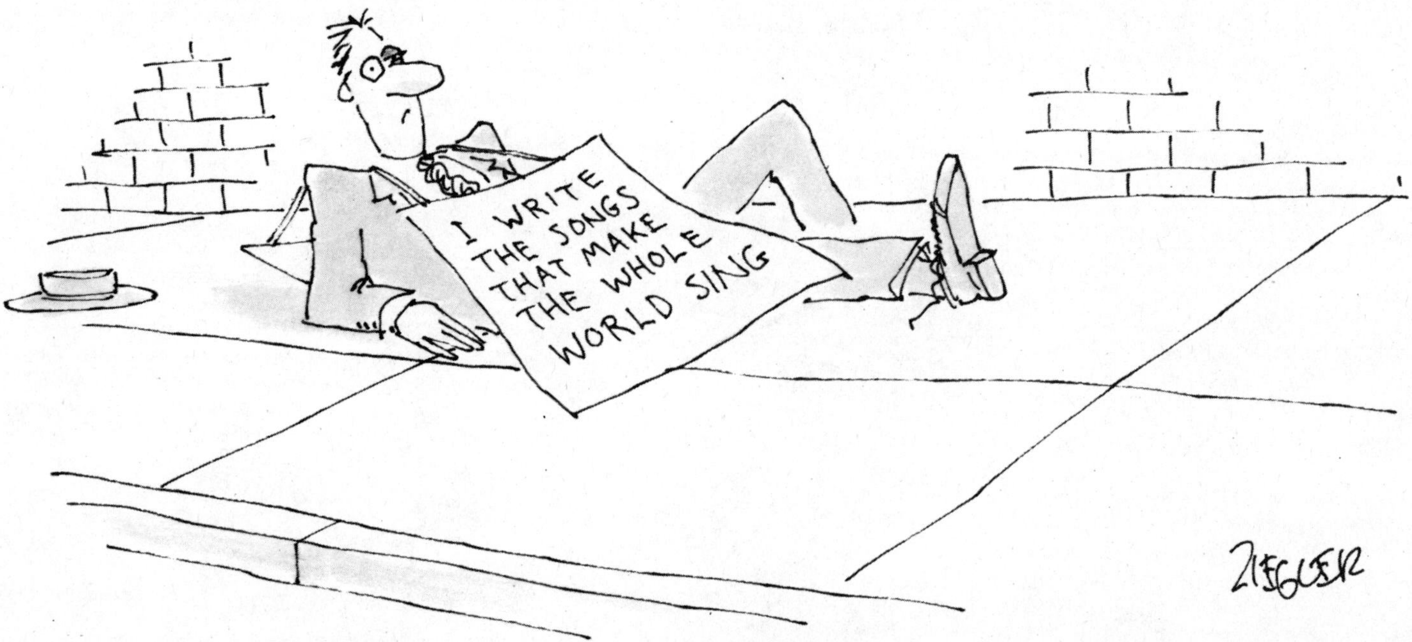
I WRITE THE SONGS THAT MAKE THE WHOLE WORLD SING
ZIEGLER

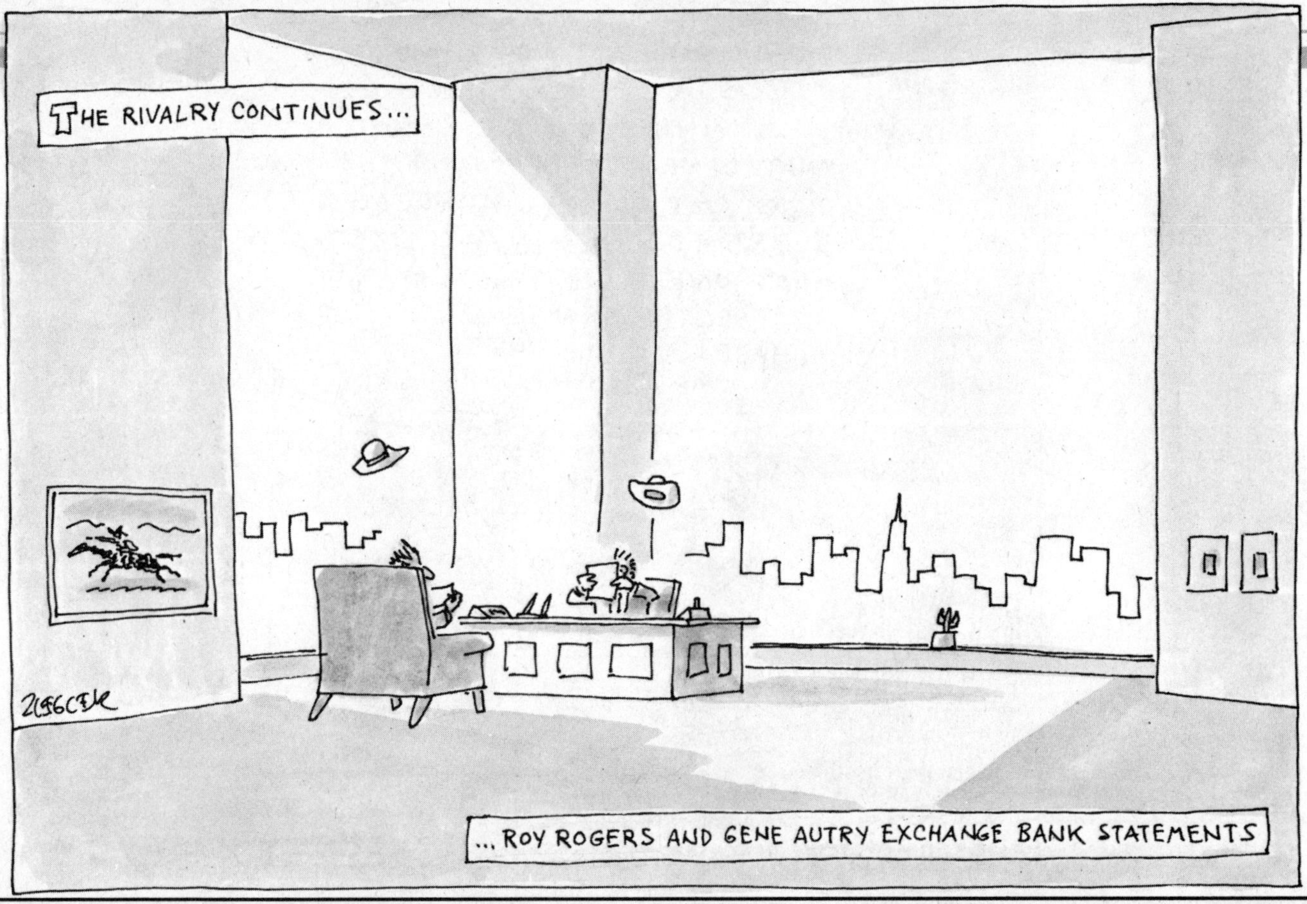
THE RIVALRY CONTINUES...
ZIEGLER
...ROY ROGERS AND GENE AUTRY EXCHANGE BANK STATEMENTS

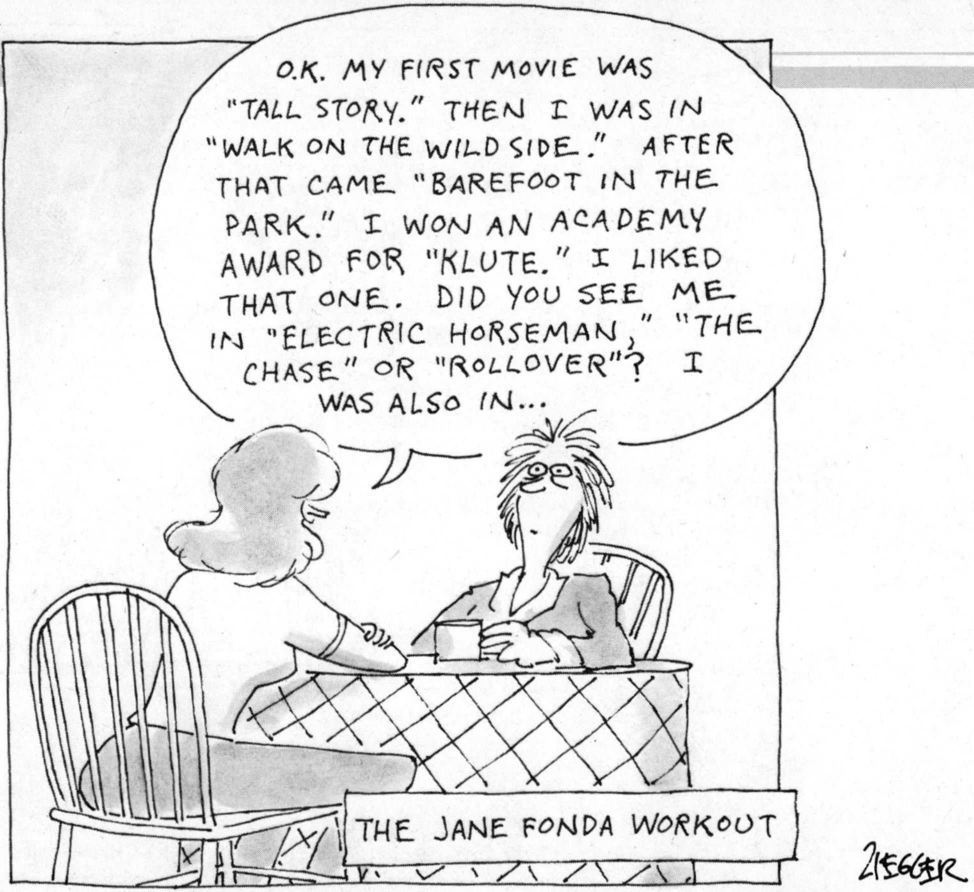
O.K. MY FIRST MOVIE WAS "TALL STORY." THEN I WAS IN "WALK ON THE WILD SIDE." AFTER THAT CAME "BAREFOOT IN THE PARK." I WON AN ACADEMY AWARD FOR "KLUTE." I LIKED THAT ONE. DID YOU SEE ME IN "ELECTRIC HORSEMAN," "THE CHASE" OR "ROLLOVER"? I WAS ALSO IN...
THE JANE FONDA WORKOUT
ZIEGLER

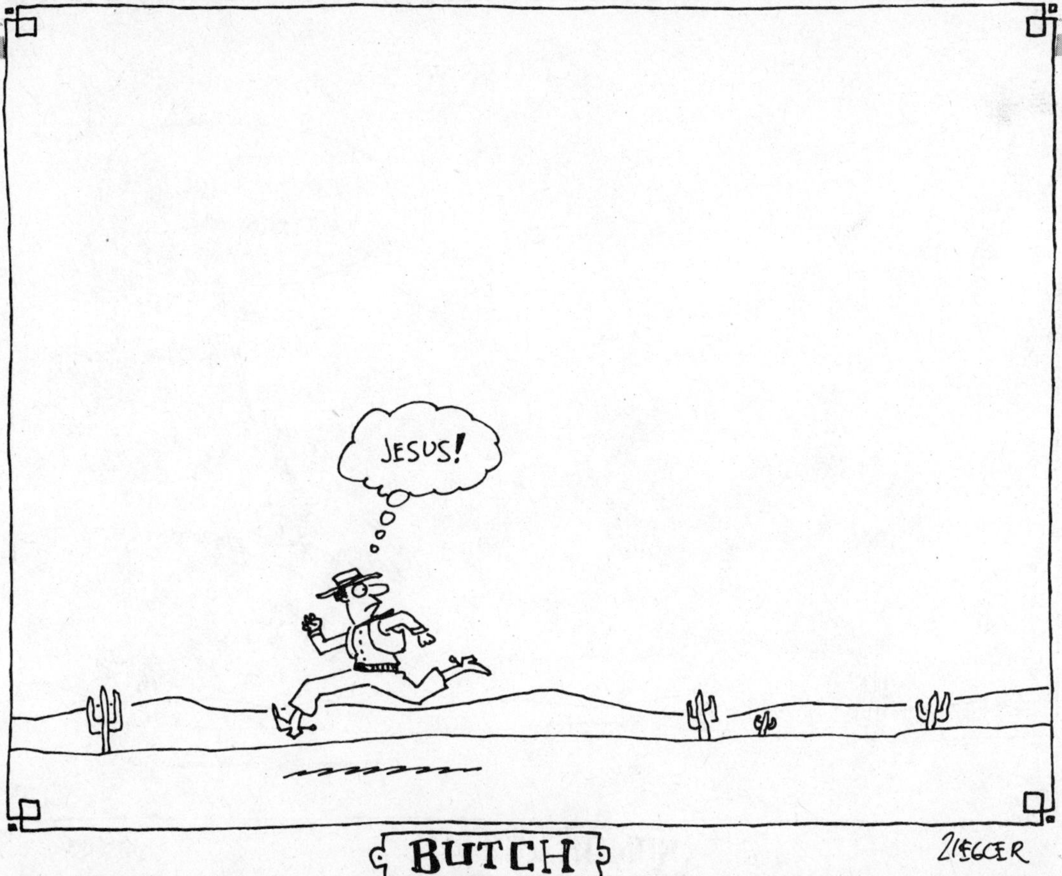
JESUS!
BUTCH
ZIEGLER

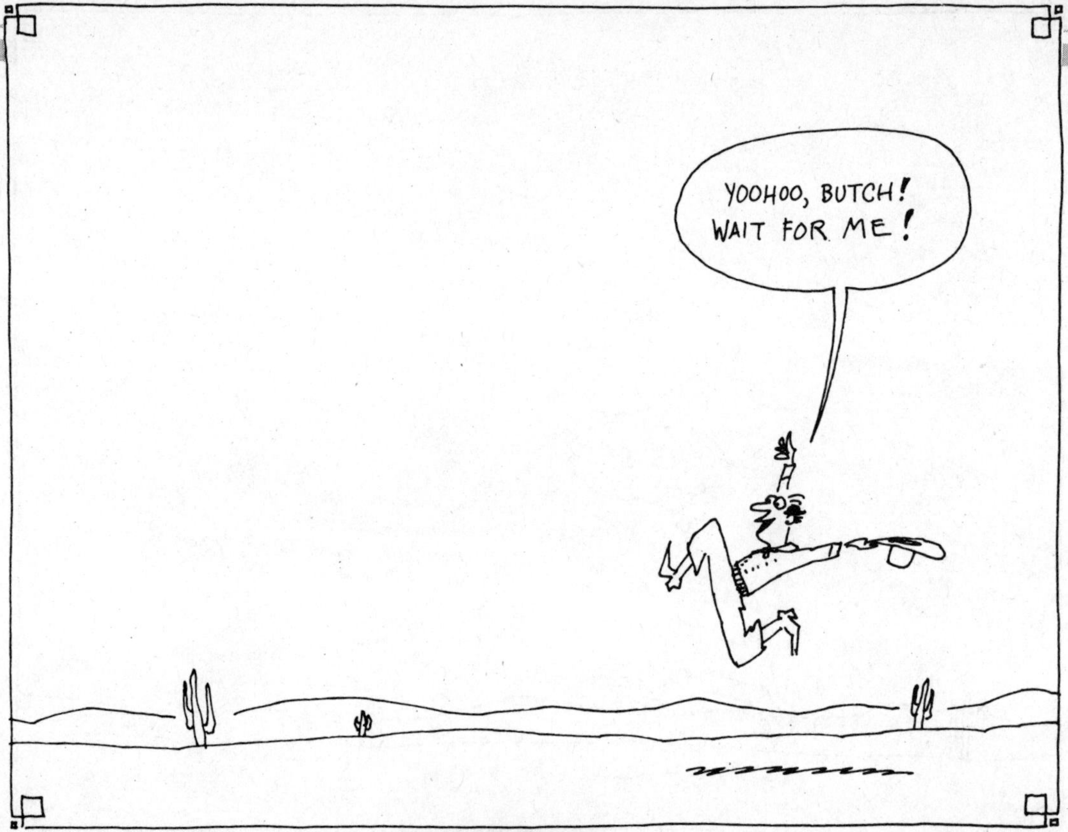
YOOHOO, BUTCH!
WAIT FOR ME!

SUNDANCE

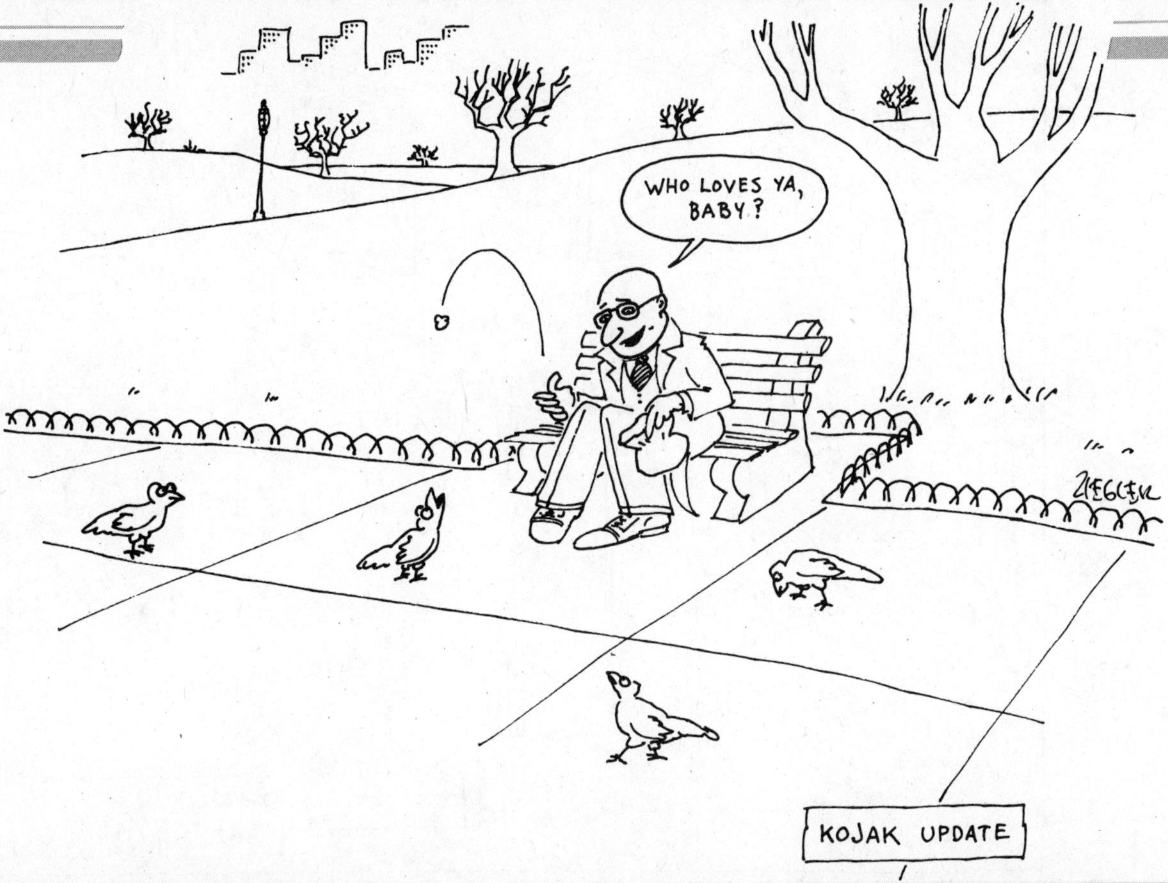
WHO LOVES YA, BABY?
ZIEGLER
KOJAK UPDATE

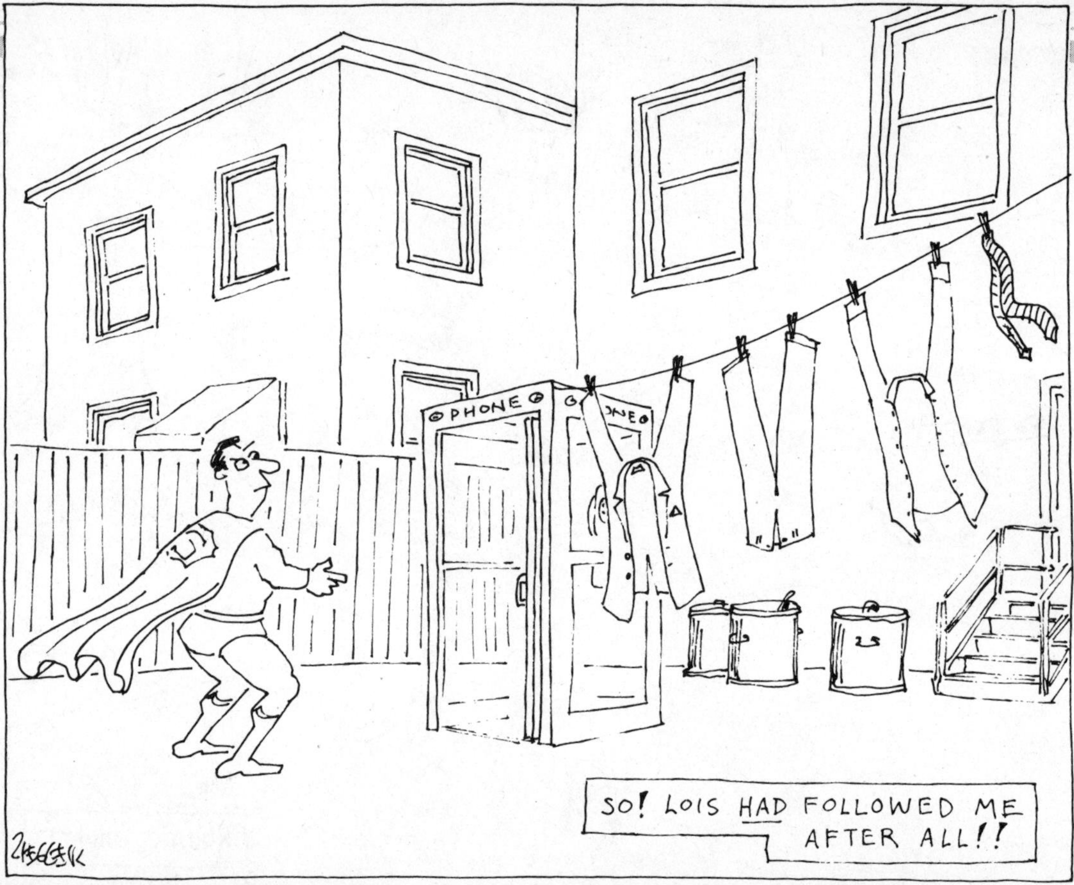
PHONE
SO! LOIS HAD FOLLOWED ME AFTER ALL!!

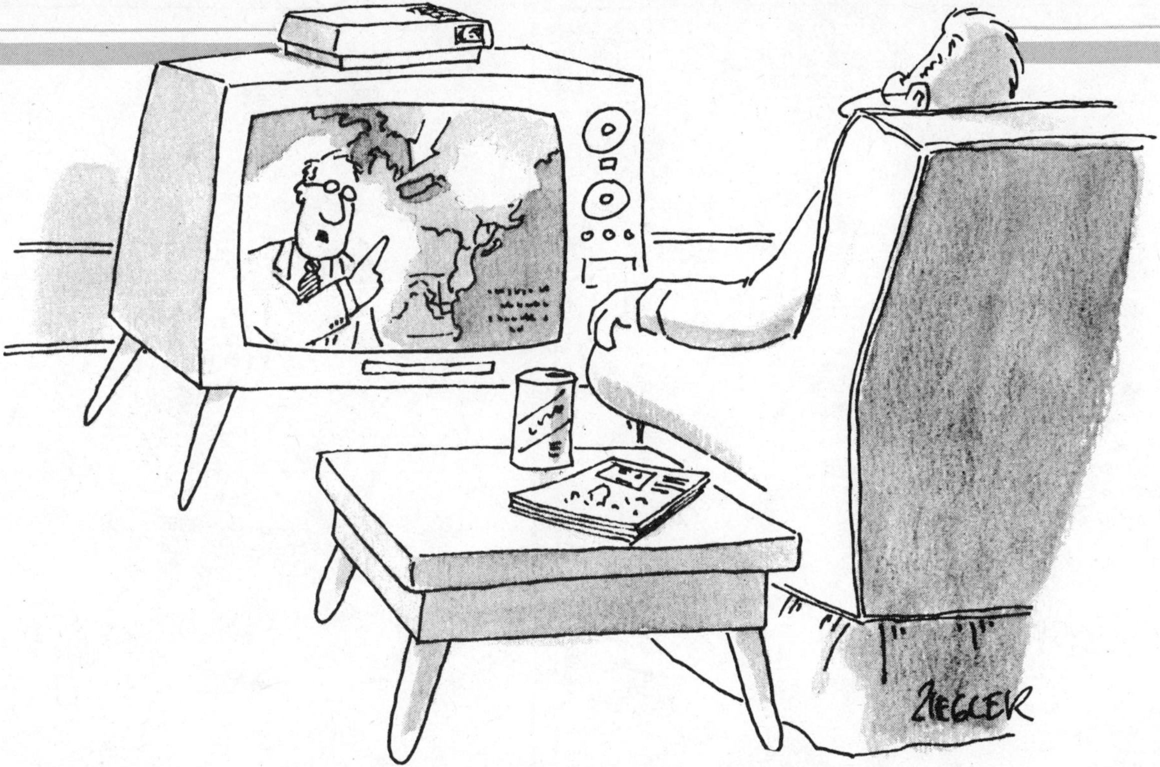
ZIEGLER

"Rain in the Northeast, clear skies to the south, while large portions of the Midwest continue to be blanketed by Shirley MacLaine's aura."

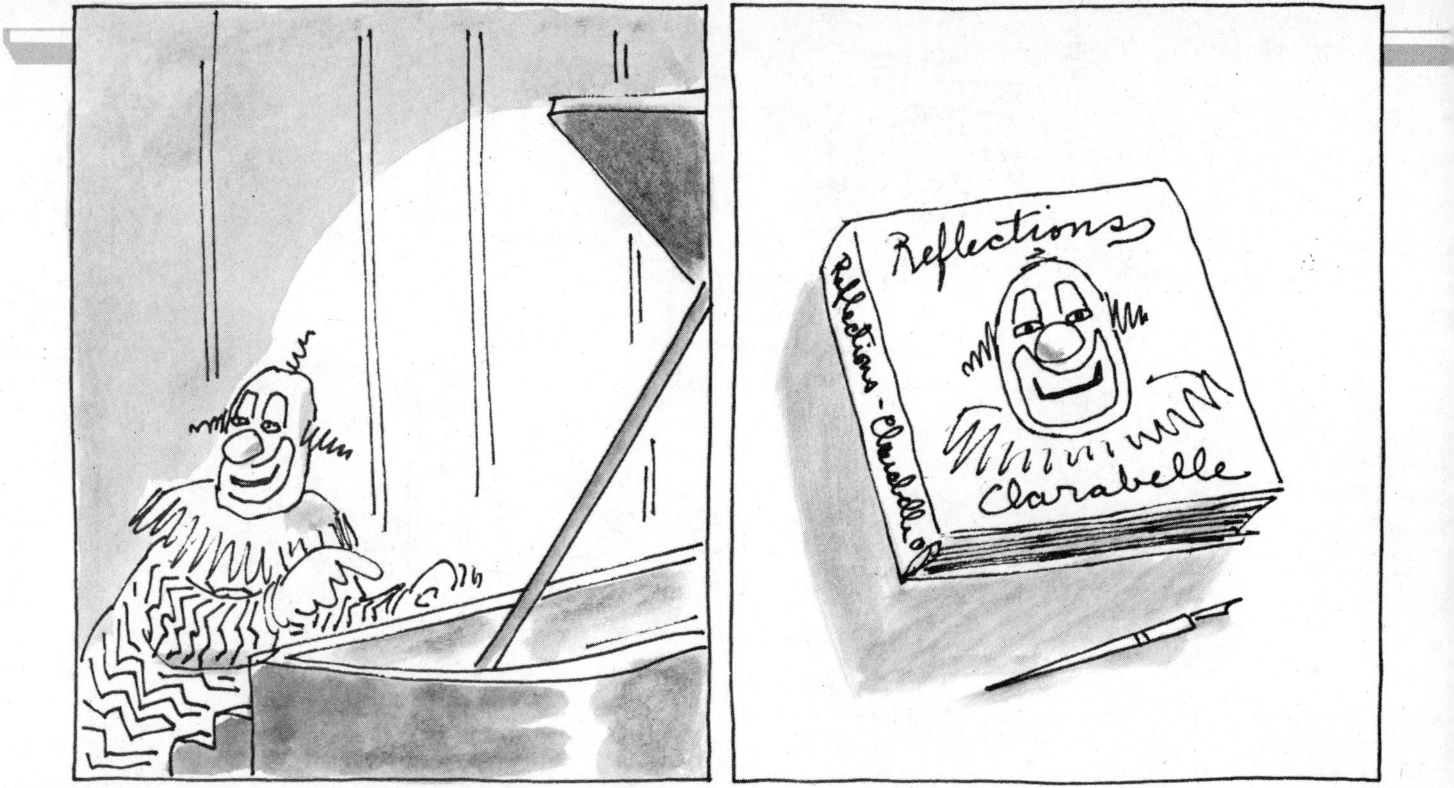
Reflections
Clarabelle
Reflections - Clarabelle

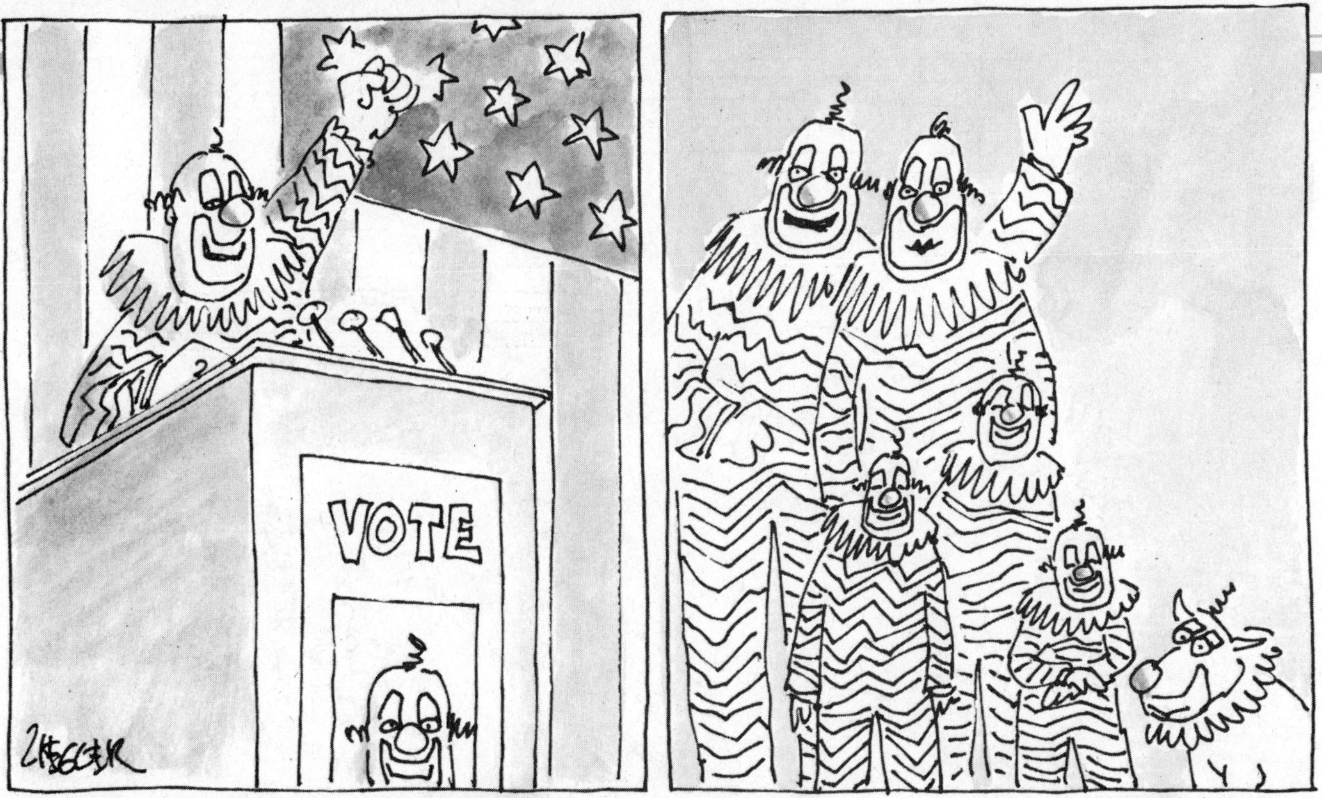
VOTE

CLARABELLE: THE YEARS WITHOUT HOWDY

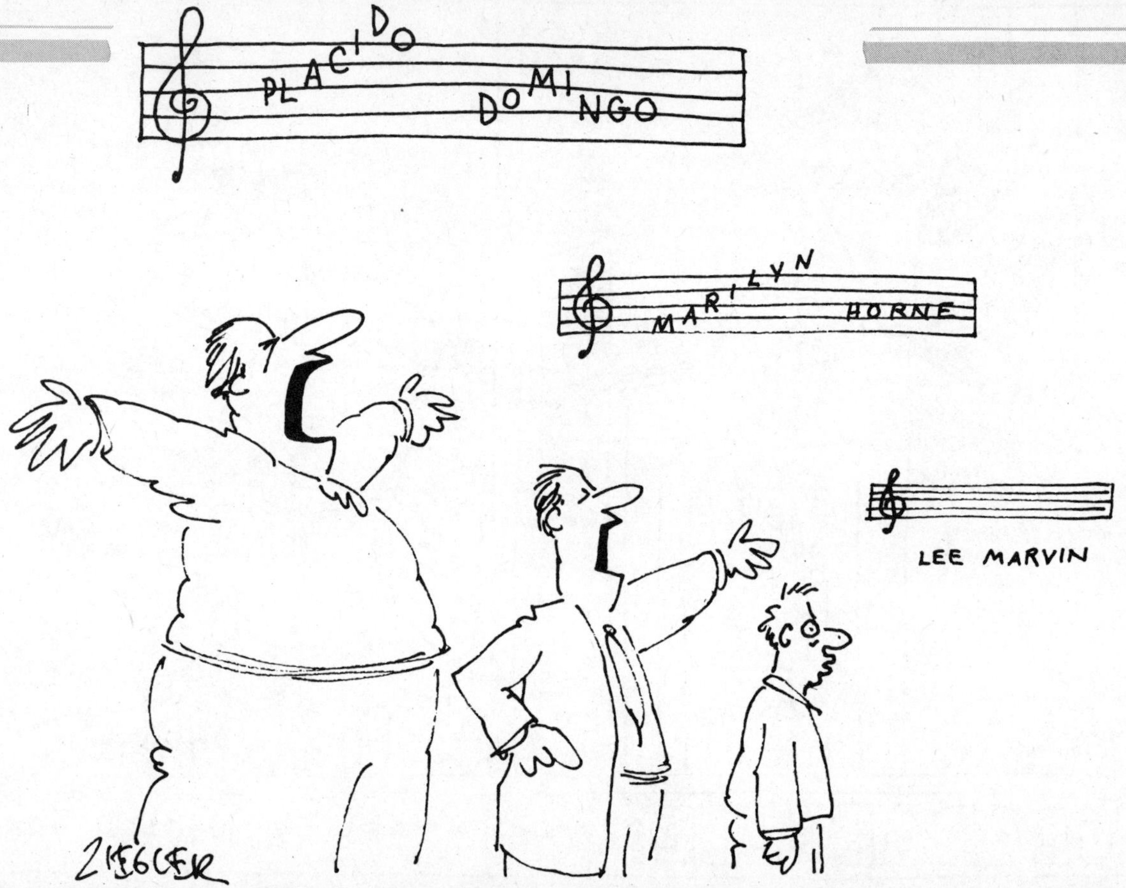
PLACIDO
DOMINGO
MARILYN
HORNE
LEE MARVIN
ZIEGLER

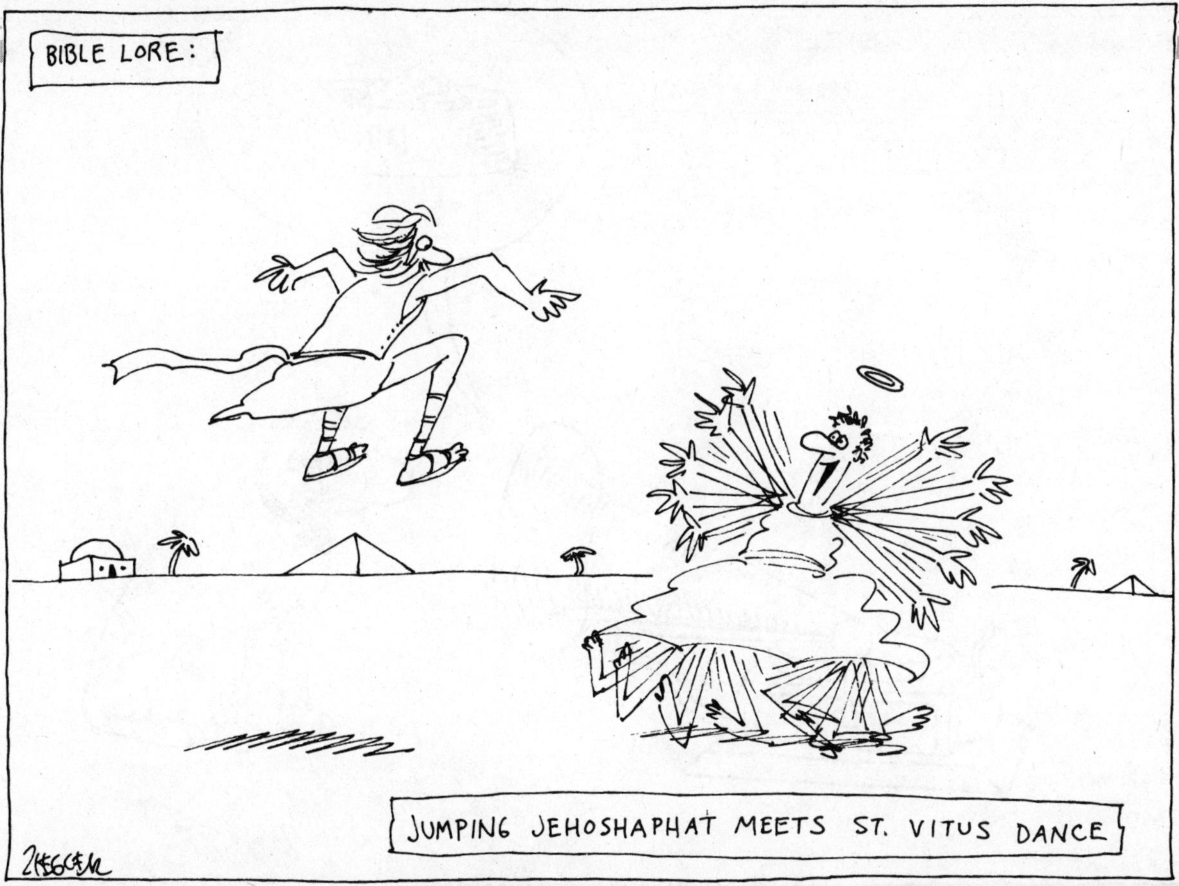
BIBLE LORE:
JUMPING JEHOSHAPHAT MEETS ST. VITUS DANCE

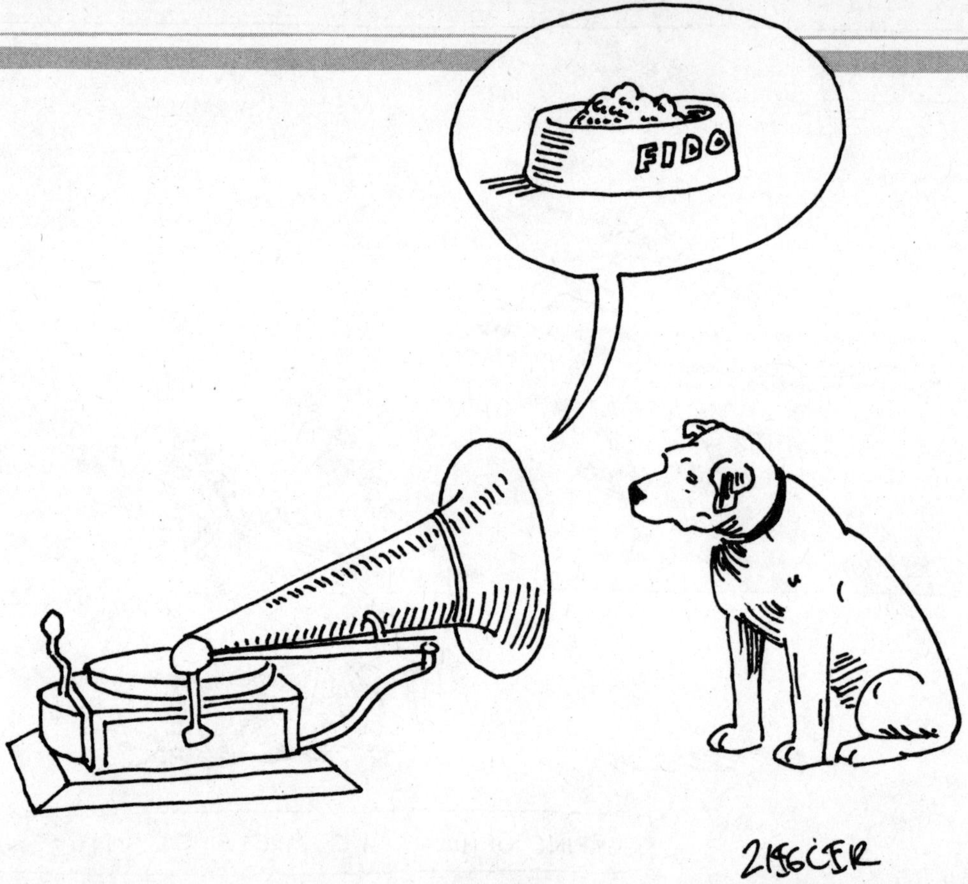
FIDO
ZIEGLER

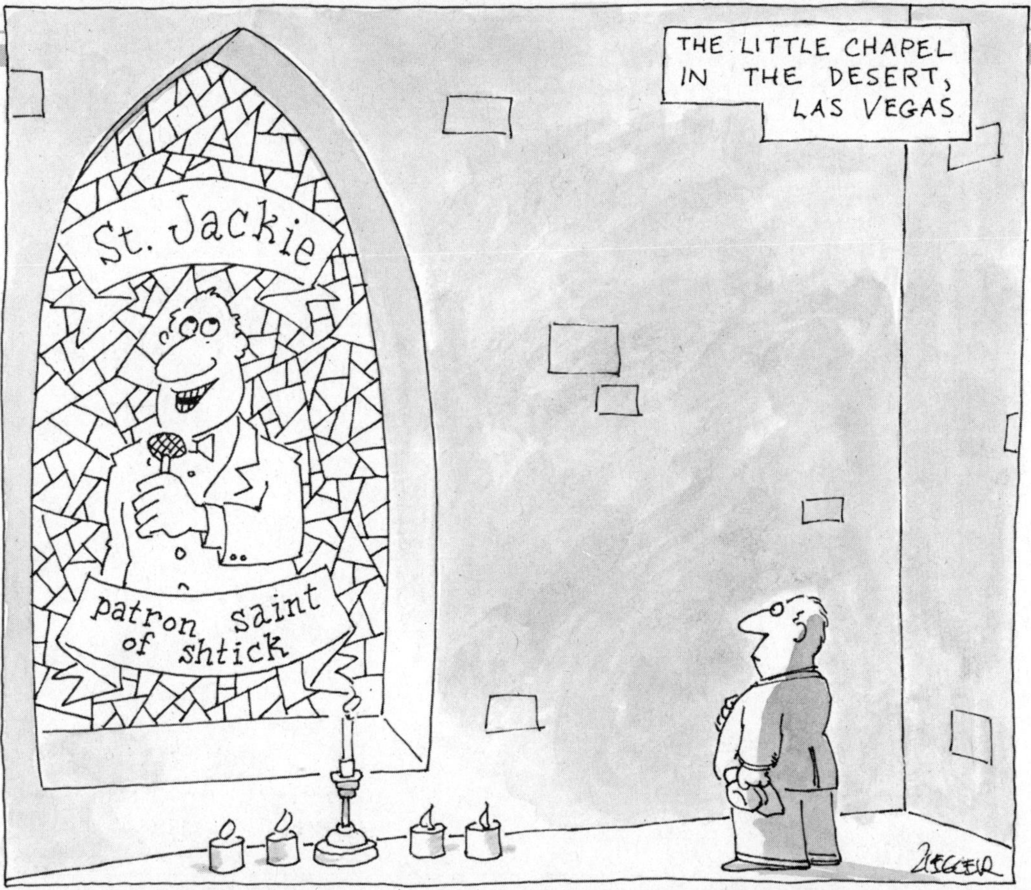
THE LITTLE CHAPEL IN THE DESERT, LAS VEGAS
St. Jackie
patron saint of shtick

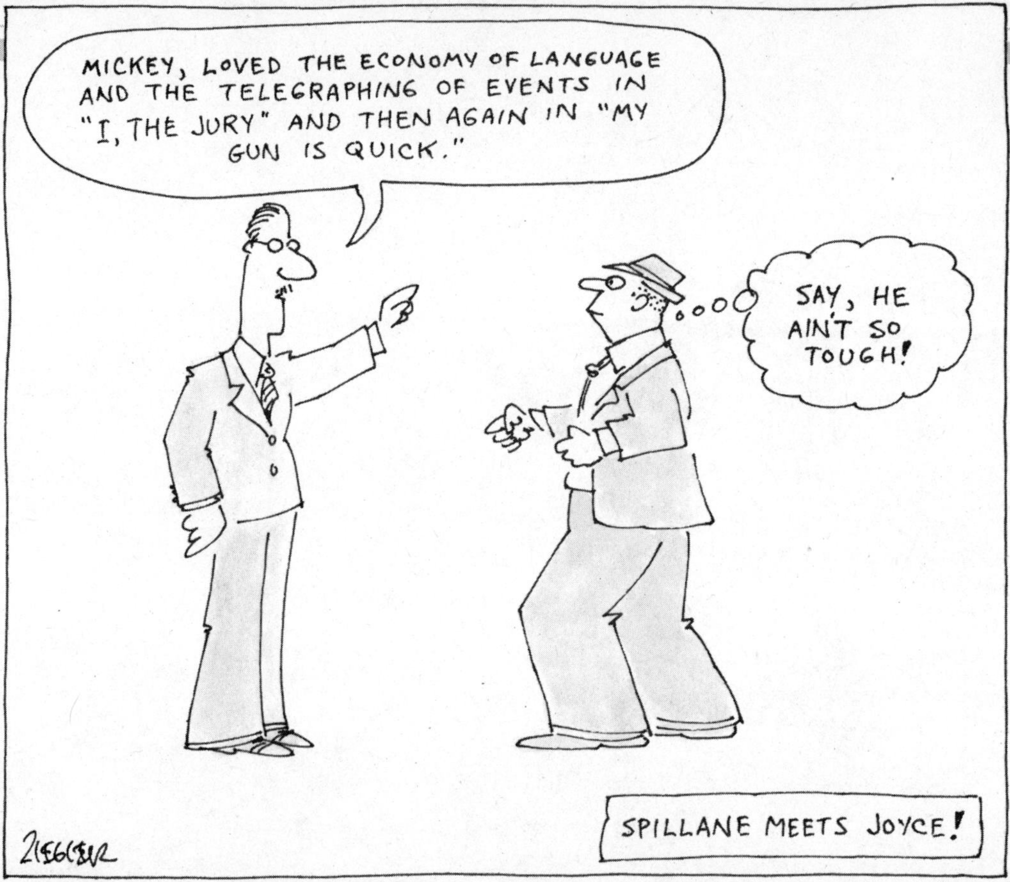
MICKEY, LOVED THE ECONOMY OF LANGUAGE AND THE TELEGRAPHING OF EVENTS IN "I, THE JURY" AND THEN AGAIN IN "MY GUN IS QUICK."
SAY, HE AIN'T SO TOUGH!
SPILLANE MEETS JOYCE!
ZIEGLER

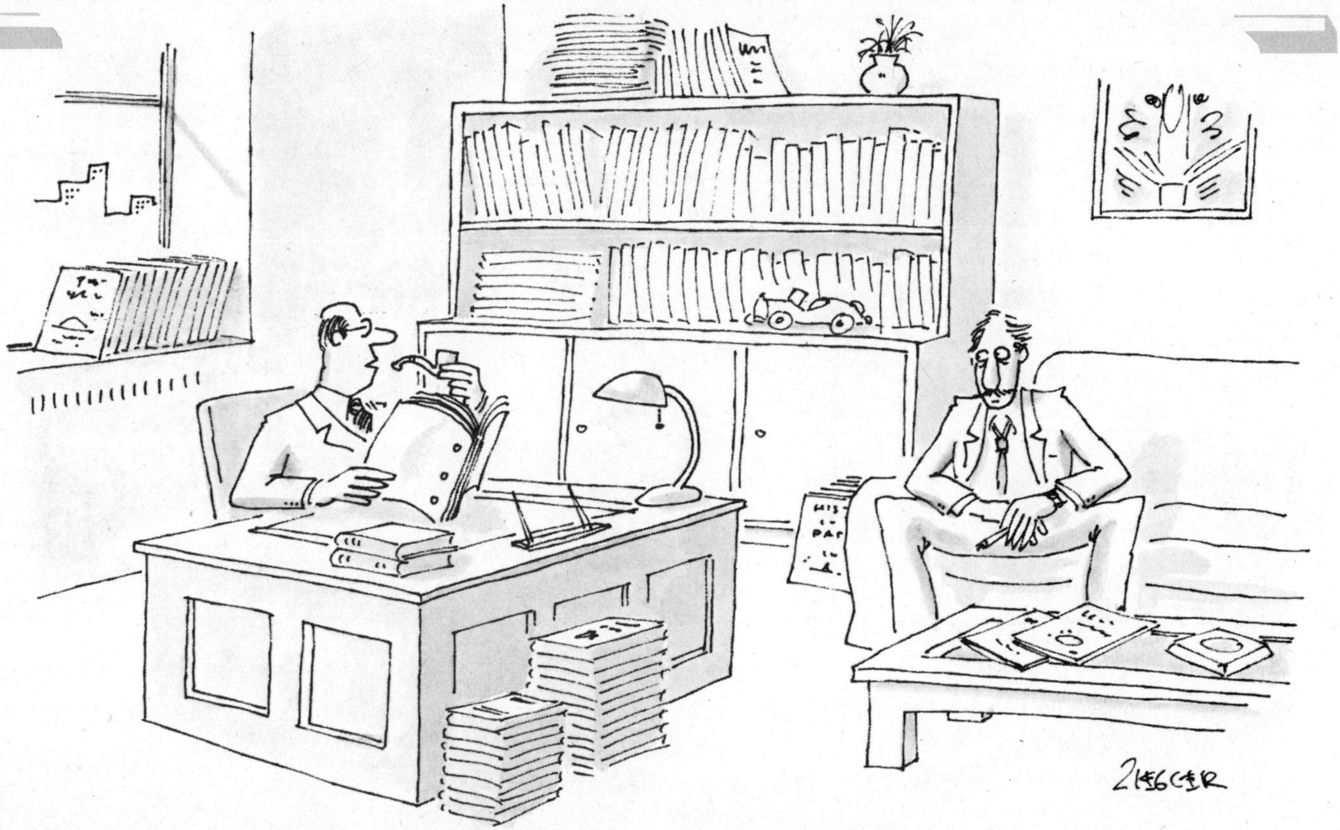

"Say, aren't these the same characters that Saul Bellow used in *his* last novel?"

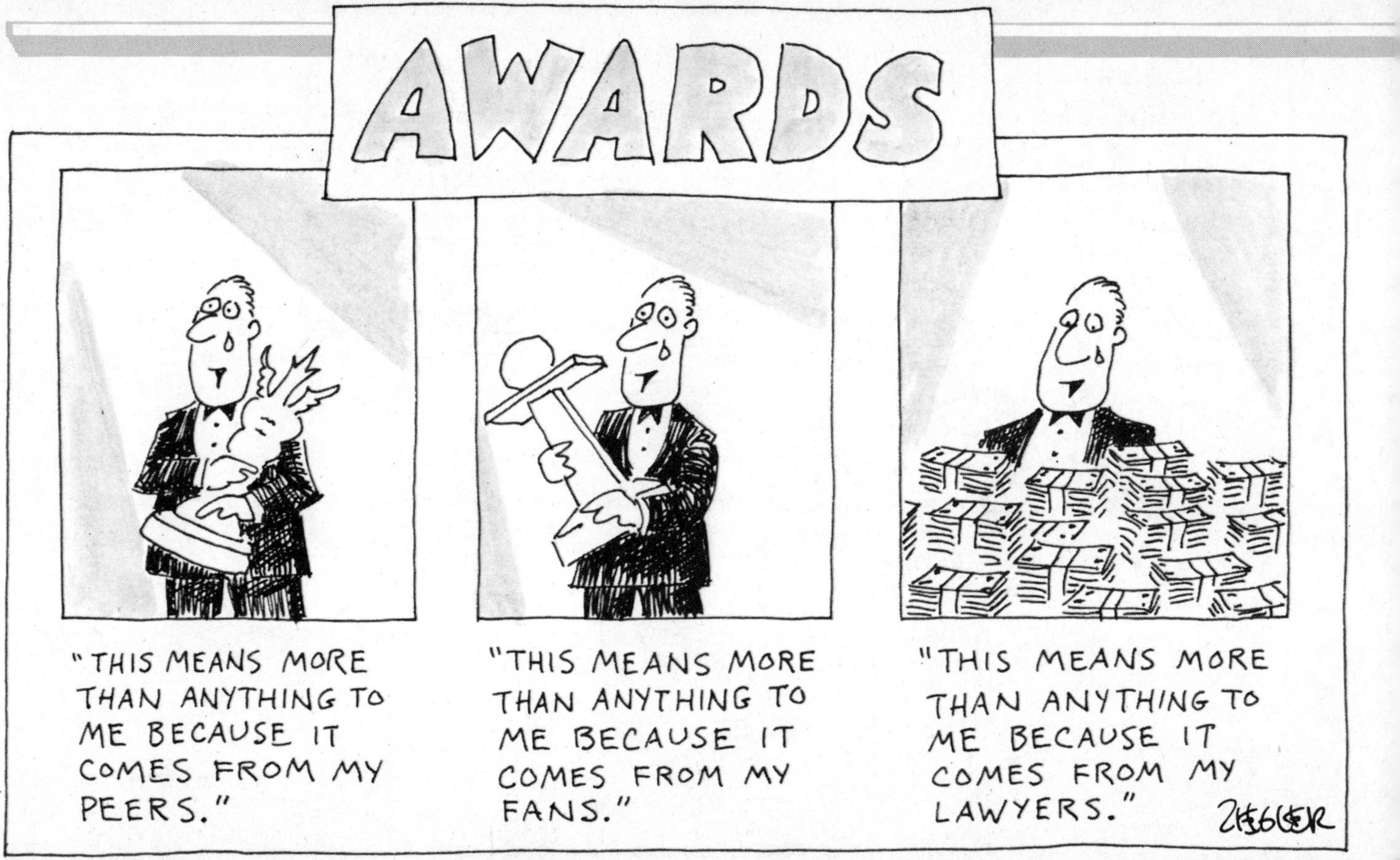
AWARDS
"THIS MEANS MORE THAN ANYTHING TO ME BECAUSE IT COMES FROM MY PEERS."
"THIS MEANS MORE THAN ANYTHING TO ME BECAUSE IT COMES FROM MY FANS."
"THIS MEANS MORE THAN ANYTHING TO ME BECAUSE IT COMES FROM MY LAWYERS."
ZIEGLER

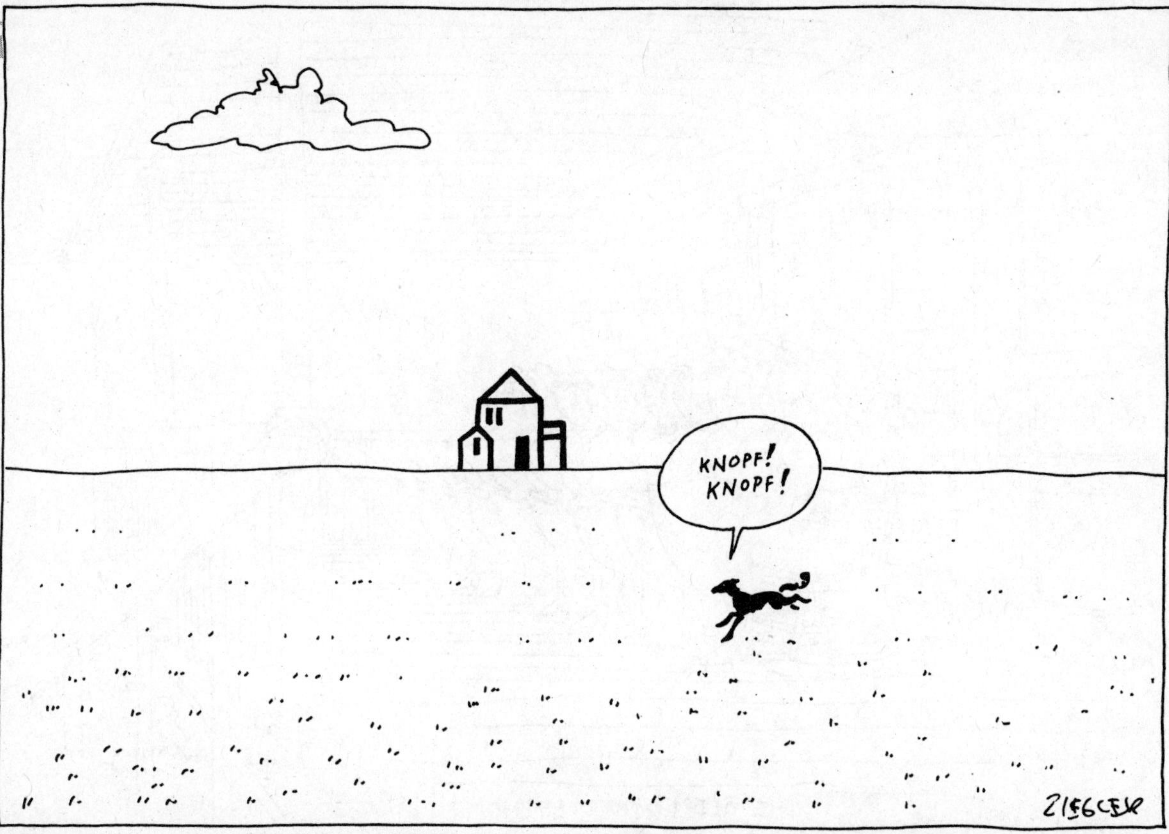
KNOPF! KNOPF!
ZIEGLER

THE RANDOM HOUSE ON THE PRAIRIE UNDER DURESS FROM SOME NEIGHBOR'S INTRUSIVE DOG

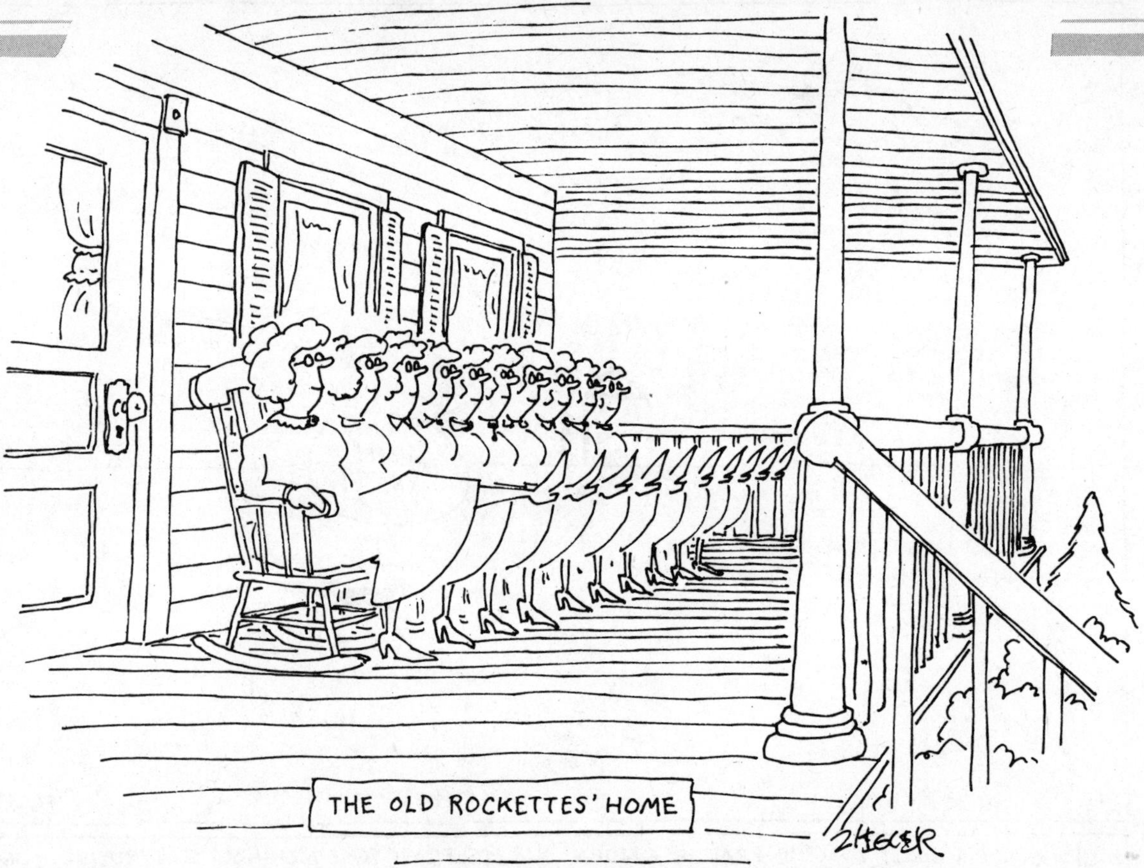
ZIEGLER

THE OLD ROCKETTES' HOME

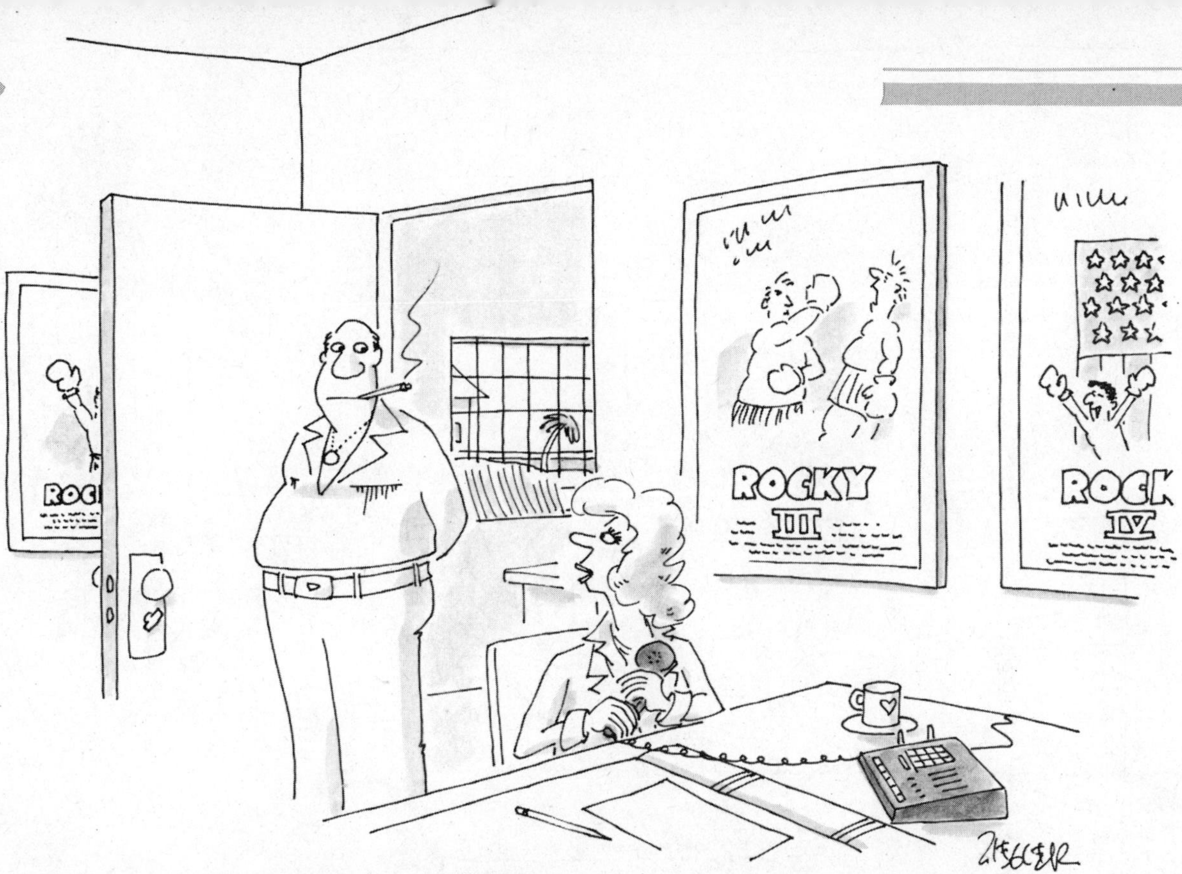
ROCKY
III

"It's Mr. Stallone. He says he has another idea for a movie."

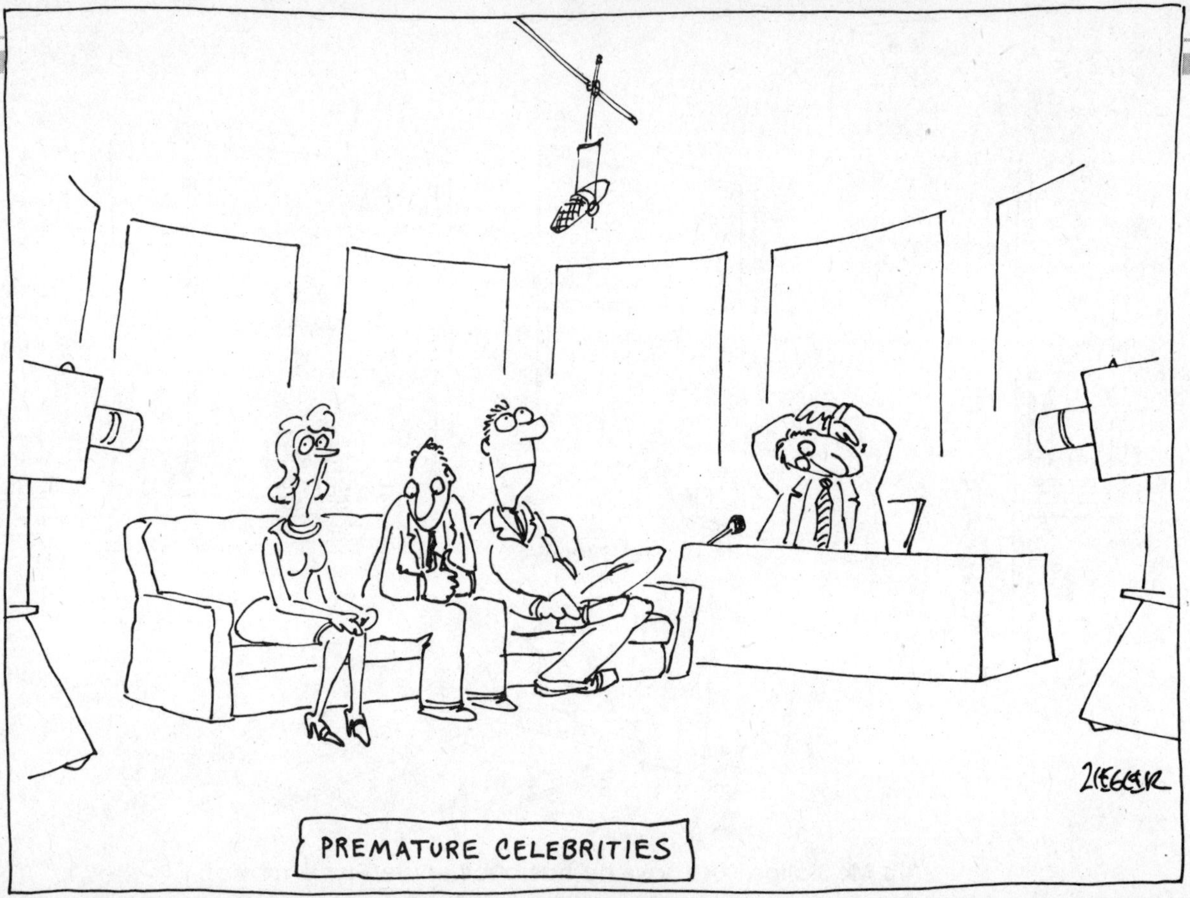
ZIEGLER
PREMATURE CELEBRITIES

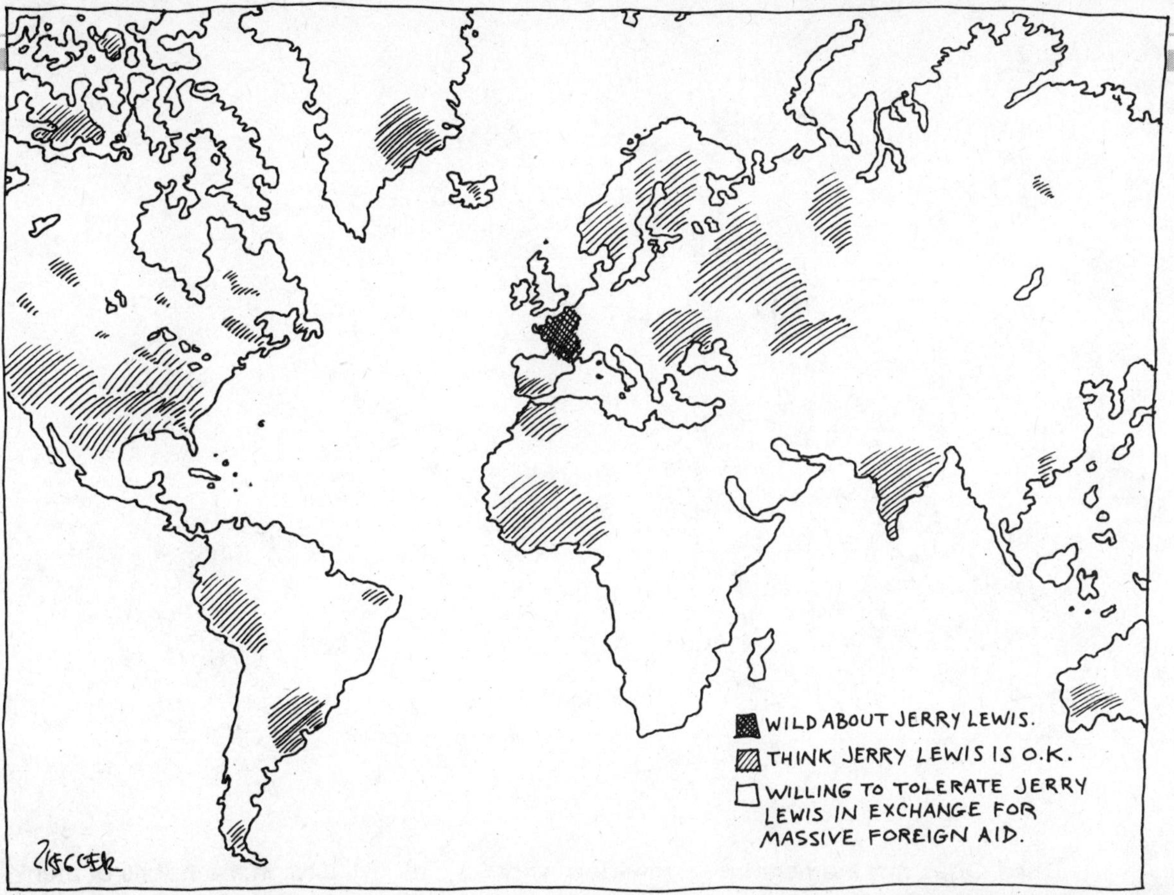
WILD ABOUT JERRY LEWIS.
THINK JERRY LEWIS IS O.K.
WILLING TO TOLERATE JERRY LEWIS IN EXCHANGE FOR MASSIVE FOREIGN AID.
ZIEGLER

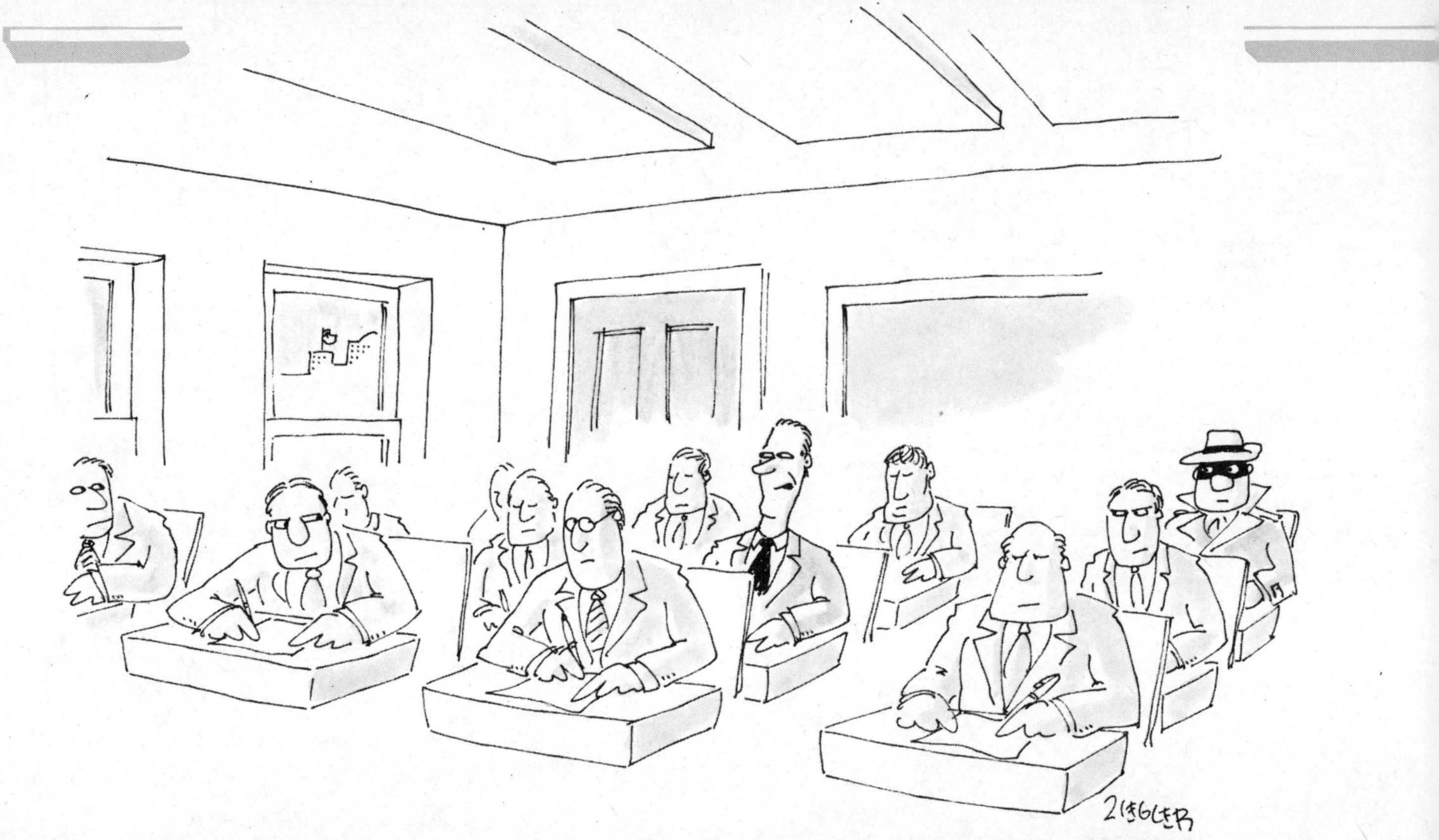
ZIEGLER

"Pssst. Does anyone here have any idea what the hell evil lurks in the hearts of men?"

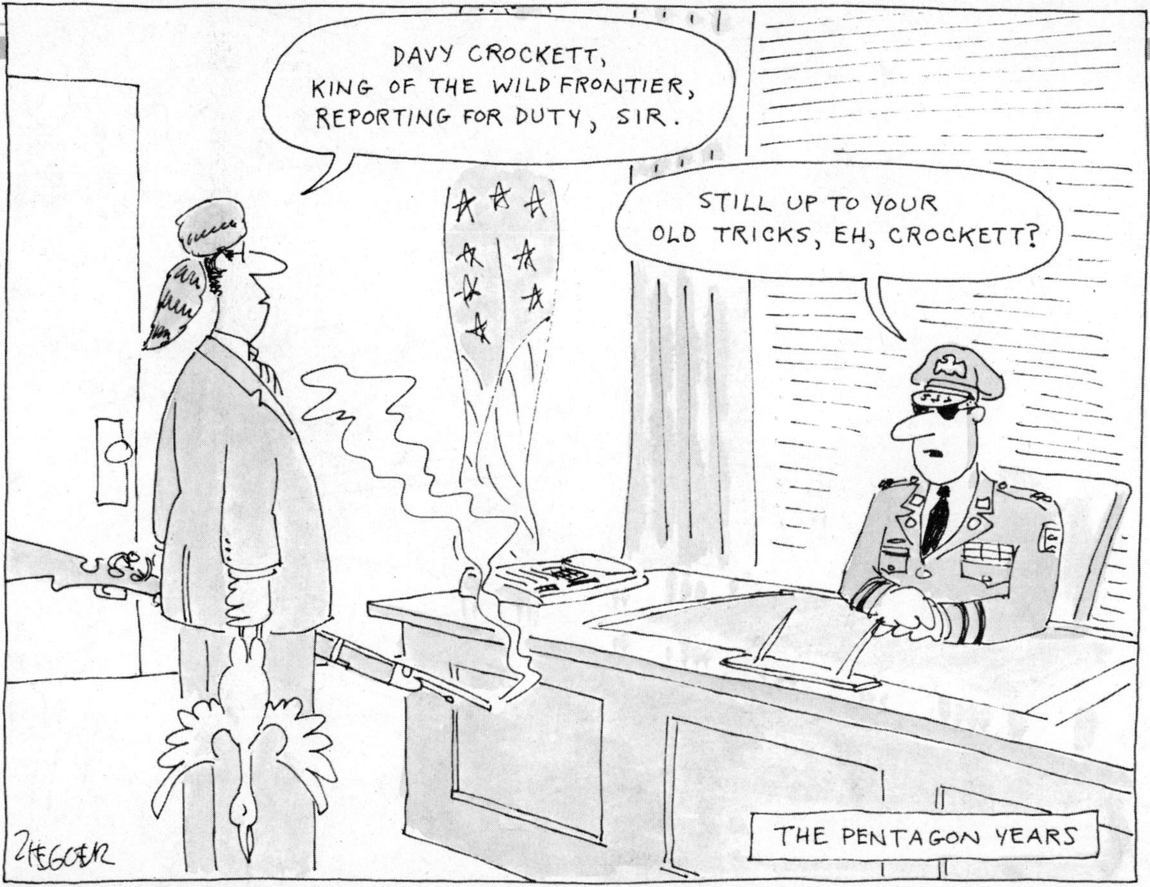
DAVY CROCKETT, KING OF THE WILD FRONTIER, REPORTING FOR DUTY, SIR.
STILL UP TO YOUR OLD TRICKS, EH, CROCKETT?
THE PENTAGON YEARS

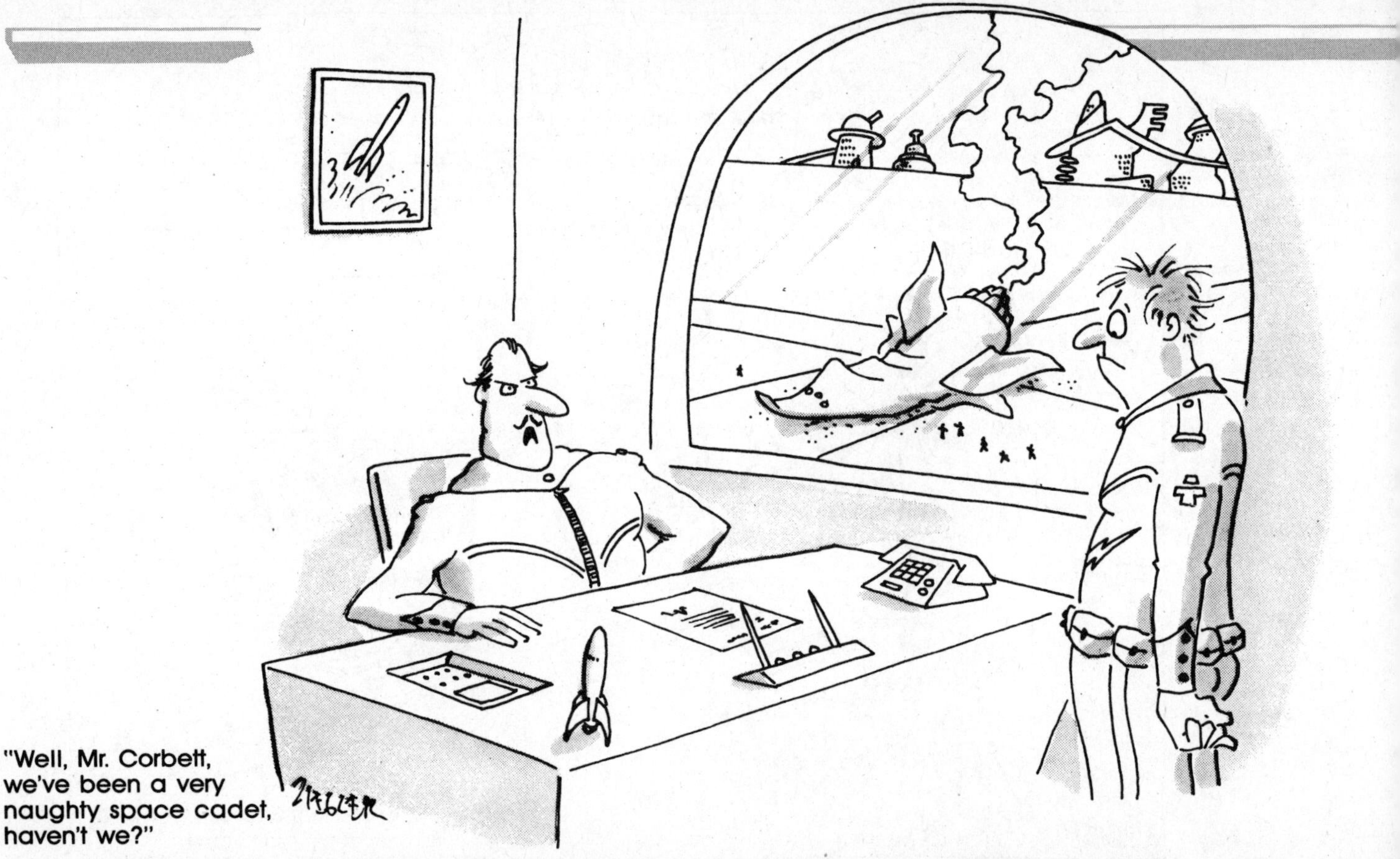

"Well, Mr. Corbett,
we've been a very
naughty space cadet,
haven't we?"

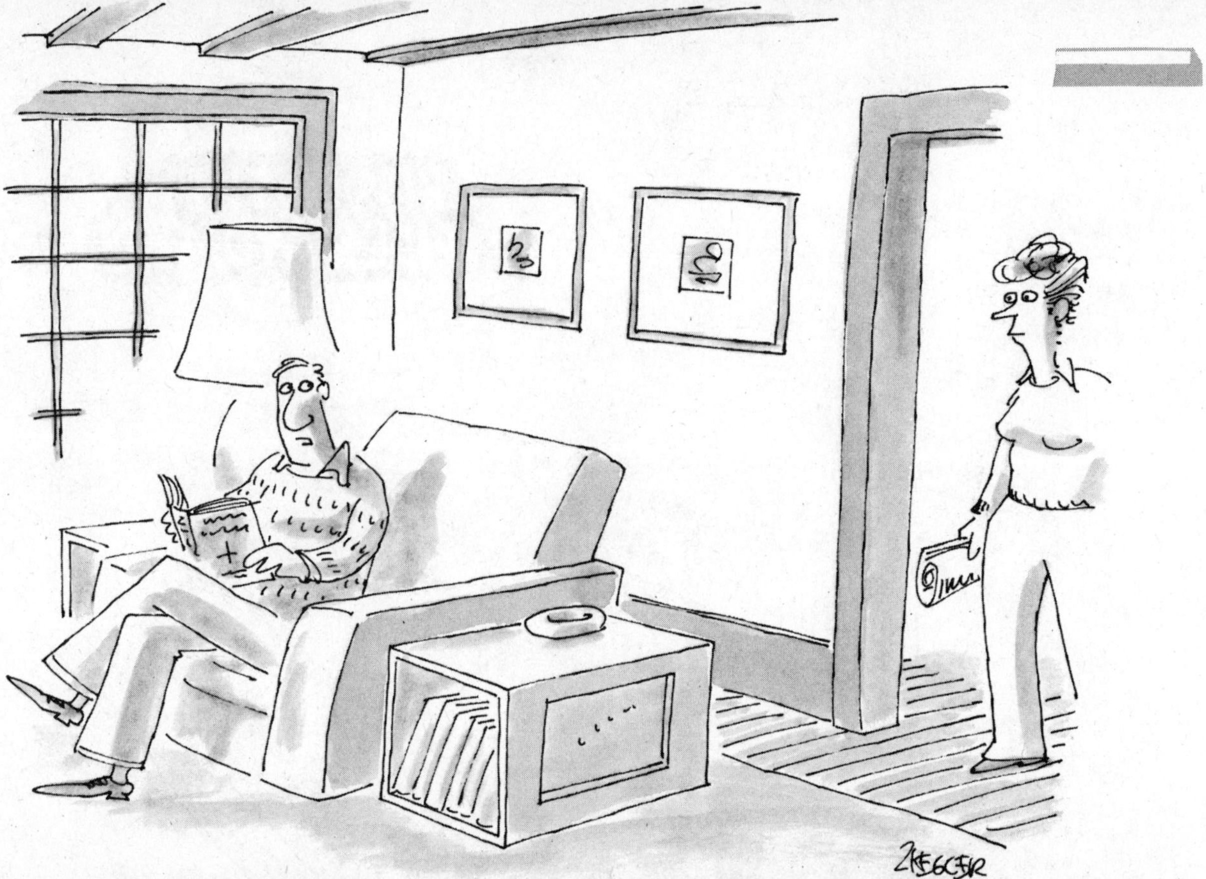

"It's by Stephen King, writing under the pseudonym of Richard Bachman, but I'll be damned if I know why."

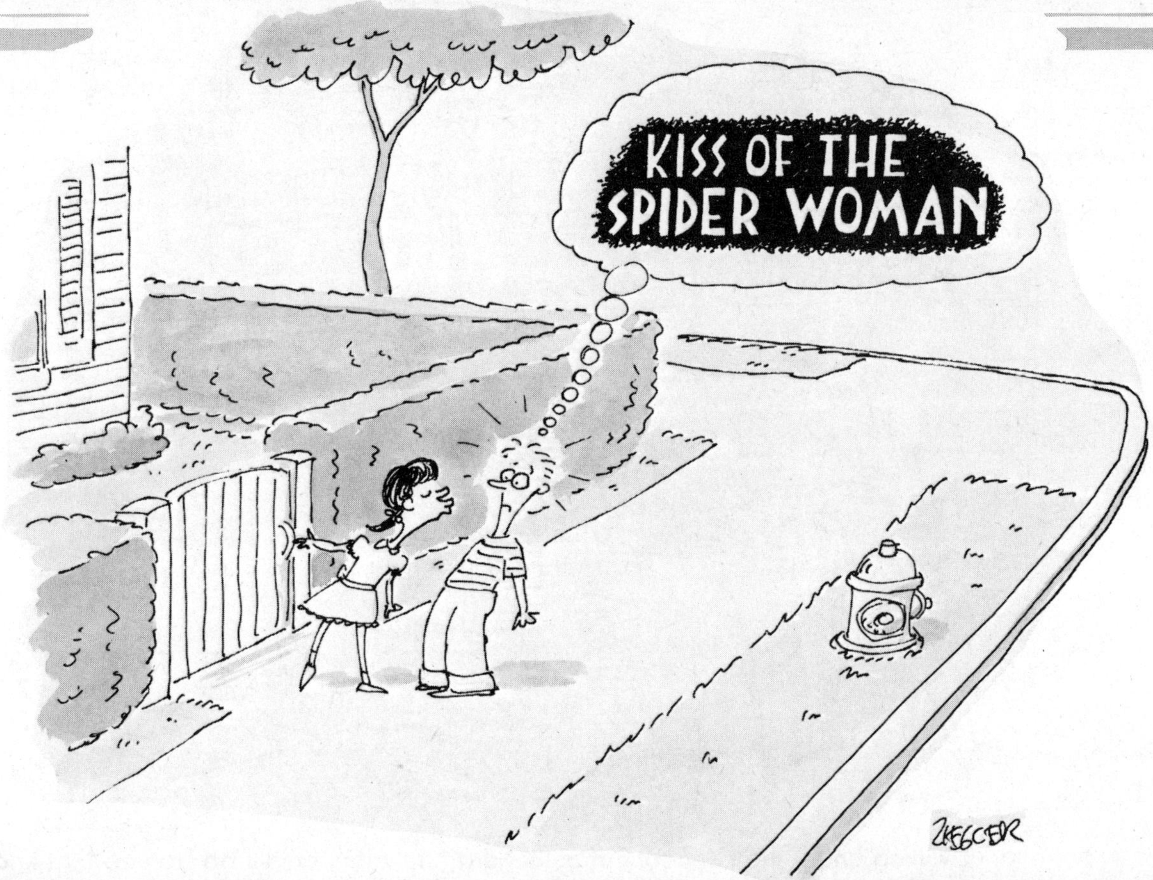
KISS OF THE SPIDER WOMAN
ZIEGLER

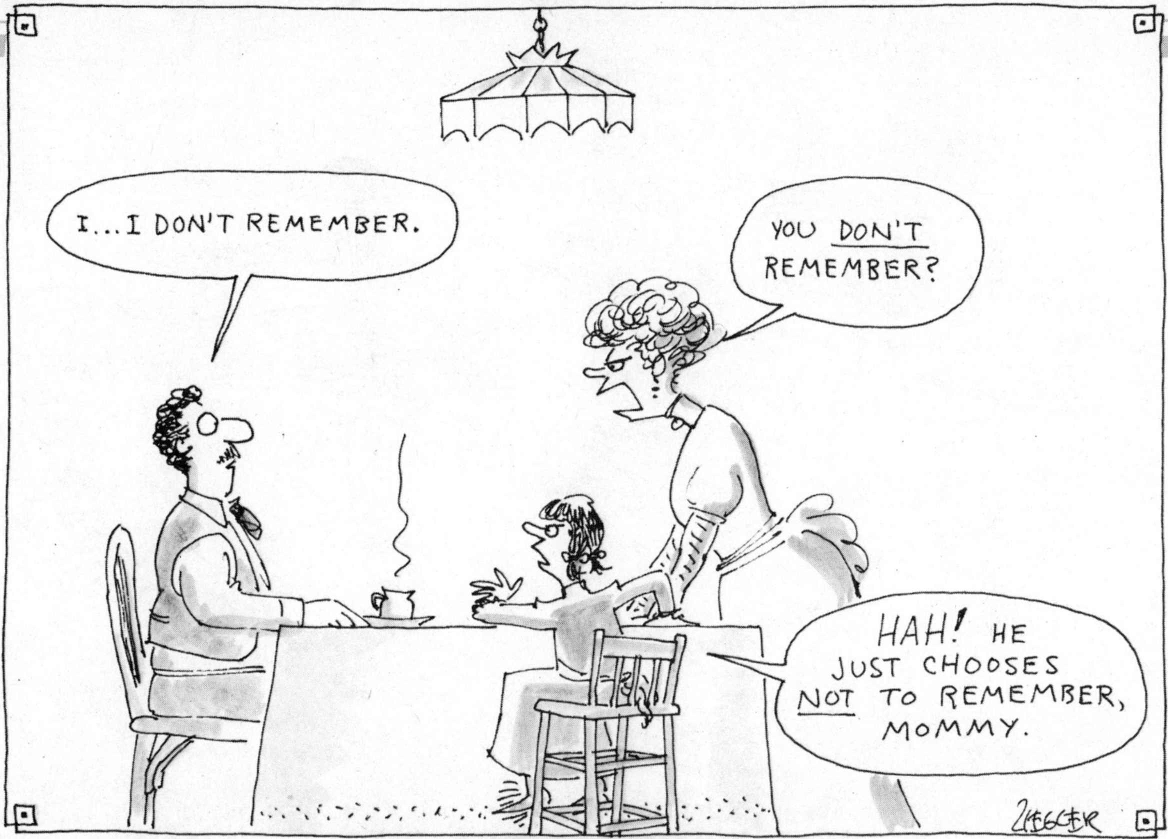
I...I DON'T REMEMBER.
YOU DON'T REMEMBER?
HAH! HE JUST CHOOSES NOT TO REMEMBER, MOMMY.
ZIEGLER

PROUST: THE WRITER WAKES

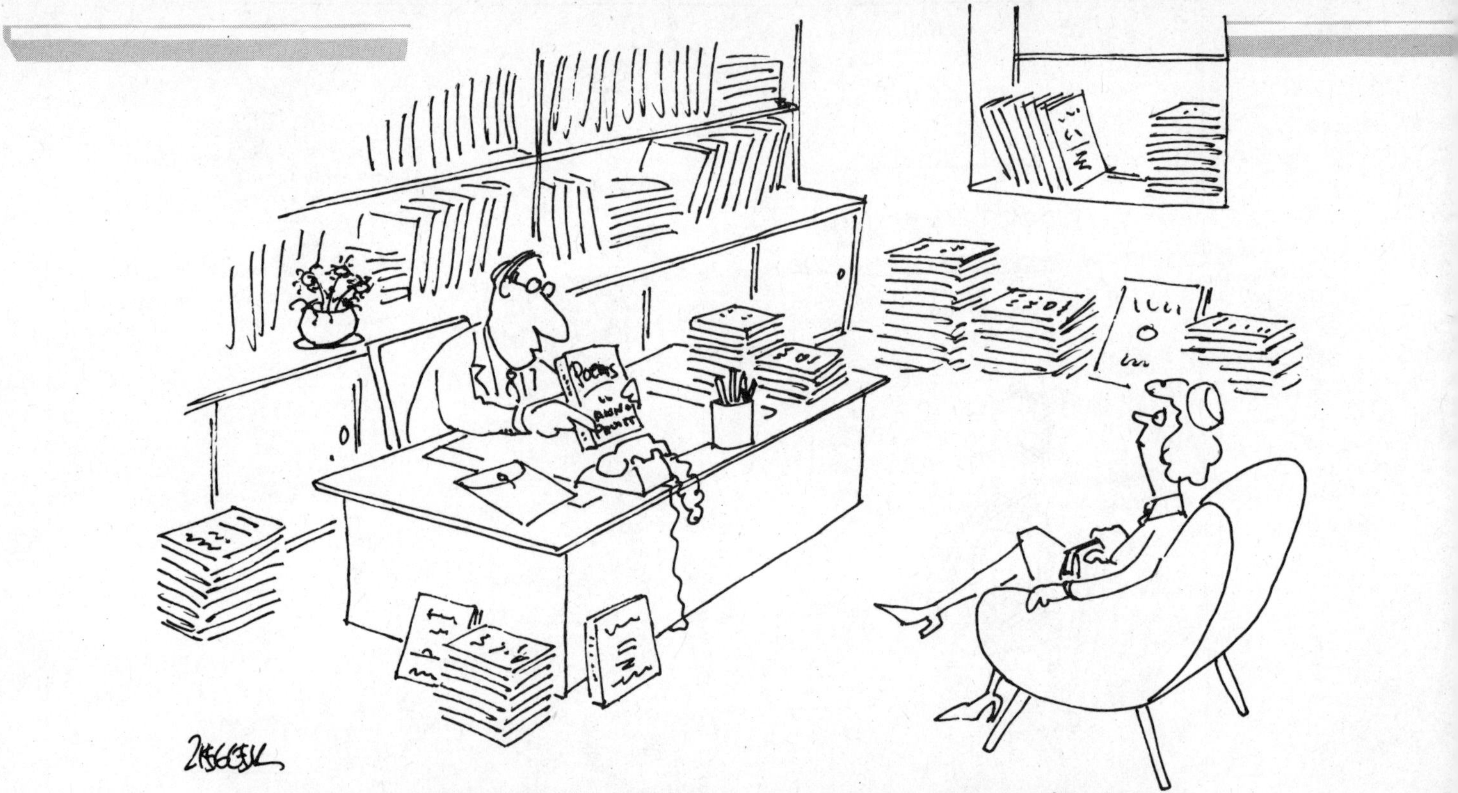

"The reason, Mrs. Pruitt, that your slender volume of poems retails for $49.95 is to help us offset the huge financial gap created by Norman Mailer's latest advance."

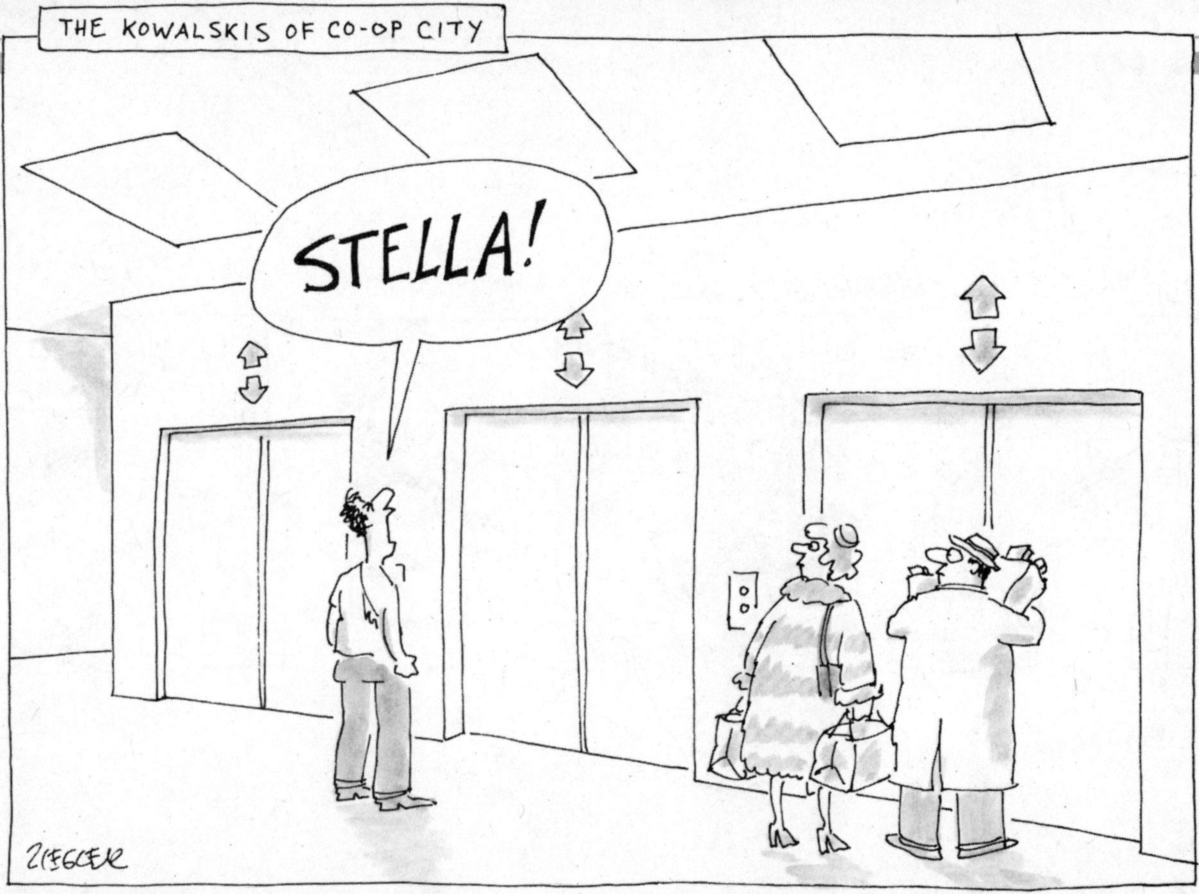
THE KOWALSKIS OF CO-OP CITY
STELLA!
ZIEGLER

Philrizzuto Phunnies

HOLY COW!
HOLY COW!
PRESS BOX
HOLY COW!
HOLY COW!
ZIEGLER

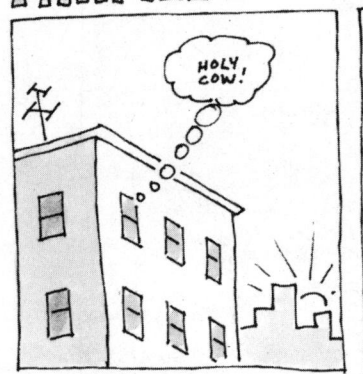

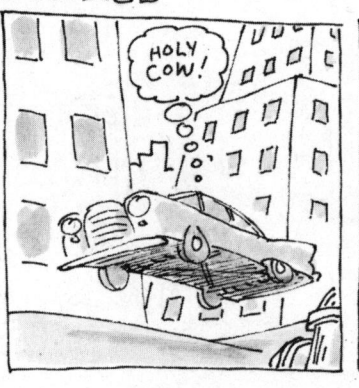

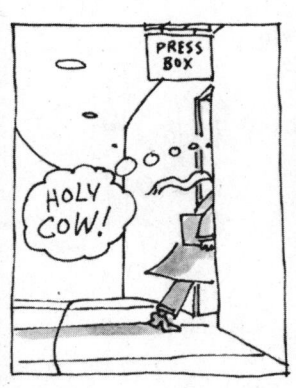

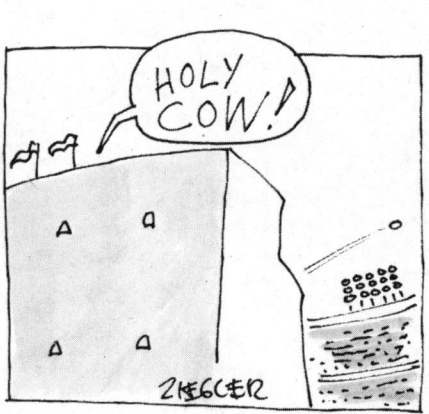

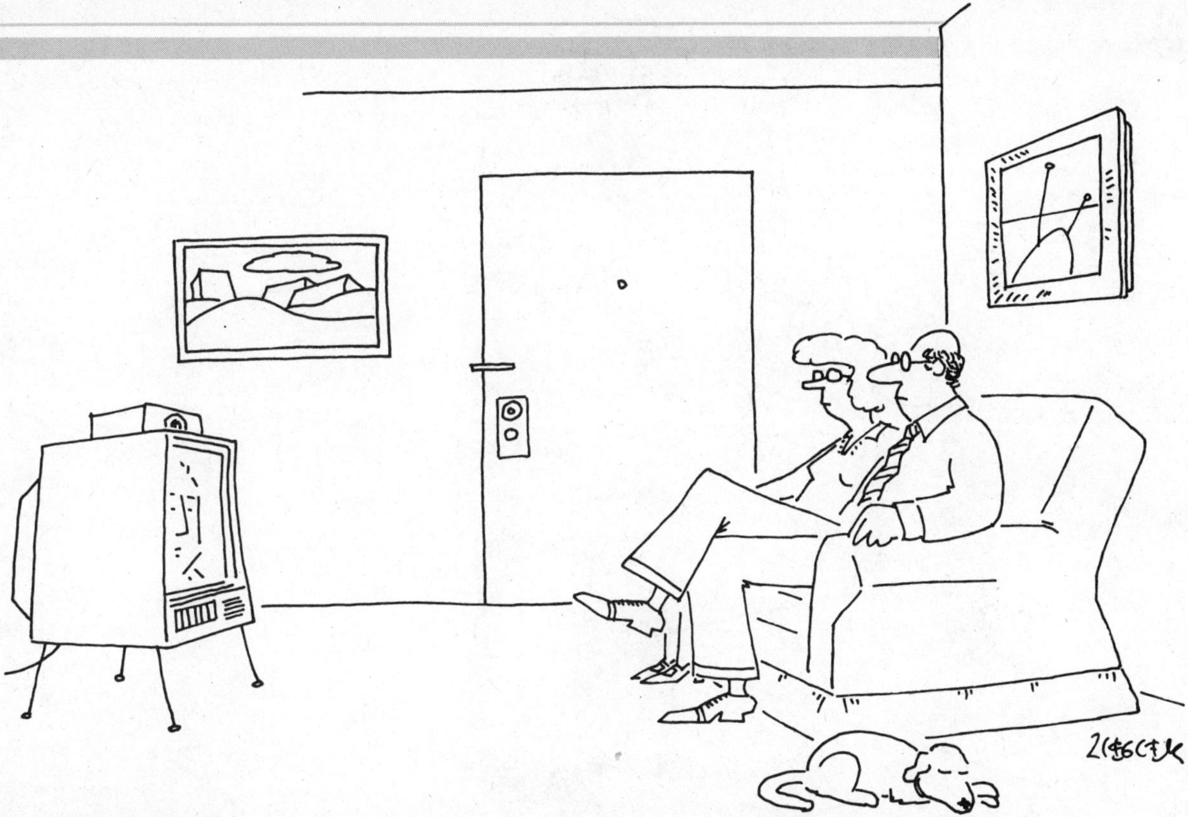

"At the top of our news this evening, once again there were no clear winners on the Phil Donahue show today."

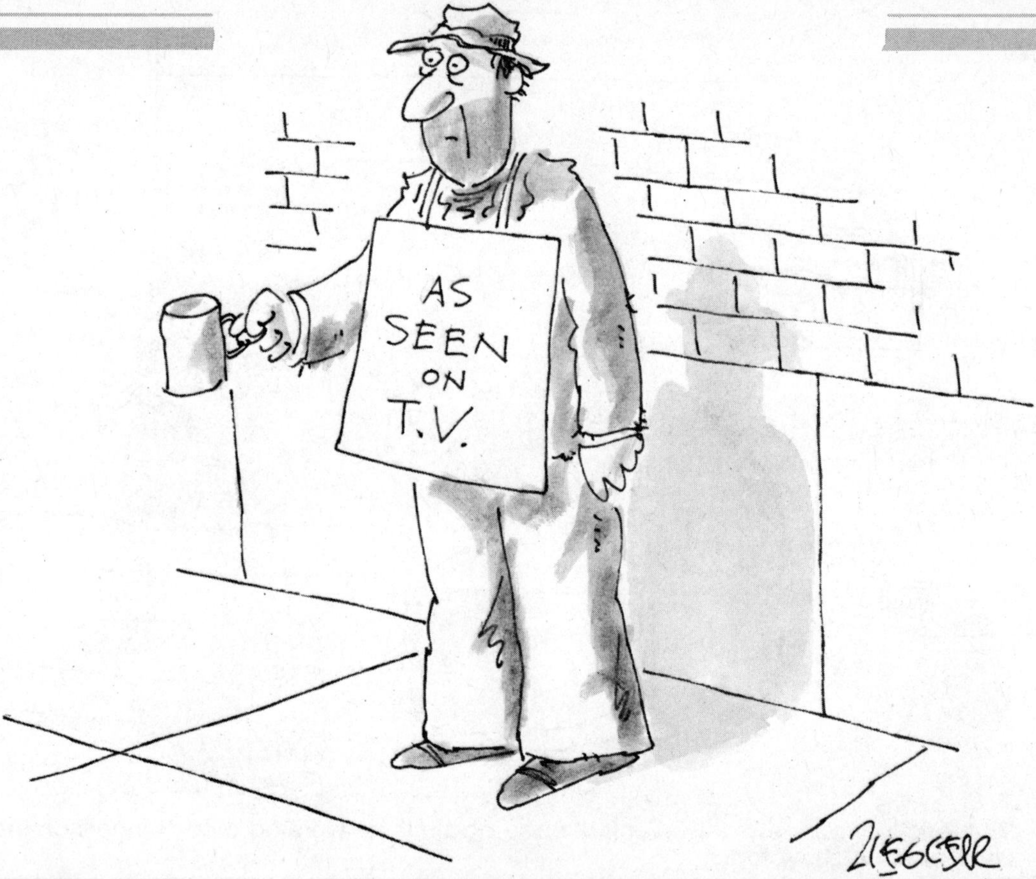
AS
SEEN
ON
T.V.
ZIEGLER

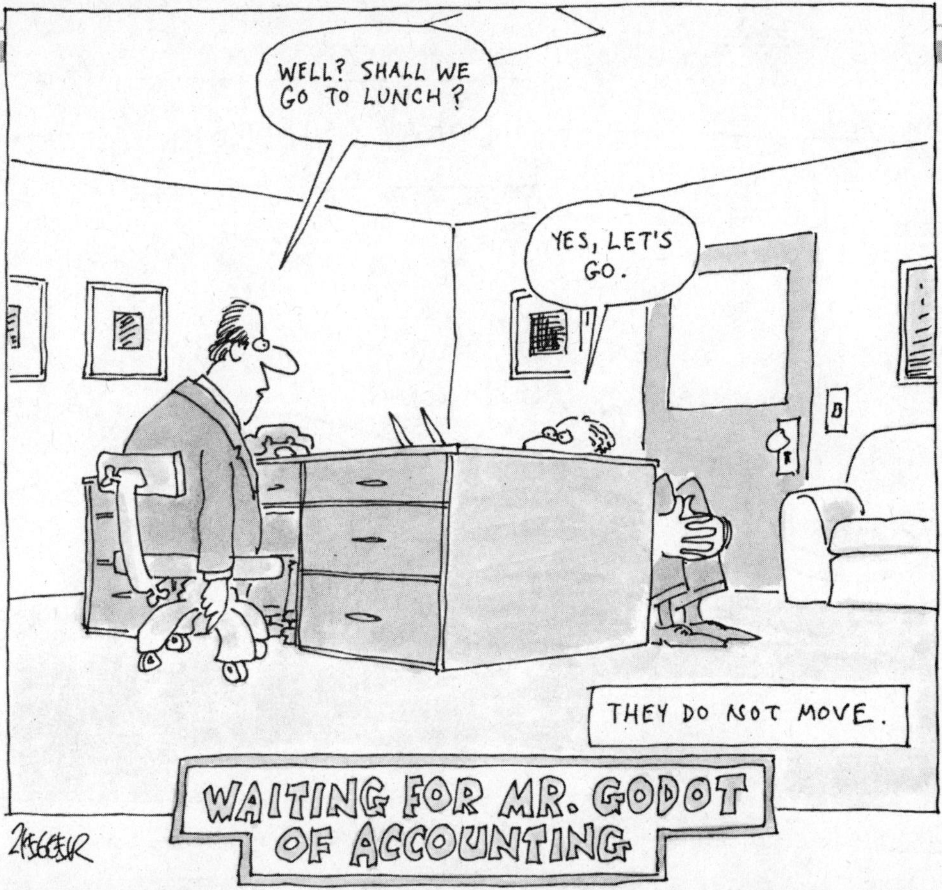
WELL? SHALL WE GO TO LUNCH?
YES, LET'S GO.
THEY DO NOT MOVE.
WAITING FOR MR. GODOT OF ACCOUNTING

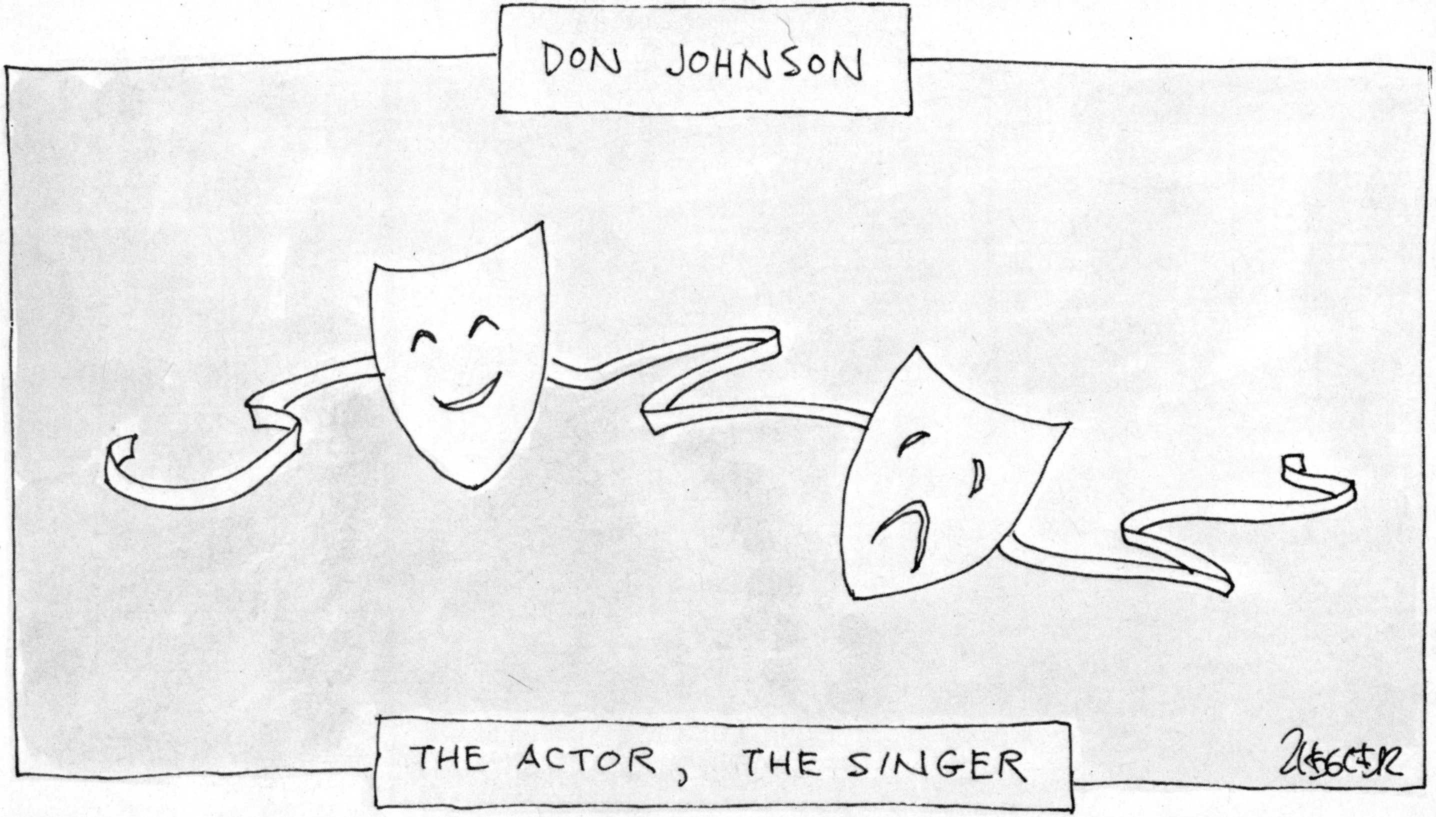
DON JOHNSON
THE ACTOR, THE SINGER

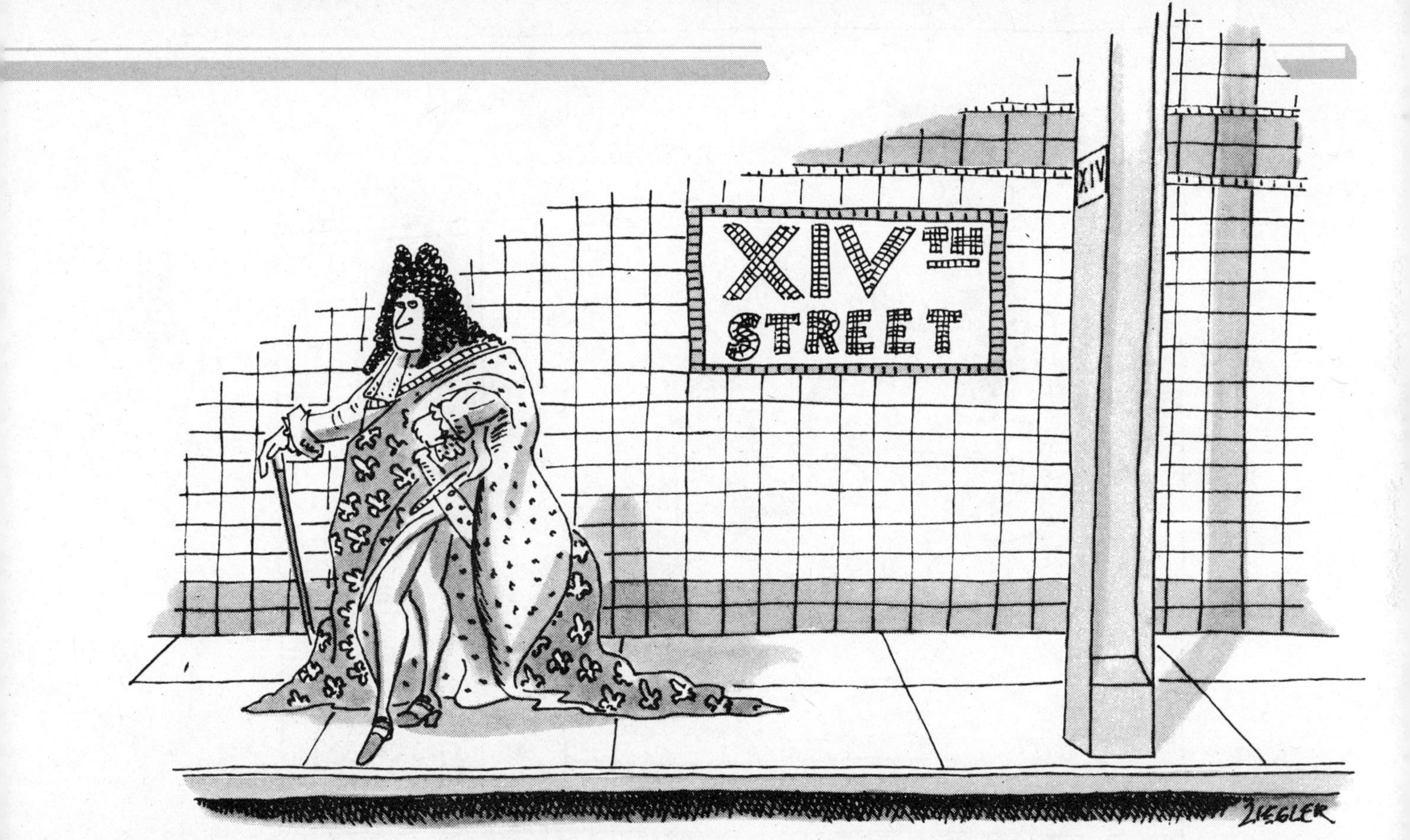
XIVth
STREET
XIV
ZIEGLER

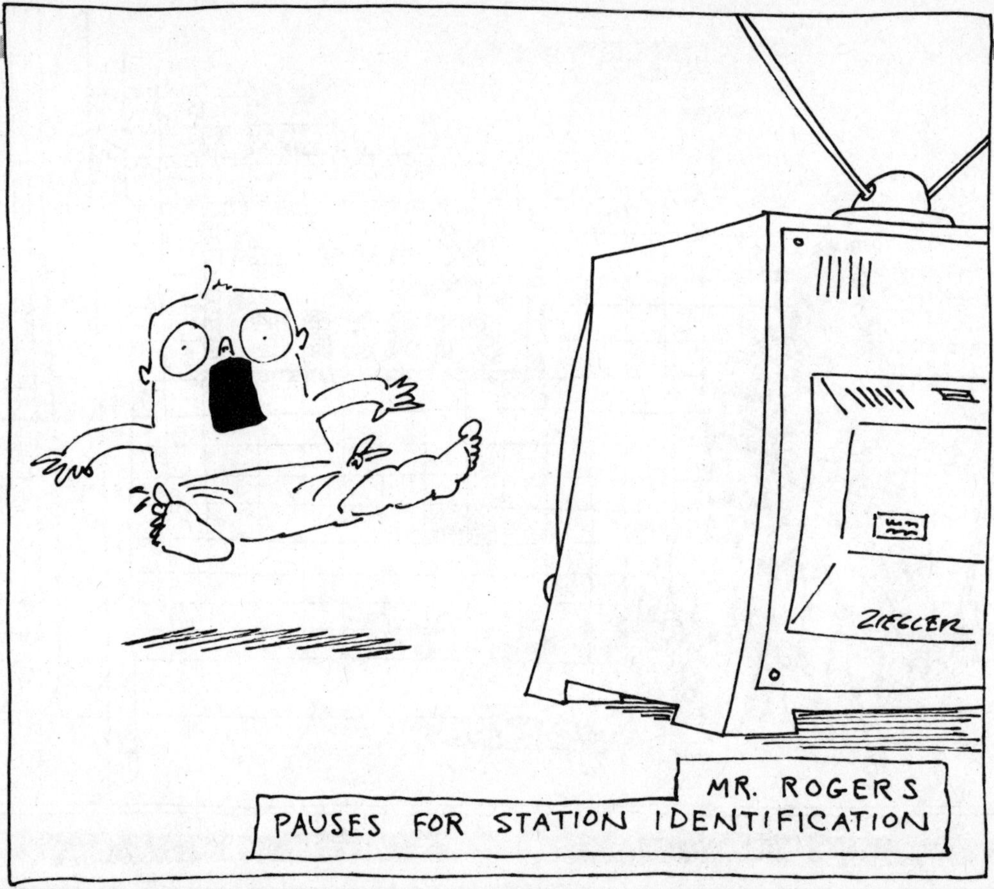
ZIEGLER
MR. ROGERS
PAUSES FOR STATION IDENTIFICATION

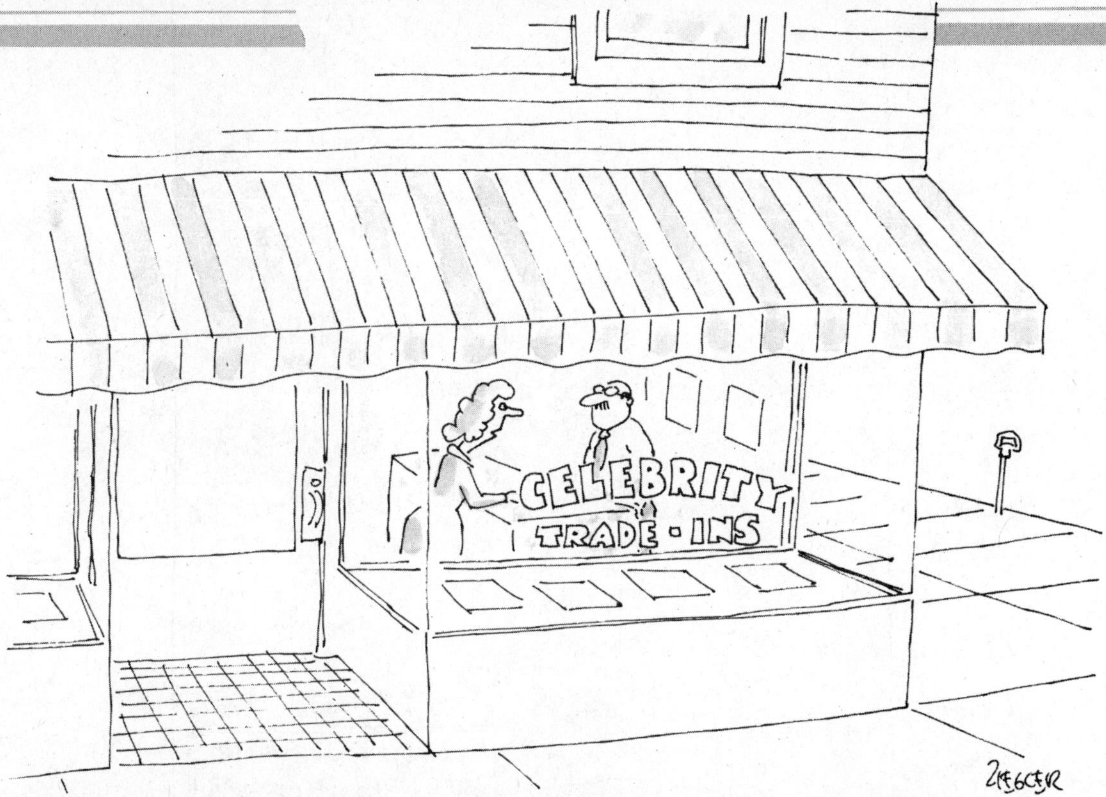
CELEBRITY
TRADE-INS

"I'm sick and tired of the likes of the Hollywood Brat Pack and Boy George. Do you have anything in a Ryan O'Neal or a Pierre Trudeau?"

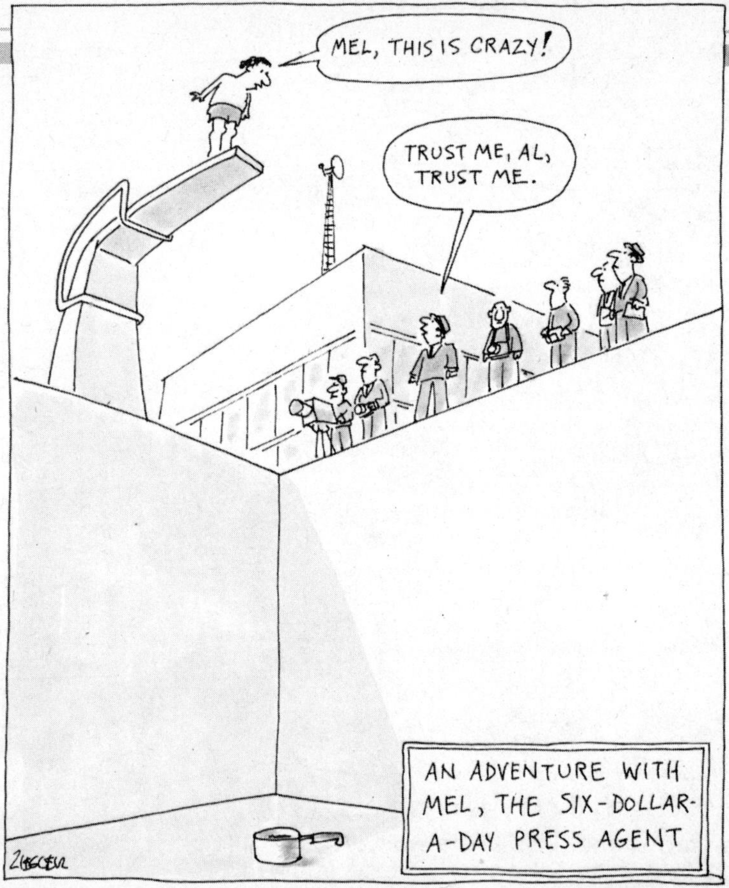
MEL, THIS IS CRAZY!
TRUST ME, AL, TRUST ME.
AN ADVENTURE WITH MEL, THE SIX-DOLLAR-A-DAY PRESS AGENT

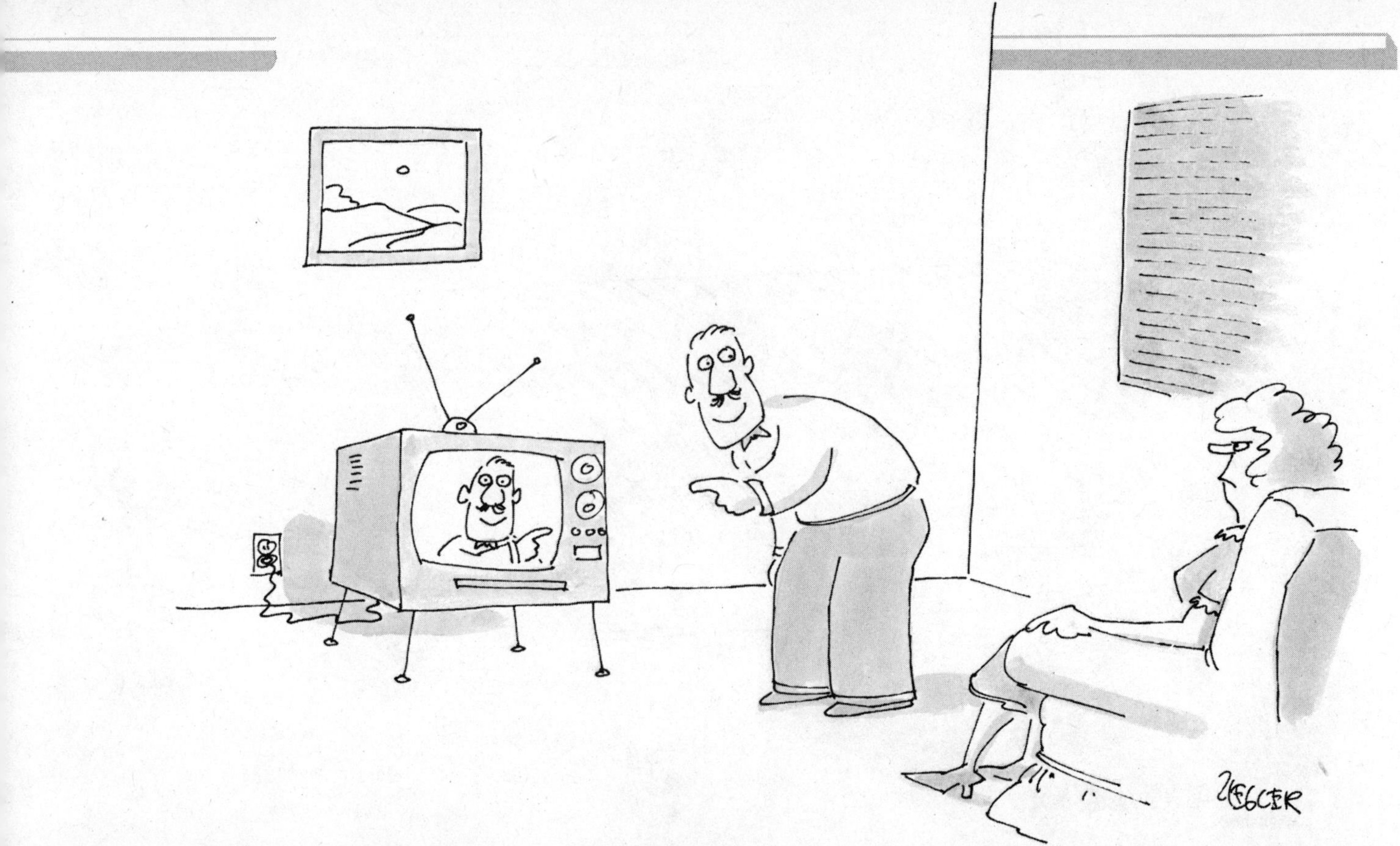

BREAD
BREAD
ZIEGLER

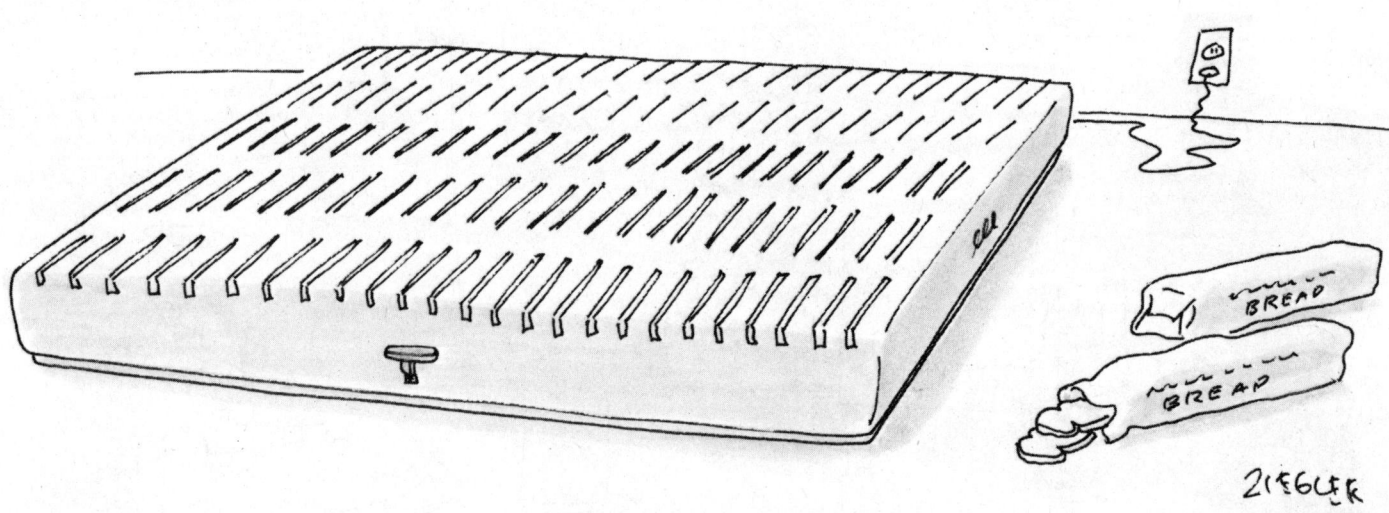

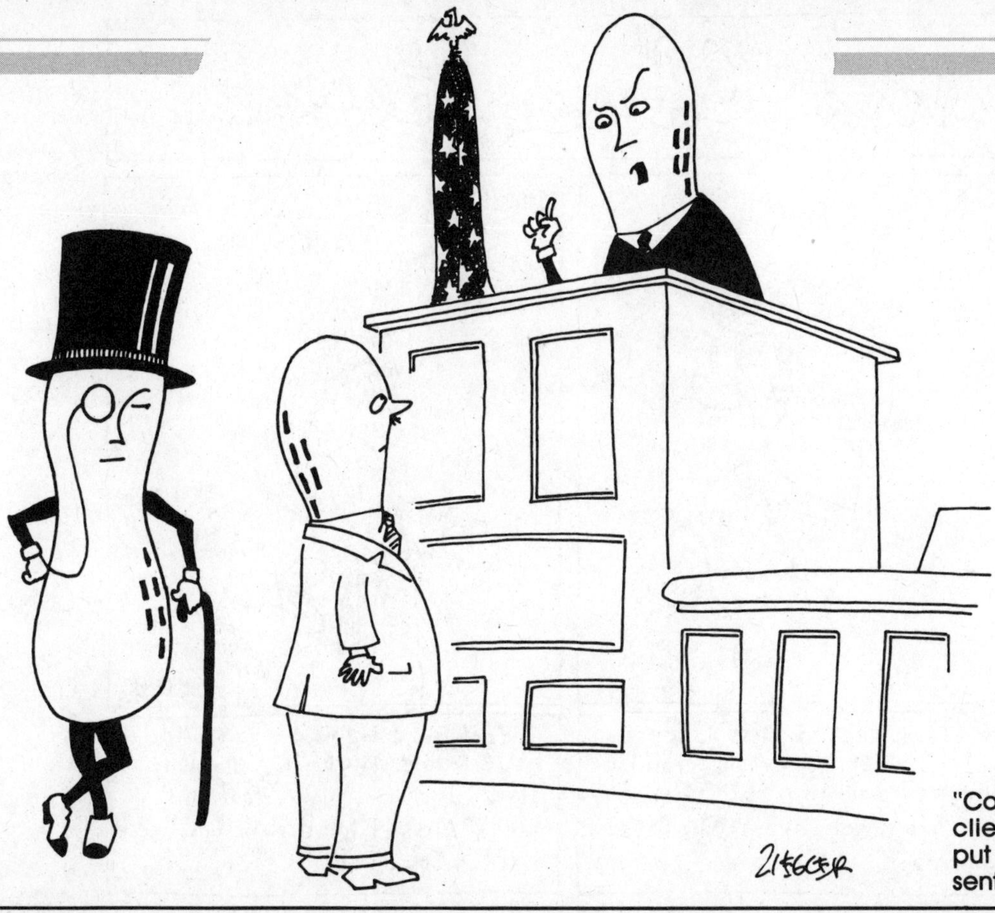
ZIEGLER

"Counsellor will instruct his client to remove his hat and put on some pants before sentencing."

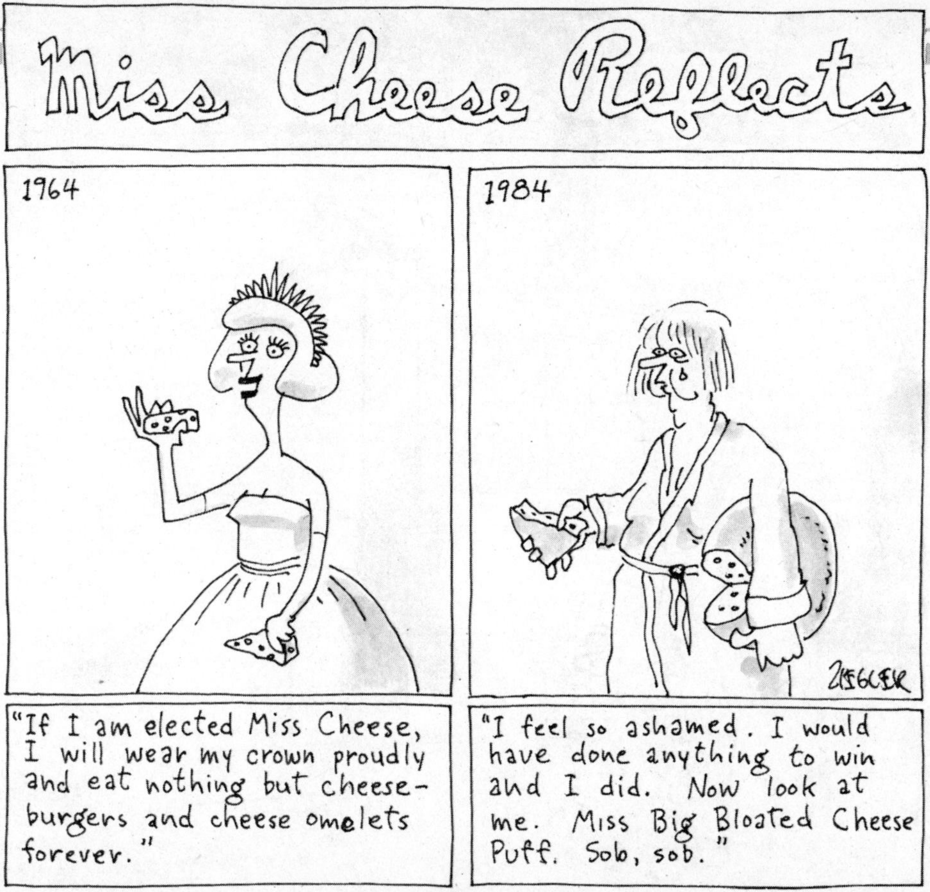
Miss Cheese Reflects
1964
1984
ZIEGLER
"If I am elected Miss Cheese, I will wear my crown proudly and eat nothing but cheese-burgers and cheese omelets forever."
"I feel so ashamed. I would have done anything to win and I did. Now look at me. Miss Big Bloated Cheese Puff. Sob, sob."

TOOTHBRUSHES OF THE RICH AND FAMOUS
JOHN TRAVOLTA
JOAN COLLINS
PIERRE TRUDEAU
CHER
TED KOPPEL
PRINCE CHARLES AND LADY DI

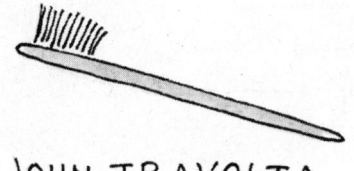

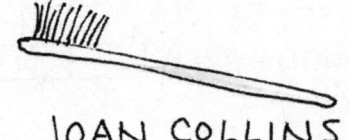

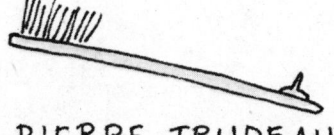

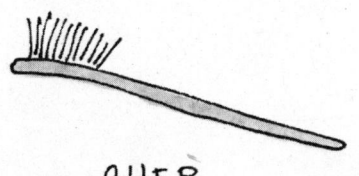

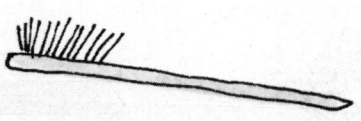

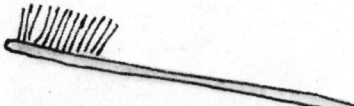

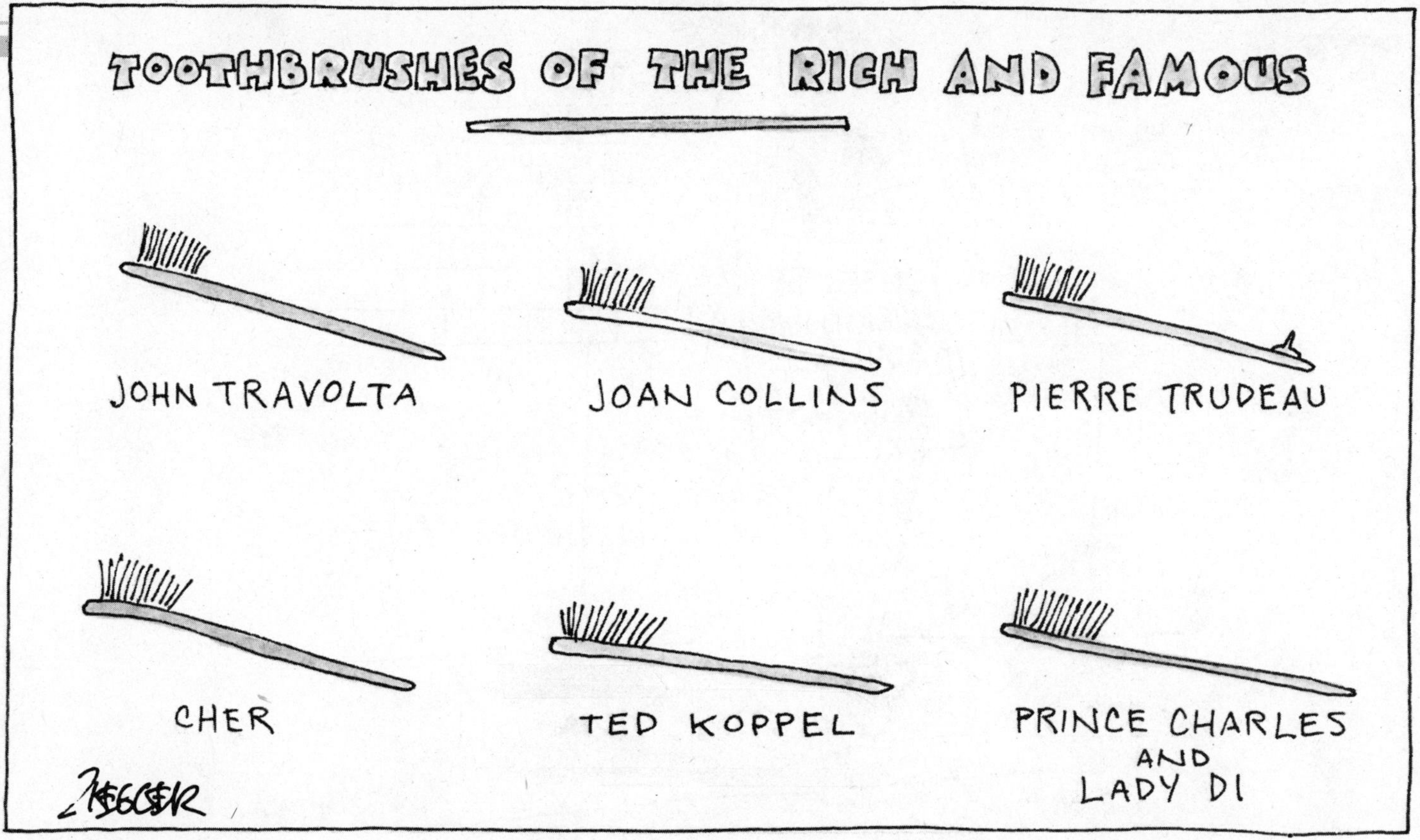

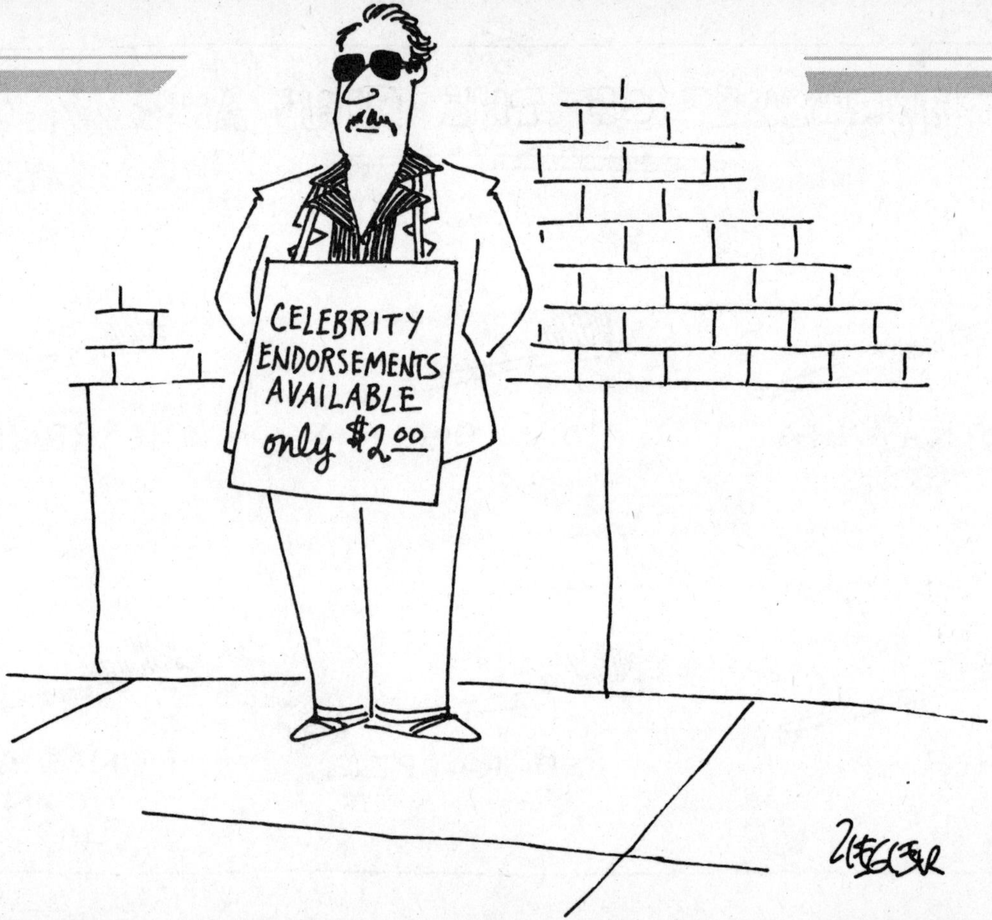
CELEBRITY
ENDORSEMENTS
AVAILABLE
only $2.00
ZIEGLER

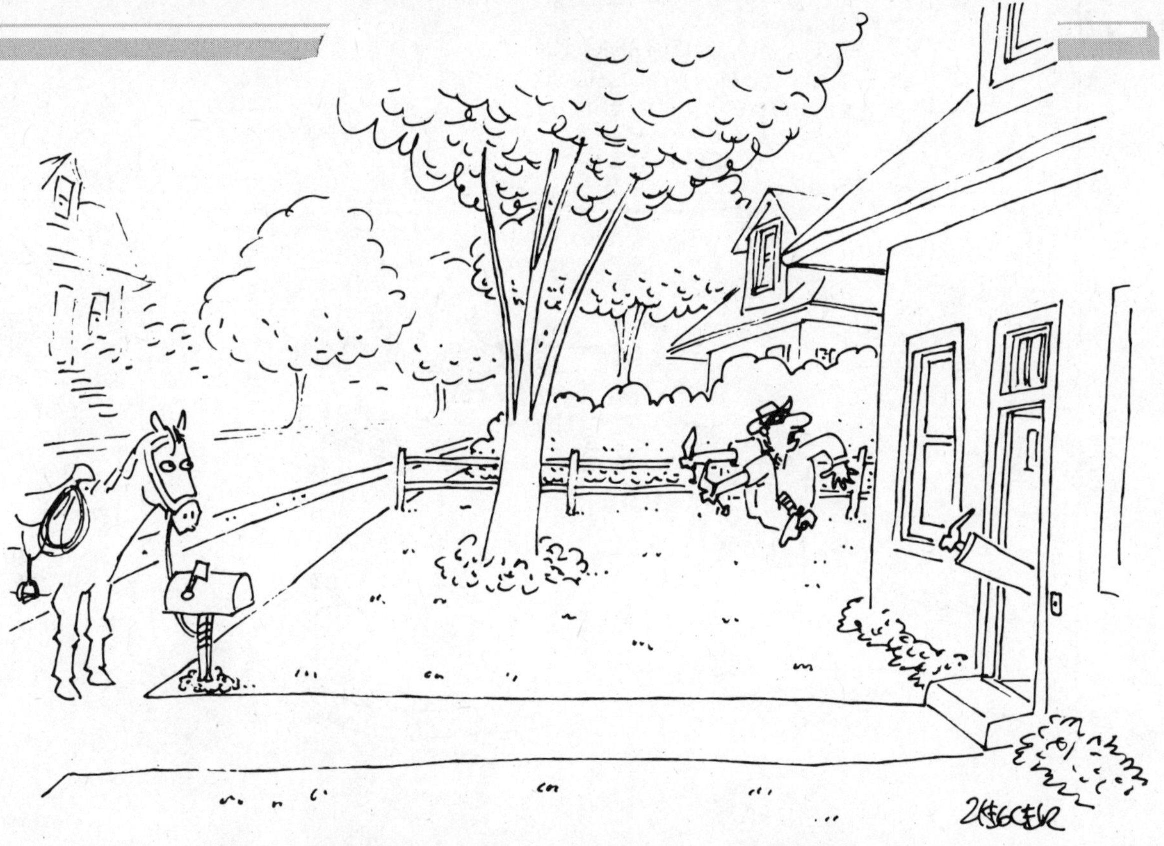

"Gee. Whatever happened to 'Who *was* that masked man?'"

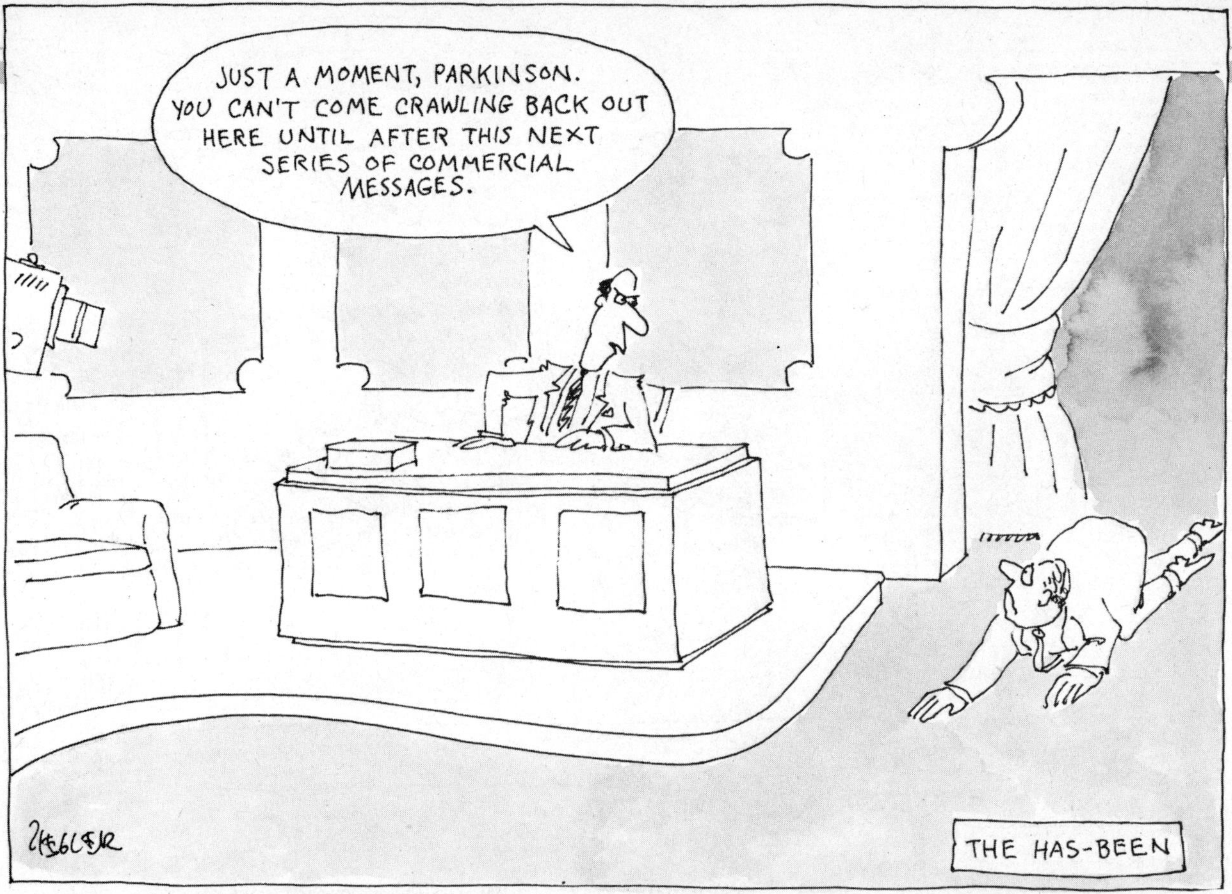
JUST A MOMENT, PARKINSON. YOU CAN'T COME CRAWLING BACK OUT HERE UNTIL AFTER THIS NEXT SERIES OF COMMERCIAL MESSAGES.
THE HAS-BEEN
ZIEGLER

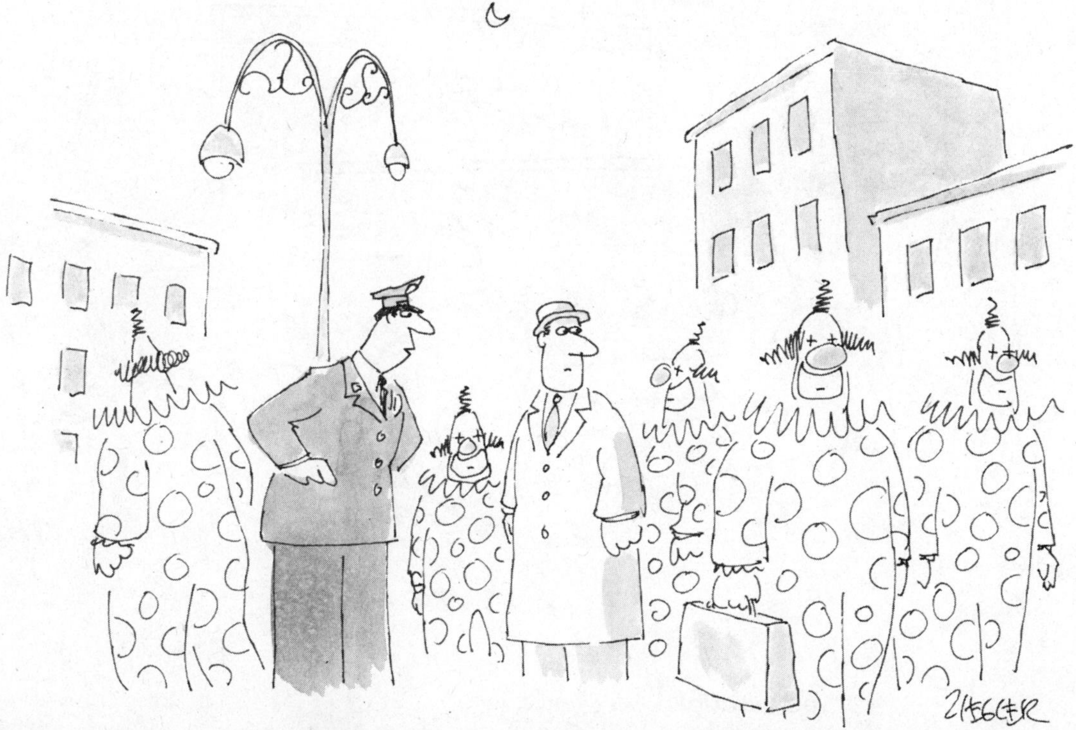
ZIEGLER

"You should have been
here last night,
sir. It was the night of the
Cybill Shepherds."

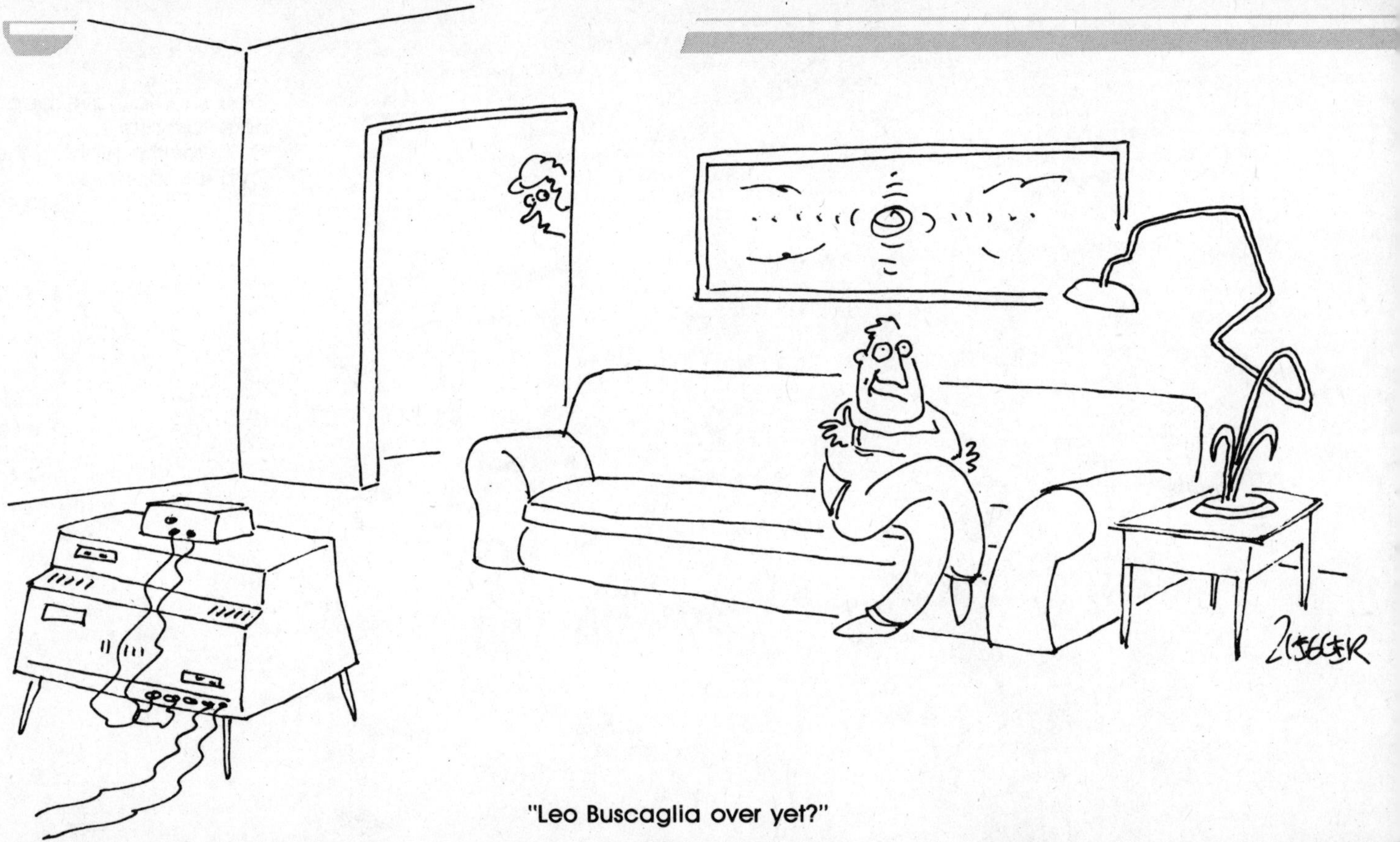
ZIEGLER

"Leo Buscaglia over yet?"

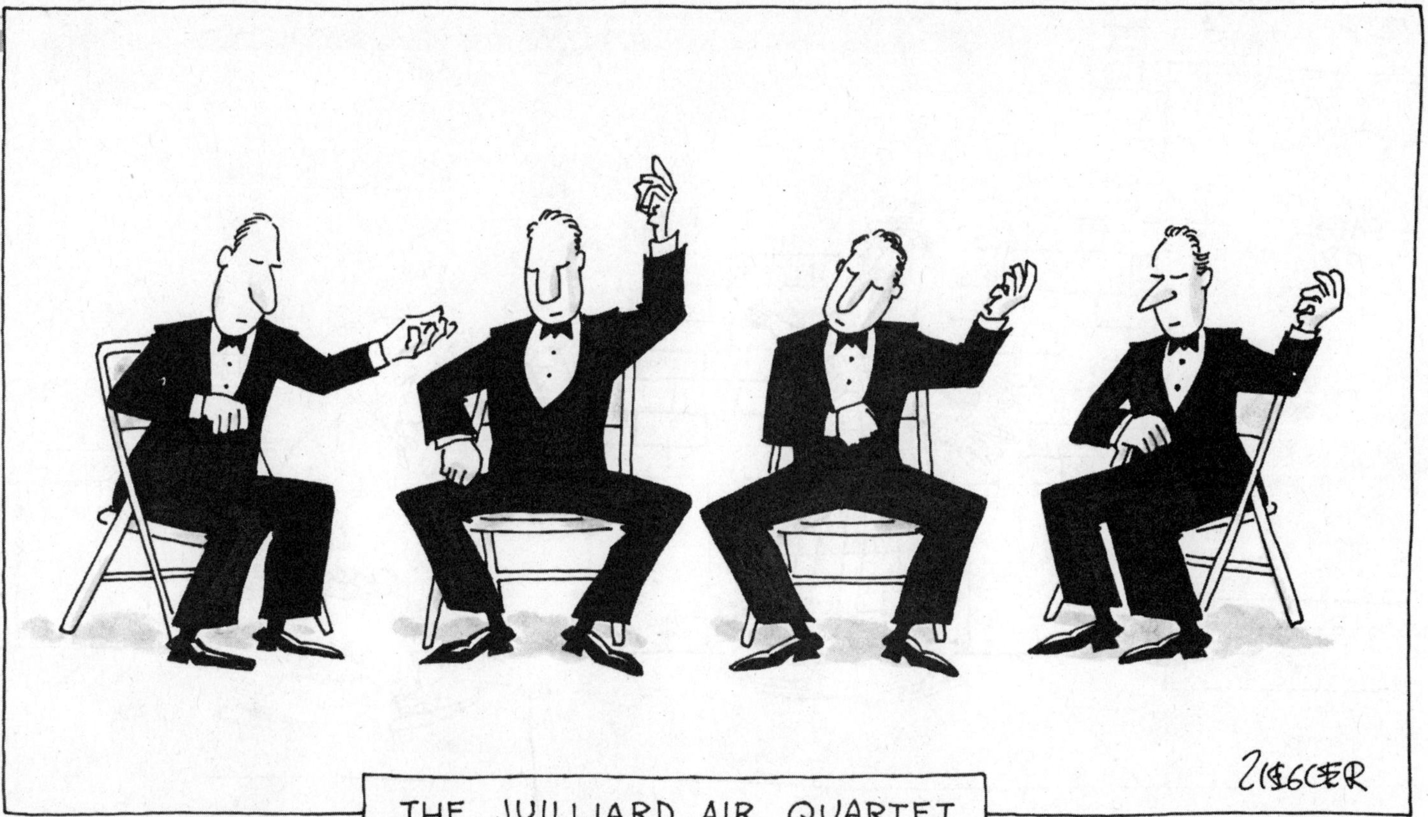

THE JUILLIARD AIR QUARTET

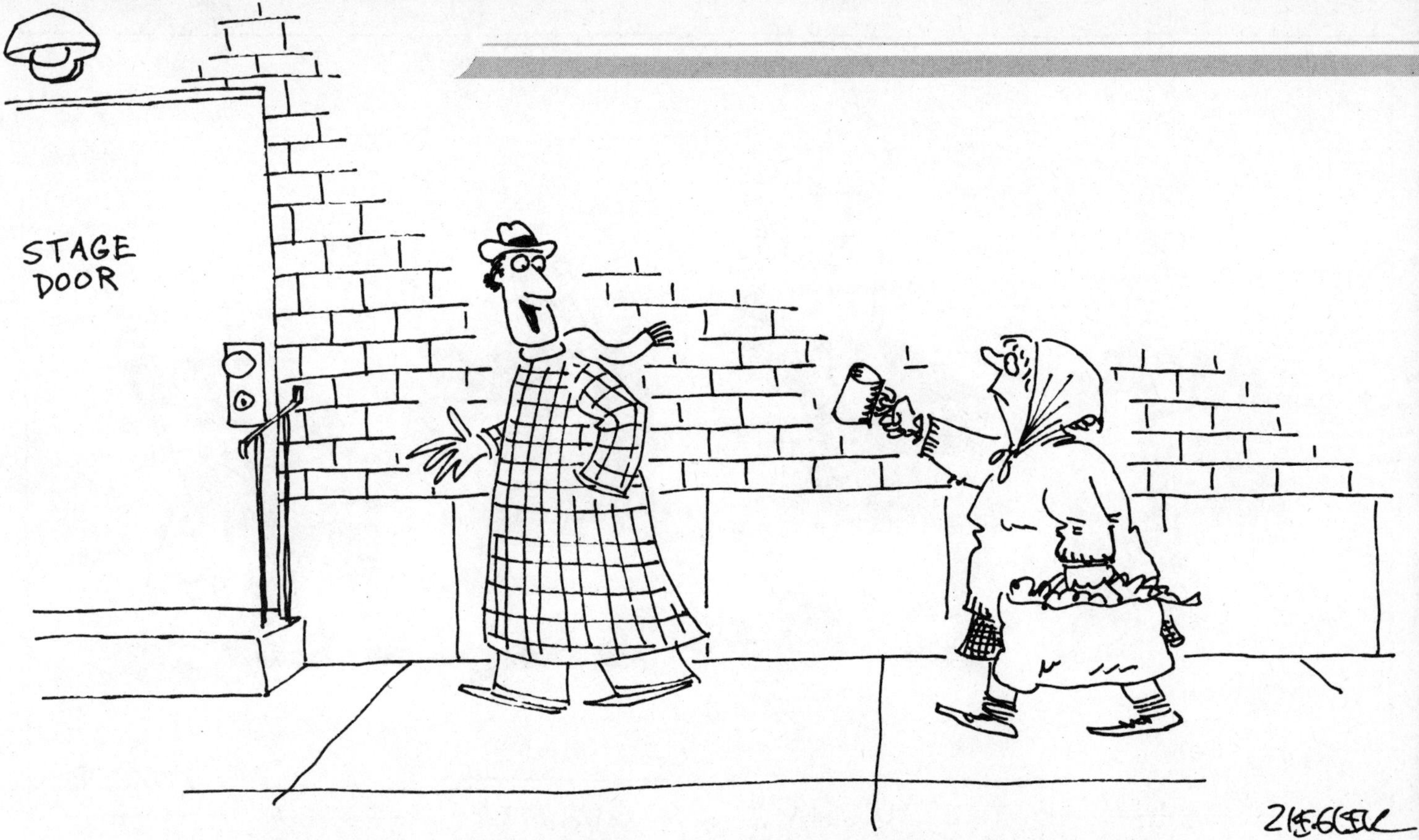
STAGE
DOOR

"C'mon, Mom. I never expected *you* to become a celebrity maven."

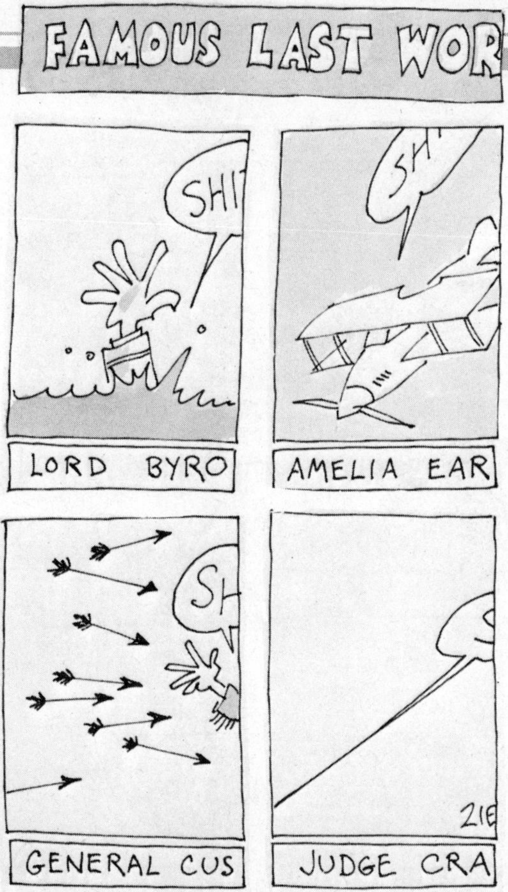
FAMOUS LAST WOR
SHI
LORD BYRO
SH
AMELIA EAR
SH
GENERAL CUS
S
JUDGE CRA

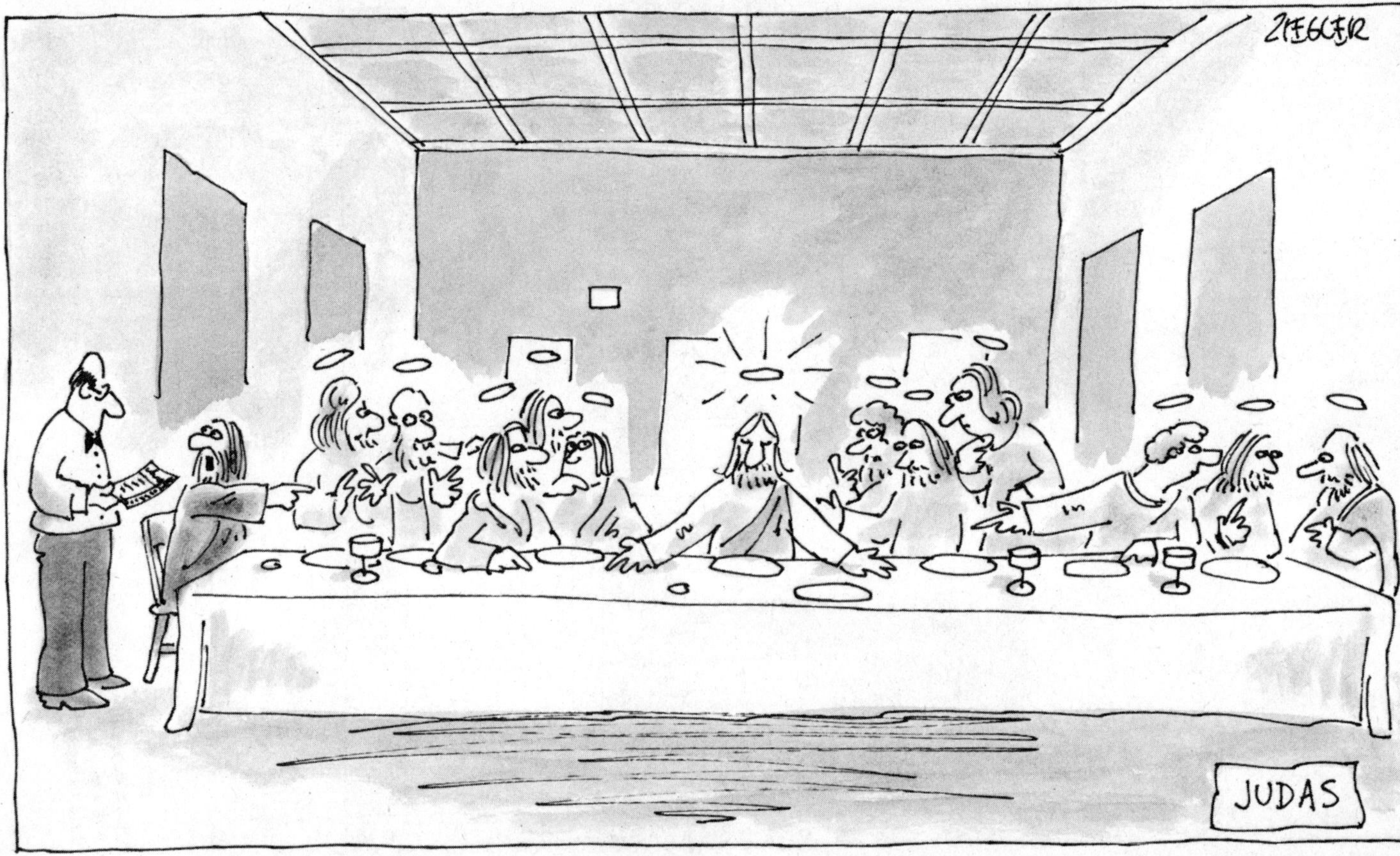
ZIEGLER
JUDAS

INDEX

Ann-Margret, *29*
Asimov, Isaac, *72*
Astaire, Fred, *56–57*
Autry, Gene, *75*

Bachman, Richard: see King, Stephen
Balboa, Rocky:
  see Stallone, Sylvester
Beatles, The, early, *27*
Bellow, Saul, *89*
Bernstein, Leonard, *22*
Bogart, Humphrey, *8*
Bono, Sonny, *73*
Brinkley, Christy, *11*
Buscaglia, Leo, *122*
Byron, George, Lord, *125*

Cagney, Christine, and
  Lacey, Mary Beth, *52*
Cagney, James, *8*
Cassidy, Butch, *77*
Cassidy, Hopalong, *68*
Charles, Prince of Wales
  (see Di, Lady), *117*
Charming, Prince, *21*
Cheese, Miss *116*
Cheetah, *63*
Cher, *30*, *117*
Clarabelle, *82–83*
Cleaver, Beaver, *24*
Collins, Joan, *117*
Corbett, Tom, *98*
Crater, Judge, *125*
Crocker, Betty, *64*
Crockett, Davy, *97*
Custer, Gen. George A., *125*

Dance, St. Vitus, *85*
Day, Doris, *16*
Dead, Grateful, *37*
Deneuve, Catherine, *13*
Di, Lady, Princess of Wales, *117*

Dickens, Charles, *71*
Domingo, Placido, *84*
Donahue, Phil, *105*
Doody, Howdy, *82–83*
Duran, Duran, *55*

Earhart, Amelia, *125*
Earl, Duke of, *51*
Einstein, Albert, *45*

Flynn, Errol: see Flynn, Errosol
Flynn, Errosol, *9*
Fonda, Jane, *76*
Frog, *21*

Garagiola, Joe, *22*
Garbo, Greta, *8*, *40*
Garfunkel, Art, and Simon, Paul, *23*
George, Boy, *111*
Godot, *107*
Gordon, Flash, *60*
Greene, Lorne, *33*

Hammerstein, Oscar, and
  Rodgers, Richard, *36*
Hope, Bob, *59*
Horne, Marilyn, *84*

Iacocca, Lee, *53*

Jackson, Reggie, *22*
Jehoshaphat, Jumping, *85*
Joel, Billy, *11*
Joffrey Ballet, The, *70*
Johnson, Don, *108*
Jones, Dow, *26*
Joyce, James, *88*
Judas, *126*
Juilliard Quartet, The, Air, *123*

Kent, Clark, *80*
King, Stephen, *99*
Kirk, Captain James T., *25*
Kissinger, Henry, *58*

Klein, Calvin, *49*
Knopf, Alfred A., dog of, *91*
Kojak, Theo, *79*
Koppel, Ted, *117*
Kowalski, Stanley and Stella, *103*

Lacey, Mary Beth, and
  Cagney, Christine, *52*
Lad of Sunnybank, *51*
Lane, Lois, *80*
Lauper, Cyndi, *62*
Lewis, Jerry, *95*
Lone Ranger, The, *32*, *119*
Louis XIV, *109*

MacLaine, Shirley, *81*
Madonna, *11*
Mailer, Norman, *102*
Mancini, Henry, *54*
Manilow, Barry, *74*
Mara, Countess, *49*
Marvin, Lee, *84*
Mehta, Zubin, *22*
Menace, Dennis the, *66*
Mormon Tabernacle Choir, The, *114*
Mozart, Wolfgang Amadeus, *42*
Murdoch, Rupert, *47*

Nelson, Willie (-ville), *12*

O'Connor, Sandra Day, *16*
Oldenburg, Claes, *44*
O'Neal, Ryan, *111*
Osmond, Donny, *41*
Ozawa, Seiji, *34*

Pavarotti, Luciano, *26*
Peanut, Mr., *115*
Penn, Sean, *11*
Pickens, T. Boone, *46*
Pilobolus Dance Troupe, *48*
Previn, André, *22*, *34*
Proust, Marcel, *101*

Rebecca of Sunnybrook Farm, *51*
Rizzuto, Phil, *104*
Rockettes, The, *92*
Rodgers, Richard, and
  Hammerstein, Oscar, *36*
Rogers, Mr., *110*
Rogers, Roy, *75*

Sales, Soupy, *10*
Savalas, Telly; see Kojak, Theo
Schubert, Franz, *39*
Shadow, The, *96*
Shepherd, Cybill, *18*, *121*
Shields, Brooke, *29*
Simon, Paul, and Garfunkel, Art, *23*
Sontag, Susan, *20*
Spider Woman, The, *100*
Spillane, Mickey, *88*
Springsteen, Bruce, *37*, *55*
Stack, Robert, *33*
Stallone, Sylvester (Sly), *5*, *93*
Stein, Gertrude, and
  Toklas, Alice B., *43*
Steinbrenner, Mister George, *69*
Stones, Rolling, *37*
Streep, Meryl, *35*
Sundance Kid, The, *78*
Superman: see Kent, Clark

Tarzan: see Cheetah
Toklas, Alice B., and
  Stein, Gertrude, *43*
Tonto, *32*
Travolta, John, *117*
Trudeau, Pierre, *111*, *117*
Trump, Donald, Tenement, *17*

Valente, Sergio, *49*
Vanderbilt, Gloria, *49*
Vitus, St., dance of, *85*

Whistler, James McNeill, father of, *31*
Wonder Woman, Ms., *67*

Yuma, Johnny, *65*

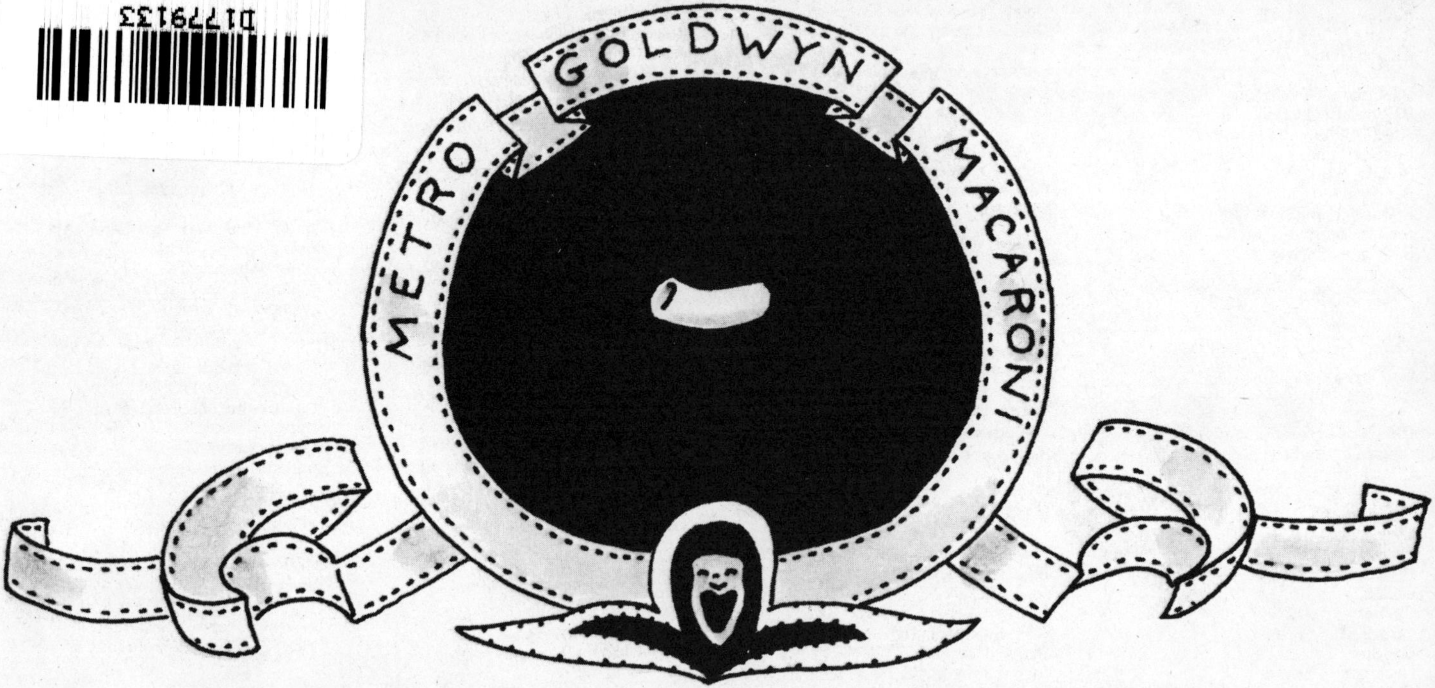
GOLDWYN
METRO
MACARONI